Praise for

Women of the Pleasure Quarters

"The geisha . . . has long been a source of intrigue. Through interviews with geisha, Downer gives her a face, heart, soul, and, most important, a voice. Comprehensive and illuminating . . . artfully intelligent . . . Part personal narrative, part social anthropology, and part good storytelling, *Women of the Pleasure Quarters* is as striking and compelling as its subject."

—THE ASSOCIATED PRESS

"If one wants to learn the facts about geisha, one should turn to Lesley Downer's *Women of the Pleasure Quarters*."

—COLUMBUS DISPATCH

"In her extensive and readable blend of reportage and history, Lesley Downer takes us into the secrets of what was once a closed world and even now, on the verge of extinction, is a veiled one."

—ATLANTA JOURNAL AND CONSTITUTION

"Downer skillfully intertwines her profiles of Kyoto personalities and tea house customs with a fluidly written geisha story that's . . . aimed at a Western audience . . . Written in dynamic, highly readable prose, the book is supported by exhaustive research."

—PUBLISHERS WEEKLY

"Lesley Downer's *Women of the Pleasure Quarters: The Secret History of the Geisha* is one of the few books to trace the history of these extraordinary women and explore the realities of life behind the flawless geisha mask."

—SALON

"Exploring the secretive geisha world, *Women of the Pleasure Quarters* looks at the unique experience of Sadda Yakko, a geisha who dined with an American President and was painted by Picasso, and probes the truths and myths of an institution caught between the past and the future."

—DAILY NEWS (London)

"A lush, seductive story book . . . A contemporary history, a diary of an age which is slowly but surely dying out."

—LONDON HAMPSTEAD AND HIGHGATE GAZETTE

women of the pleasure quarters

The Secret

History

of the Geisha

Lesley Downer

women

of the

pleasure

Quarters

Broadway Books · New York

BROADWAY

PRINTED IN THE UNITED STATES OF AMERICA

BROADWAY BOOKS and its logo, a letter B bisected on the diagonal, are trademarks of Broadway Books, a division of Random House, Inc.

Visit our website at www.broadwaybooks.com

First Broadway Books trade paperback edition published 2002

Book design by Maria Carella

The Library of Congress has cataloged the hardcover as:
Downer, Lesley.
    Women of the pleasure quarters: the secret history of the geisha / Lesley Downer.— 1st ed.
       p.   cm.
    Includes bibliographical references and index.
    1. Geishas.   I. Title.
  GT3412 .D68 2001
  792.7'028'0952—dc21   00-049409

ISBN 0-7679-0490-7
10 9 8 7 6 5 4 3

To the memory of my father and mother

Gordon Downer

and

Lilian Downer

Also by Lesley Downer

On the Narrow Road
The Brothers: The Hidden World of Japan's Richest Family

contents

acknowledgments

First of all I would like to thank the many Japanese women who have, over the years, befriended me and opened their world to me and with whom I have spent many hours enjoying women's pursuits, women's talk, and women's life. I should also record my debt to Arthur Golden and his wonderfully evocative novel, *Memoirs of a Geisha.* It inspired me to look again at Japan, its women and their history, and made me curious to meet the real geisha and look into the living reality today.

In researching the world of the geisha I was immeasurably helped by the work of many great scholars. Like everyone who studies the geisha, my first step was to turn to Liza Dalby's brilliant anthropological analysis, *Geisha,* the bible of geisha studies. Ms. Dalby generously offered suggestions and encouragement in e-mails and phone conversations.

One important source in examining the background and the rise of the geisha was Cecilia Segawa Seigle's marvelous *Yoshiwara,* a fascinating work of scholarship which provides huge amounts of detail about the Yoshiwara and evokes it very colorfully. Searching out details of the hidden history of the geisha I scoured many other scholarly works, beginning with the classic texts by the grand old men of Japanese studies,

Donald Keene and Edward Seidensticker. I was fortunate to have access to the unparalleled collections of the School of Oriental and African Studies library at the University of London and also the fine collection at International House in Tokyo; both include many rare and wonderful Victorian volumes.

Hiroaki Sugita, recently retired from the *Kyoto Shimbun* (newspaper) and author of many scholarly works, was a fount of knowledge on the history of the geisha. He introduced me to Sadayakko, loaded me down with books, and took me to tiny historical nooks in Gion connected with the geisha.

Many Western scholars of Japan offered friendship, suggestions, introductions, and inspiration. I am particularly grateful to Patricia Fister, who shared time and friendship as well as her great scholarship with me, and also to Monica Bethé (thank you for recommending the book on *kabuku*!), Richard Emmert, Drew Gerstle, who kindly read through the historical section of the first draft (though all errors, of course, are my own), Peter Grilli, Gaye Rowley, and Timon Screech.

In Japan many friends, both new and long time, were unfailingly kind and also helped to provide introductions.

In Tokyo I should like to record my debt of gratitude to Yutaka and Kazuko Aso and to Julia Boyd, who kindly introduced me to them; to Koichi Tsuzuki, maverick author, who provided a mobile phone as well as friendship; Johnny Walker, Svengali of my Tokyo social life; and Junko Koshino, who kindly introduced me to Toshiki Takahashi of the Wachigaiya. My old friend Seiko Taniguchi of the Japan National Tourist Organization introduced me to Mr. Mochizuki of Ryokan Sadachiyo in Asakusa, who in his turn introduced me to Shichiko (to whom much gratitude for friendship as well as help). Junichi Yano and Kazuko Koizumi-Legendre of the Foreign Press Center provided sterling backup. I am also grateful to Takashi Azumaya, Shi Yu Chen, Mr. Fukumoto and Mr. Kubota of All-Wave Productions, Toshiaki Honda of Tokyo Video Center, Keisuke Muratsu, Kiyoha, Iwamoto-san, Donald Fontayne (even though we failed to meet) and the geisha of Shimbashi, Asakusa, Akasaka, and Mukojima who were very generous with their time and hospitality. Many of these people became my friends and played a huge part in the making of this book. I hope they are pleased with it. Thanks also to Bernard Krisher and my old friends Michihisa Kitashirakawa and Yukiko Shimahara.

I have fond memories of all the people who were kind to me in Kyoto, starting with Mr. and Mrs. Sawai, whose inn became my home away from home, and the master and mistress of Suzuya, where I breakfasted. Many of the geisha, older sisters, and house mothers of Miyagawa-cho, Gion, Gion Higashi, and Kamishichiken were exceedingly generous of their time and hospitality and I am very grateful to all of them. I would like to express my thanks to Haruta-san, Imae-san of Daimonji teahouse in Kamishichiken, Ishihara-sensei of Yamato hairdressing salon, Takae Kaida, Koito, Komae-san of Komaya, and many more members of the geisha world whom I do not name in order to protect their privacy. I am very grateful to all of them for their friendship and open-heartedness. Thanks also to my old buddy Hal Gold, Malte Jaspersen, Reiko Kato of Shoho-in temple, Alex Kerr, Ritsuko Kishi, Satoshi Kita, Kanji Mori, Yasuyoshi Morimoto, Kojiro Sakai, Satoyu, Seto-san, Mr. and Mrs. Shimofuri of Kazurasei, Kyoko Sugiura, Toshiki Takahashi of the Wachigaiya, Zenzaburo Yamamori of Kyoto City Tourist Association, and Mr. Kimura, my wonderful tea ceremony teacher.

In Osaka, my old friend Narito Sasaki of the New Otani was, as always, bubbling with ideas. In Kanazawa, Mr. Keiichiro Yagi and Mr. Yoshihisa Kita of Yagi Corporation were my kind hosts.

Many thanks to my two helpers, Sarah Roche in Kyoto and Chieko Tsuneoka in Tokyo, who read books fast and furiously and put up patiently with all my demands.

Kyle Crichton applied a critical and expert eye to the first draft, for which I am enduringly grateful. Thanks also to Carolyn Watts, who provided many invaluable suggestions as well as being responsible for the author photograph.

I owe a bottomless debt of thanks to my wonderful agent, Bill Hamilton of A. M. Heath in London, who insisted that I embark on this project and has been there all the way through, offering wise advice and support. My agent in New York, Ellen Levine, has also provided wonderful support and been a staunch ally. Many thanks also to Lauren Marino, Cate Tynan, and everyone at Broadway Books, who have been full of enthusiasm and offered many wise suggestions. This book would not be what it is without their contribution. And thank you to my extremely supportive network of friends, in London, New York, and Tokyo, who have continued to be my friends despite my refusal to take phone calls while working.

Lastly I would like to remember my mother, who was Chinese-Canadian, and my father, also Canadian and Professor of Chinese, first at the School of Oriental and African Studies in London, then at the University of Leeds. Both passed away within a year of each other while I was working on this book. They are sorely missed. This book is dedicated to them.

Note on Geisha Names

Like sumo wrestlers, geisha have only one name, a professional name like a pen name or an actor's name. These names are quite different from Japanese women's names and immediately recognizable as professional names. The name also indicates a geisha's relationship with her "older sister"; the names of the two have at least one element in common.

Usually only one person at a time bears a particular name in a particular district. In order to preserve the privacy and discretion of women who very kindly spoke with extraordinary openness to me, I have used pseudonyms—ordinary Japanese women's names—for some of them and blurred their identities by, for example, not specifying the geisha district where they live. One Shimbashi geisha told me that if it was known that she had spoken with such openness to me, she would never work as a geisha again. I have taken precautions not to betray these women's trust.

Note on Pronunciation

Japanese words are pronounced as they are spelled, with each syllable distinct and with clean vowels and nonaspirated consonants, rather like Italian. All syllables are equally stressed. Thus *karaoke* is pronounced *ka-ra-o-ké* and *mizuage mi-zu-a-gé*. The word *geisha,* incidentally, is pronounced not *gee-sha* or *guy-sha* but *gay-sha*.

introduction: through the looking glass

When I see the first new moon
Faintly in the dusk
I think of the moth eyebrows
Of a girl I saw only once.

        Anonymous poem[1]

      On a Kyoto backstreet one sultry May evening, I caught my first glimpse of a geisha. She came flitting toward me with a faint tinkling of bells, an extraordinary vision like an apparition from another age. Her face, smooth and impassive as a mask, was an immaculate white oval with the sides of the nose and the eye sockets shaded in pink. Her eyes were outlined in black, her eyebrows two moth wings of feathery brown, and her lower lip a startling crimson crescent; her upper lip, disconcertingly, was white. Her hair, piled into gleaming black coils, was teased and lacquered into an undulating landscape of hills and valleys adorned with flowers, dangling silver pins, ribbons, and combs. Swathed in an ornate kimono in shades of blue and gold, she clattered by on preposterously high wooden clogs, her long sleeves swaying as she walked.

As darkness fell, white lanterns began to glow, lighting up the shadows. She was a vision made for darkness, for an era when geisha used to flit through the gloom of unlit teahouses, glimpsed only by flickering candlelight. Their painted faces transmuted them into shamanesses who could transport men into another world, a world of dreams.

She passed with a rustle of silk, revealing a breathtaking expanse of exquisitely white-painted back. I had not realized that geisha wore their kimono quite so shockingly low. It was like a décolletage in reverse, enormously erotic. At the nape of the neck, which Japanese men find especially sexy, was a titillating fork of naked, unpainted skin, shaped like a serpent's tongue. It was the most mesmerizing of all, a reminder that behind the alabaster mask, beneath the layers of silk and brocade, was a real flesh and blood woman.

Breaching a Secret World

It was nearly sunset when I got to Kyoto that mild May evening. I had to ask the taxi driver to drop me off at the end of the lane where I was to stay; it was too narrow for cars to squeeze through. I lugged my suitcase the last hundred yards to the inn, over the doorstep, through the door, then up a couple of dark, very steep wooden staircases to my room.

It was bright, airy, and wide open to the elements. One wall was barely a wall at all but a rickety wooden balcony with flimsy slatted doors which you could slide shut to close off the room when it was hot, cold, or rainy. The tatami matting of the floor was moth-eaten. On it sat a dumpy bandy-legged wooden table, a worn flat cushion, and a doll's house–size dressing table perilously supporting a tall thin mirror with a piece of ancient brocade draped over it. In one corner was a wobbly wooden frame with a few hooks for hanging clothes.

Bamboo blinds attached under the eaves created the illusion of a fourth wall, flapping and banging in the slightest breeze. Standing on the balcony I peeped through at the vista of gray tiled rooftops interspersed with telegraph poles and a mad cat's cradle of wires. The road below was lined with little wooden houses very similar to the one I was in. In the house opposite a couple of women were silhouetted behind the blinds. Voices, laughter, and the jangling plink plonk of the shamisen, a banjo-like instrument, hung in the air. Women pattered up and down the street, pausing to bow and greet each other in high-pitched coos.

Having spent many years in Tokyo, I had come to the ancient city of Kyoto in search of geisha. Once the capital of Japan, it was still the country's cultural heart, home of temples, palaces, gardens, and theaters and the place where the classical heritage was most fiercely preserved. The picturesque streets of the geisha districts, the old pleasure quarters, looked more like the Japan portrayed in nineteenth-century woodblock prints than anywhere else. Kyoto was also the only place where the strict geisha training continued and the geisha traditions were handed down.

I wanted to meet the real women behind the painted faces, the charming chit chat, and the eternal mysterious smile. The geisha, it seemed to me, were purveyors of dreams. Theirs was a misty world of romance created for the enjoyment and entertainment of men, in which the most browbeaten office worker could be king. It was not my intention to spoil the illusion or dispel the mystery. But as a woman, I wondered out of what past the geisha had come. Who were the women who, in modern Japan, had chosen to live this life? For men it was a dream world; but who were the women whose job it was to create this dream?

I had lived, talked, traveled, and daydreamed my way through a couple of decades in Japan, filtering my experience of a country which was often shockingly ugly through the prisms of its past. I absorbed myself in the passionate stories of heroes, villains, and beautiful temptresses recorded in its spare but evocative poetry, drama, and literature—like the tale of the all-time femme fatale, Ono no Komachi, the most beautiful woman in the world; or Narihira, the great lover, who cut a swathe through women's hearts; or the Heian courtiers of the tenth century who made love into the essence of life, to be studied, cultivated, and perfected as an art form. The geisha were the heirs to this romantic heritage. I hoped I would find that they prospered still, that the past had not faded completely into the realm of imagination and dusty scholarly tomes.

But at the dawn of a new century, was there a place for geisha in the land of Nintendo, Sony, Nissan, and Honda? Persistent reports in papers and magazines had suggested that they were an endangered species, if not already extinct. Although I had come across geisha in the small provincial town where I had lived when I first arrived in Japan, for years I had barely glimpsed them. And if I did succeed in befriending any, would they be "real" geisha or mere shadows, play-acting at being the real thing?

Before I had even reached Kyoto I had discovered that there was something strangely unsettling about the very notion of geisha. On the plane on my way to Japan, I had mentioned to the man next to me that I was planning to do some research on geisha. Suddenly he changed from the mild-mannered mustachioed academic he had seemed—he had told me he was a specialist in car ergonomics—and poured out a torrent of abuse.

"Fujiyama," he foamed, spitting out the word which foreigners mistakenly use when speaking of Mount Fuji and a symbol to Japanese of our inability to muster even the faintest understanding of their country. " 'Fujiyama', 'geisha'!" he snarled. "Stereotype, prejudice!"

I had said nothing about my attitude or approach to geisha or why I was interested in them. The very idea that a foreigner would dare to even think of writing about them filled him with rage.

At least one foreigner had already done so—Arthur Golden, whose novel, *Memoirs of a Geisha,* took a generation of Western readers inside the geisha world of 1920s Gion. The book, at that time, had yet to be translated into Japanese. The West, meanwhile, had been swept by geisha fervor. Inspired by Golden's heroine, Sayuri, the fashion world rediscovered the allure of femininity. The collections of 1999 were full of kimono-like creations which wrapped and concealed the body, hinting at the mysteries beneath rather than revealing them. That summer Madonna appeared at the Grammies in an extraordinary outfit described as a kimono, with long flapping sleeves and a plastic obi. It would be hard to imagine anything further from the traditional garment. Nevertheless it was the talk of Tokyo.

My neighbor on the plane was not just an eccentric. To my amazement, confiding in Japanese men that I was planning to look into geisha and their culture exposed me to my first experiences of rudeness in this country of protocol and courtesy. Enraged, they laid into me for taking an interest in such a trivial, old-fashioned, and banal aspect of their culture. A Japanese woman who, as a teacher of the shamisen, lived her life on the borders of the geisha world, asked me with gentle puzzlement why I wanted to look into the "dark, bad side of Japan." And when I went to bookshops, I found intriguingly little on the geisha.

When I mentioned geisha to friends and acquaintances in Tokyo, many said (with, it seemed to me, unnecessary forcefulness) that no, they did not know any. But some did. They took me aside, sat me down, and explained that geisha were dancers, musicians, entertainers, and conversationalists who filled a specific niche at the highest levels of Japanese society. They were absolutely not prostitutes, high class or otherwise. That established, they suggested particular geisha that I might care to look up and, most important, indicated that I might mention their name.

First Days in Kyoto

On my first morning in Kyoto I was woken by a strange shouting, like the cry of an animal. Sunlight was streaming into the small room where I slept on the floor, sending motes of dust sparkling and spinning. Purely by chance I had ended up staying in one of the geisha areas, in a house which had until recently done service as a geisha house. When I finally met geisha, I learned that they lived in bare little rooms as poorly furnished as mine.

I went in search of breakfast and found a coffee shop along the street. Inside, mellow jazz emanated from the speakers. The master of the shop, nervy and balding, tapped his fingers on the counter while he brewed up coffee in a glass percolator. The mistress, warm, plump, and smiling in a pink-and-white-checked apron, prepared industrial-size slabs of cotton-woolly toast. The shop was full of women sitting over breakfast, flicking through newspapers or chatting.

Later, wandering the neighborhood, I found myself in a warren of alleys lined with wooden houses pressed so close together that only the occasional shaft of sunlight pierced the gloom. Every now and then a motorbike or scooter skidded past but mainly there was silence. I had never been anywhere in Japan so untouched by the passage of time. It was as if I had stepped back into a preindustrial era.

There were five geisha areas or *hanamachi* (flower towns), of which three clustered together on the eastern side of the River Kamo which rolled, wide and brown, a couple of minutes walk away from the inn where I was staying. These three—Gion, the most famous and classy, Gion Higashi (East Gion), and Miyagawa-cho—were bordered to north and south by two thoroughfares, Sanjo and Gojo (Third and Fifth) streets. Cutting through the middle, the nerve center of the area, was Shijo (Fourth) Street, crammed end to end with shops dealing in all the paraphernalia of the geisha world—hairpins, tortoiseshell combs, dangly hair decorations, fans, clogs, kimono fabric, white face paint, sticks of safflower lipstick, hair wax, camellia oil, and small beautifully molded cakes of sugar, rice, and beans.

The river divided this small alternative universe from the modern city with its snarled traffic, air-conditioned department stores, clashing neon, and bustling people. Across the river from Gion was the fourth of the five *hanamachi,* Pontocho, a tiny picturesque alley lined with restaurants which in summer were extended at the back to make platforms lined with reed matting where one could dine, sip sake, and enjoy the cool breezes above the rolling waters of the Kamo. It was several days before I visited the fifth, Kamishichiken (literally "Seven Houses to the North"), in the northwest of the city. To my mind it was the most charming of all, a couple of quiet intimate lanes lined with dark prosperous houses, many with a lantern glowing outside, meandering in a gentle curve up to the stone lanterns and plum trees of Kitano Shrine.

That evening I was to have my first appointment with one of the *grandes dames* of the geisha world. I had mentioned on the phone that I was a friend of a friend, an important and powerful businessman whom I will call Mr. Suzuki, and hoped that that would smooth my way. Far from seeking publicity, the geisha shun it. Their whole profession depends on their ability to keep secrets. Many have been the friends of the nation's most powerful men, often for a lifetime. Such men choose to entertain at geisha houses because they can trust these women to keep their lips sealed, no matter what they see or hear. But I also knew that in Japan as elsewhere the most important thing is who you know. With the help of introductions from friends I had made over years of living and working in Japan, I was confident that little by little I could breach this closed world.

At the end of an alley I pushed open a door and found myself in a small brightly lit room. There was a bar along one side and some leather sofas arranged to make a couple of alcoves. A small, regal woman in a kimono greeted me, offered me a whiskey, then turned back to banter with a group of noisy elderly men. Rather awkwardly I perched on a stool at the bar and began to chat to the barman. Finally the woman came to perch alongside me.

"So you are here through the introduction of Ken-chan," she said, using the affectionate, diminutive form. "I've known him for years, since he was a little boy. I used to bounce him on my knee."

It was hard to imagine the leathery Tokyo businessman I knew being bounced on anyone's knee. Added to which, if that was the case, I realized with surprise, she had to be in her seventies. She was as tiny and frail as a butterfly, with the kind of looks that become, if anything, more beautiful with time—a fine-boned, delicate face, perfect skin without a trace of lines. Dressed in a modest indigo-blue kimono with a subtle pattern woven through it, her hair drawn back into a pristine bun, she sat very upright, poised and gracious.

"So . . . what would you like of me?" She spoke in Kyoto dialect, ineffably polished and stylized, where everything is hinted at and nothing is said directly. Fresh from Tokyo, I found it difficult to pick up every nuance.

Clumsily I launched into an explanation. As she knew, I was a writer. I was hoping to write about the geisha world. Hopefully I could meet geisha, some young, some at the height of their career, perhaps even spend time in a geisha house living among geisha like one of them, seeing life from the inside. I gathered she might be able to help me. I'd be very grateful if she could do so.

I stumbled to a close. She sat in silence, looking straight ahead.

"Mmm," she said slowly after a long pause, pursing her lips. "But how can you ever understand our *shikitari*?"

"*Shikitari?*" I prided myself on my spoken Japanese but this was new to me.

"You see?" she smiled, tight-lipped. "You do not even know the word."

Many of the customs and practices in the geisha world, I was to learn, have their own terminology, a sort of jargon known only to insiders, incomprehensible to most Japanese. Other words which they regularly use—such as *shikitari*—are rare and sound rather archaic to the Japanese ear. It was only after considerable research that I discovered that *shikitari* means "customs, practices, the way of doing things." It was indeed the *shikitari* which I wanted to learn about, among much else.

"How long are you planning to stay in Kyoto?" she went on.

"Several months," I replied uncomfortably, adding hastily, "but I've lived in Japan for many years. I first came more than twenty years ago . . ."

"I have been to London many times," she snapped. "I have met all the top people—the aristocracy, musicians, singers . . . But you would still say that I cannot understand England, would you not?"

I had to confess, I murmured as politely as possible, that that was not exactly the way that English people thought. For a start, she said, ignoring my response, geisha were of different sorts and different status. Some, like her, had been born in Gion. She herself was third generation; her mother and grandmother before her had been geisha. Then there were those—here there was the faintest, barely perceptible curl of the lip—who had come in from elsewhere. They, she implied, were a different class altogether. Of the five *hanamachi,* Gion, Pontocho, and Kamishichiken had long histories. They had always been geisha districts. But I must bear in mind that East Gion and, worse still, Miyagawa-cho were different, unspeakably low, in fact quite beyond the pale; in the past, prostitutes—she breathed the word with distaste—had lived there.

"I would not like to see Miyagawa-cho written about in the same breath as the others," she said emphatically.

Even Gion, Pontocho, and Kamishichiken were all completely dissimilar, with entirely different histories and *shikitari.* She had met many Westerners, she concluded, writers and journalists, who had come to Kyoto on the same quest as mine. They had all failed. They had all given up and so should I.

"No matter how long you are here you will never understand the intricacies of our system."

Gloomily I took another sip of whiskey. I had never met a Japanese woman so formidable and steely. In the alcoves the men were shouting and laughing. Ties were loosened, faces flushed.

"Mama!" shouted one. With the indulgent smile of a mother for a naughty child, the mama-san—my hostess—slipped away to join them, topping up their drinks and admonishing them teasingly. One, rather the worse for wear, came over to try his English skills on me.

At that moment the door opened. With a rustle of silk and brocade, a creature like a painted doll appeared.

"Okasan, oki-ni!" she cooed in breathy, high-pitched tones using the Kyoto word for thank you: "Mother, thank you." Tottering unsteadily into the room on clogs a good four inches high, she stood nodding, smiling, and giggling, covering her mouth with her hand.

"She has just become a maiko," explained the mama. "This is her third day."

I was dumbstruck, as many people are, on coming face to face with a maiko. (Maiko literally means "dancing girl" but is usually translated "trainee geisha" or "apprentice geisha.") Later, as the days and months passed, I was able to see the childish faces underneath the thick white paint. But that time, I could not stop myself staring in amazement and curiosity at this extraordinary confection. I was not the only one. For a moment there was silence before the chatter started up again.

She was wearing a sumptuous black kimono with an intertwined design of bamboo leaves and stems in browns, whites, and greens around the hem. The kimono sat flatteringly low on her shoulders, revealing a layer of brilliant red brocade at the throat which I took to be an under-kimono; in fact it was a separate under-collar. Around her waist, wrapping her like a corset from armpit to hip, was a thick cummerbund—the obi—of pale gold embroidered with flowers.

She was not so much a woman as a walking work of art, a compilation of symbols and markers of eroticism, as far removed from a human being as a bonsai is from a natural tree. Geisha have been described as icons of femininity. If that is the case, it is a very stylized image of femininity, following conventions utterly different from Western notions of beauty and sexiness. There was certainly not the slightest pretense that this was a real woman. She was an actress, painted up to play a role; it would be as absurd to confuse the girl with the role as to assume that the star of a soap opera actually was the character she was playing.

Rather unsteadily, with much rustling of fabric, she perched on the edge of one of the sofas; the enormous obi prevented her from sitting any further back. I glanced at the mama, hoping that I might slip over and join the group; but with a barely perceptible pursing of the lips she indicated that I should keep quiet and stay where I was. So I watched and listened, curious to see what this painted creature might have to say.

"When were your parents born?" began the stringy, gray-haired man next to her, basking in her presence.

She smiled, giggled, covered her mouth with her hand.

"Showa twenty-nine," she trilled, using the Japanese calendar in which years are numbered according to the ruling emperor (1944 by the Western calendar).

The man roared appreciatively as if she had just uttered a scintillating witticism.

"Showa twenty-nine, same as my son!" he beamed.

Smiling, she picked up one of the bottles of beer which littered the table and offered to fill his glass. One by one she moved from guest to guest, filling their glasses, giggling, repeating *"Oki-ni!"* Her job, it seemed, was just to be there. Chatting was an optional extra. Soon the men had reverted to talking among themselves.

Time passed. She rose to her feet. Bustling and clucking like a mother hen, the mama tugged, pulled, and patted her kimono into place and adjusted the heavy gold obi until the two long ends which crossed one over the other and hung to her feet were perfectly symmetrical.

"Oki-ni! Oki-ni! Okasan, oki-ni!" sang the girl. Bowing and giggling, with a clatter of clogs and a tinkle of bells, she backed out of the door and was gone. The room seemed a little duller, a little gloomier without her.

It seemed an auspicious beginning. But as the days and weeks passed, I began to fear that I would never get any further than this. I could see the geisha, I lived among them. But I was always an outsider, I could never step through the looking glass. And the more curious I became, the more the geisha world presented me with a blank face.

Every connection I thought would be hopeful turned out to be a dead end. From time to time I was introduced to women who I knew were ex-geisha and the proprietresses of geisha houses.

"I wonder if I might meet the geisha and maiko in your house," I would murmur tentatively. "Would it be possible . . ."

"Much too busy," they would snap. "Geisha are busy all day. They go to classes, they appear at parties. They certainly wouldn't have the time to talk to you. But call me next week, I'll see what I can do."

Hardly daring to hope, I would call them the following week. The answer was always the same.

But on the fringes of the geisha world I was making friends. Every day I went to the coffee shop for breakfast. By now the motherly owner and her jazz-loving husband were used to my eccentric foreign ways. Instead of the tiny container of cream substitute which they served to everyone else, they gave me, smiling at the oddness of it, real milk to top up my coffee and indulgently cut me thin slices of toast instead of doorstop-thick slabs. Sometimes I wrote my diary; sometimes I chatted to the owners or the other women.

Then, tape recorder and notebook in bag, I would set off. Sometimes I would drop in to see Mr. Ishihara, the hairdresser. Maiko usually came in to have their hair done in the morning. I would sit in a corner and watch. He would start off with a long thick mane of hair and, while the maiko pored over a teenage magazine, he would smooth it with curling irons, comb in gobs of wax, part and knot and tug and tie, slip in a tail of yak's hair and wads of stuffing, then add ribbons and string and pins until the hair had been transformed into an immaculate gleaming coiffure. He was not so much a hairdresser as a sculptor who worked in hair. Between customers he would sit down to chat. He knew everything one could ever want to know about geisha and their hairstyles, the history and the meanings of the different styles, and had written four books on the subject.

As much as I could I absorbed the geisha arts. The word *gei-sha* literally means "arts person"; perhaps it could be translated "artiste." Maiko spend five years studying dance and music before they graduate, and fully qualified geisha continue to study for the rest of their lives, honing and perfecting their technique. As I walked the streets I would hear the plangent plink plonk of shamisen riffs being practiced over and over again.

Soon after I arrived the Pontocho geisha gave a series of public dance performances. The small theater, tucked on one side of the narrow lane which made up the Pontocho district, was packed out with women in dark-toned kimonos who looked much like the owners of geisha houses and their elderly escorts, who might have been husbands, friends, or patrons. While the spectators fluttered their fans, the all-female troupe gave an abbreviated performance of *Chushingura* (The Tale of the Forty-Seven Ronin [Lordless Samurai]), a drama as familiar as a Shakespeare play or a performance of Swan Lake would be to a Western audience. For the geisha of Kyoto it was a particularly appropriate choice, for the most moving scenes take place in Gion's Ichiriki-tei, the most famous and venerable teahouse in the country.

Little by little my ear was becoming attuned to the melodies and rhythms of the music, at first rather dissonant for Western taste, while my eye was becoming sharper, better able to perceive the quality and crispness of the movements. One way of stepping inside the geisha world, I thought, might be to sit in on some of the maikos' music and dancing classes. But to do this I needed an introduction. Taking a deep breath, I called the formidable mama, thanked her very much for her kindness, and asked if I might come and see her again.

"Of course," she replied, all icy politeness.

Whenever you visit anyone in Japan you take a gift, beautifully wrapped in the shop's brand-name paper and presented in the shop's carrier bag. A mere glance at the choice of shop communicates to the recipient your savoir faire and your degree of respect. So it was an urgent priority to find a suitable gift. Should I take cakes or, as a Westerner, expensive French wine? Several guidebooks recommended a celebrated cake shop on Shijo with a long pedigree. So I went along, asked for their most famous cakes of the season, and bought a boxful. The cakes were of rice paste filled with red bean jam, beautifully molded.

Carrying my offering, I arrived at precisely the appointed time. The bar was silent, dark, and empty apart from the barman, who was leaning on the counter, smoking a cigarette.

"Wait a while," he said, turning on some lights, and offered me a drink. He had a swarthy, rather flat, melon-seed face and sharp, watchful eyes. He might have been anything between thirty and fifty but had become fixed forever in the ageless role of "boy." There were plenty of men around but they were all adjuncts, "employees" as one aging geisha put it, servicing the geisha—shopkeepers, barmen, men whose job it was to help the geisha dress, men who worked in the geisha unions.

The barman seemed unnervingly knowledgeable about me and the difficulties I was having.

"The geisha world is not a yes/no society," he said, apropos of nothing in particular. "You offer a maiko a cake and she just says, 'Oki-ni.' She doesn't say, 'Yes, please,' or 'No, thank you.' "

I understood what he was driving at. If I made a request, no one would ever say, "No, that's impossible," neither would they say, "Yes, I'll do that, I'll help you." They would always make encouraging noises and tell me to call them again, any time, and they would see what they could do. But no matter how many times I called, nothing would ever come of it.

The mama was a case in point. I had heard from others that she was one of the most powerful geisha in Kyoto. She had been, like her mother before her, a famous beauty. Indeed, she was still extraordinarily lovely. Rumor had it that she had a *danna,* a patron, effectively a husband, who supported her whole enterprise. "They've been together for decades," the innkeeper's wife had told me. Yet I wondered where that steely core came from. In my decades in Japan I had met many Japanese women, almost all of them married, who were strong, confident, yet also eager to befriend me, a foreigner. I had never before encountered such suspicion and intransigence. It was as if these women had built a self-sufficient world in which I was just a flea, an irritation. They had no need of me; they wanted to brush me off.

When the mama appeared, as exquisite and tight-lipped as ever, she took my carefully chosen cakes with barely a glance and put them aside, then asked me what I wanted to drink.

"*Ocha de mo ii desu,*" I said. "Tea will be fine."

"That's rude!" she snapped, rounding on me fiercely. "You say, '*Ocha o itadakimasu,*' 'I'll have tea, please.' "

Biting my tongue I apologized profusely and thanked her for being so kind as to correct me. There were no concessions to the fact that I was speaking a foreign language. The geisha were unforgiving of the tiniest error. Trying to communicate deference and humility with my body language, nodding, keeping my head bowed, I waited for an appropriate moment when, with the utmost politeness, I could put my request to her. I thought it would help my research, I explained, using the most formal and polite Japanese I could manage, if I was able to sit in on some classes at the Kaburenjo, the "Music and Dance Practice Place," which housed classrooms, a theater, and the union offices and formed the nerve center of the district.

"Let me teach you," she said, suddenly kind. "Last time we met, you asked too many things—you wanted to meet geisha, meet maiko, stay in a geisha house, do this, do that. You must learn to be patient. Take it step by step."

"Step by step," echoed the barman, who seemed to have more authority than one would have expected.

"When you meet maiko, you do not ask, 'Why did you become a maiko? What is your training?' In a gentle way, you say"—putting on a piping little girl voice—" 'If you don't mind, could I ask . . . ?' And only one thing at a time. You ask too much!"

Taking out one of her business cards, she penciled a few neat characters on to it.

"Take this to Mr. Kimura at the union offices in the Kaburenjo," she said. "We will practice what you will say. I will run through it with you."

"Well," I said, "I guess I'll introduce myself, tell him that I've lived in Japan, show him my books, then say that I want to sit very quietly and watch some classes, maybe meet maiko and talk to them, talk to the teachers . . ."

"No, no," she said. "Just say something very modest: 'I did these books, there's others too but this is all I have; if possible it would be really wonderful if I could sit in on a dance class . . .' And don't say anything else. Then the next time you make your next request. You see?"

I repeated the words after her in my best high-pitched little girl voice, full of deference and self-deprecation, inserting thanks and apologies after every few words. I was beginning to understand. Within the geisha scheme of things, I was right at the bottom of the pecking order. Here I was, a female, trying to swim along within the geisha community yet ignorant of all their codes. Had I been a man, it would have been natural for me to be an outsider. I would have fitted neatly into the category of customer. The geisha would have indulged me, flirted with me, overwhelmed me with charm and attentiveness. But in this closed, secretive world of women, there was no place for a female who did not know the proper way to behave. My experience must have been akin to that of a new girl entering a geisha house. I was undergoing the most basic geisha training such as would be given to a raw recruit fresh from the countryside.

And—though she probably disagreed with me—I felt I was learning. Living among the geisha, dealing with them on a day-to-day basis, I found their ways beginning to rub off on me. I found myself carrying my body differently, walking with dainty steps, bowing, nodding, smiling until my face hurt. Most disconcertingly, when I called Japanese who had nothing to do with geisha or the geisha world, I found myself talking with exaggerated politeness in sweet, high-pitched velvety tones: "Oh, that would really be too kind, thank you so, so much!"

The next day, full of anticipation, I went along to the large concrete Kaburenjo carrying the precious business card. It was a rather unprepossessing building to house such an august body as the geisha union. My hopes rose when I discovered that Mr. Kimura was really quite young, maybe only forty or fifty. He had clipped hair, glasses, and an office worker's suit. He took me off to a small side office and asked me brusquely what I wanted. I repeated my speech in my most unctuous tones, being as modest and undemanding as it was possible to be.

"No chance," he growled. It struck me that, for all my efforts, neither the mama nor anyone else in authority bothered much with politeness at all.

"I'll ask them upstairs, but I'm sure they'll say no," he said, scowling, and showed me the door. "You can try again next week if you like," he added, which I now understood to mean "Forget it." Downcast, I went back to my small sunny room to lick my wounds and ponder my next step.

The Best Cakes

Whenever I had time, I went to tea ceremony class. The teacher, a comely, charismatic young man, had two faces. When he was conducting the class he wore *hakama,* the formal starched and pleated men's kimono, and took on the persona of the *sensei* (teacher), barking orders and correcting the smallest mistake. Off duty he was a hip young man who worked as a stylist for a glossy magazine.

Tea ceremony is a series of precise choreographed movements performed in a spirit of stillness and concentration which also involves the serving and consuming of food and drink. It is somewhere between tai chi and the Roman Catholic mass but on a very small, intimate scale. Being very rusty, I was at the bottom of the class and had to be coaxed to remember even the most basic things, such as to hold my arms as if there were an egg tucked into each armpit. Fortunately the teacher belonged to the same school that I had studied before, so at least I did not have to relearn details like the folding of the silk napkin.

"For the name, Ippodo; for the history, Kamibayashi; for the taste, Koyama—that's what we say in Kyoto," he told us one day, naming the three most famous tea shops in the city. Then he listed the four most famous cake shops. To my relief, the shop where I had bought the mama's cakes was among them.

"Do you know Kanshindo?" he added, glancing at me. "You should go there this season. It's very old, it's where the geisha buy their cakes. It's famous for its mizu yokan [a bland slab of red bean paste jelly eaten in summer]. It's very difficult to find, only Gion people know it. If you take them Kanshindo mizu yokan, the geisha will be very surprised and impressed. Shall I tell you where it is?"

And he drew me a small sketch map.

I needed to report back to the mama and take her a gift to thank her for her kindness in introducing me to Mr. Kimura; it was irrelevant that it had not been a success. I called her, made an appointment to visit, and went in search of the cake shop. I walked down Shijo Street, looking carefully. There were plenty of alleys off the main road but nothing where the teacher had indicated. Then I noticed a gap between two buildings just wide enough to slip through. It led to a dark, narrow path lined with blank walls and the closed doors of bars. Halfway along was a small stall, not even a shop, with wrapped slabs of bean jelly in a display case. I bought a couple, wrapped in Kanshindo paper, and carried them off in the Kanshindo carrier bag.

That evening I went to see the mama. As always, I was precisely on time. As always, she was not there. When she finally appeared, I offered her the cakes, bowing and murmuring in self-deprecating tones, "This is really nothing at all, but please take it."

She took the bag and gave me a warm smile.

"The most delicious cakes!" she said. "You're learning, little by little."

I had also learned to ask no more. I thanked her profusely for her very great kindness and for teaching me so much, apologized for my shortcomings, chatted inconsequentially for a while, then left, feeling pleased with myself.

I had never guessed that cakes would make such a difference. After that, whenever I was to visit anyone, I always made a pilgrimage to Kanshindo. I became a regular customer. The two apron-clad women who ran the shop took to asking how I was and I always stopped for a chat. And when I proffered my cakes, the geisha would exclaim with delight or nod approvingly and look at me as if to say, "Aha, I can see you know what's what." I had found one of the keys to the door.

Doors Open

There was another key lying around waiting to be found—or maybe it was a door opening rather than a key.

One day I was walking home when a geisha caught up with me,

scurrying along on her silk-covered sandals. She was tall and slender with a dancer's long neck and a striking face, handsome rather than beautiful, with a long chin, high cheekbones, thoughtful eyes, and a wide sensuous mouth. She was wearing, as geisha (as opposed to maiko) do, an elegant, understated kimono in shades of pale mauve, with a plain obi, and her hair was swept back. Perhaps it was because she was wearing heavy makeup (though not the white face paint of the maiko, which geisha wear only on formal occasions) that I failed to recognize her though, to my embarrassment, she seemed to know me well.

"Going home, are you? Or dropping in to the coffee shop?" she asked gaily. Then she mentioned that she was on her way back from Tokyo where she had been performing in an *odori-kai,* a convention for professional dancers, and suddenly I realized who she was.

Whenever I had seen her before, I had always taken her for a university student or a secretary. When I went for breakfast she was often there, a quiet, serious girl with large owlish glasses who sat at the far end of the counter reading her paper. She usually wore a dress or a simple blouse and skirt over slim bare legs and had short neat hair and a scrubbed clean face. I had always been rather curious about her. She looked like a bit of a bluestocking, very far removed from a geisha, as if, like me, she was an outsider, not really part of this world at all.

I knew that she was a talented dancer. But plenty of women learned *Nihon buyo* or *jiutamai,* the forms of traditional Japanese dance practiced by geisha, as a hobby. It had never occurred to me that such a serious-looking, intellectual young woman might be a geisha herself.

The following day at breakfast she was not there. By now it was midsummer, approaching the season of the Gion festival. All the geisha had had fans made of hand-crafted paper shaped like gingko leaves and inscribed with their professional names in beautifully brushed black characters, which they handed out as souvenirs. The master and mistress of the coffee shop had a whole collection, pinned up in rows across the wall.

"Look," said the master, reading some of the names to me. "And see this one? That's our Fumiko. You know her. She's famous, she's one of the top dancers in the district."

I looked blank.

"She sits just over there. You know, with the big glasses!"

Something was changing in my perception of the coffee shop and its customers and in their perception of me. For weeks I had gone there simply to have breakfast. Sometimes I chatted to people, often I didn't. Sometimes some of the older ladies engaged me in conversation. And as I became a familiar face, the plump, motherly owner would inquire how I was getting on with my research.

I looked at these women I knew so well, with their unmade-up faces, in their slacks and blouses, some still in flimsy nightgowns, with their piled up helmets of lacquered hair. How could I not have realized? All this time I had been scouring the district, making phone calls, using connections, trotting here and there with cakes, when I was already right inside the geisha world.

In fact it was just as well that I had been so oblivious. For instead of behaving like a journalist and alienating everyone by bombarding them with questions, I had, entirely by accident, done exactly the right thing. I had sat quietly, not being obnoxious, not asking nosy questions, speaking when spoken to, just eating breakfast, day after day. It was a bit like stalking wildlife. They were used to me. I had won their confidence.

I still did nothing. I was well trained by now. I had plenty of people to meet and places to go. Then several days later the owner leaned across the counter and said in confidential tones, "You wanted to find out about geisha, didn't you? Hara-san says she'd like to talk to you."

I knew Hara-san well, a warm rather beautiful woman in her mid-seventies with a pile of snowy-white hair, large, luminous eyes and a smile which lit up her face. It turned out that she was the *okami-san*—the owner-mistress—of a teahouse a few doors away from my inn. The word "teahouse," incidentally, is a literal but rather misleading translation of *ochaya*. Geisha live in a "geisha house" *(okiya)* and work in a "teahouse" *(ochaya)*, where there is music, dancing, partying, sometimes food, and always plenty of alcohol; tea is the last thing you would expect to find there.

I went off to visit Hara-san, taking, of course, Kanshindo cakes. Talking to someone so familiar was an entirely different experience from quizzing a geisha who barely knew me. With childlike innocence, she poured out her heart, showing me photographs of herself as a beautiful, grave-faced young geisha.

Suddenly doors were flying open. I traipsed in and out of houses with my notebook and tape recorder, listening to stories. Some were uneventful, others extraordinarily moving. I was amazed at the openness with which women would reveal the most harrowing experiences of their youth.

Now, a good two months after I had first arrived, when I walked down the street maiko recognized me. They stopped to bow and say *"Ohayo dosu!,"* the quaint geisha phrase for "Good morning," or *"Oné-san, oki-ni,"* "Big sister, thank you!" The ones I knew would whisk me off on shopping expeditions, clattering along beside me on their clogs, taking my arm to make sure I was not swept off my feet by one of the lethal passing motorbikes, sheltering me with their oiled paper umbrellas when it rained, chattering and giggling sweetly. I felt pampered, protected, charmed, and hugely honored that they had chosen to befriend me. It was easy to see how beguiling such behavior must be for the wealthy businessmen who were their customers.

As a single woman, I had always been something of an oddity in Japan. People would ask why I was not married and had no children until, as I passed some unspoken but recognizable age, they became embarrassed even to ask. None of the geisha was remotely interested. After all, they themselves were not married. Some had children, some not. Those who had were single parents. No doubt they assumed that I had the occasional lover, as they did. As I lived among them it began to dawn on me that I—a modern Western career woman—was not far removed from a geisha myself; though when I put this theory to the geisha I knew, they looked distinctly dubious. Perhaps that was the answer. Perhaps they were the original liberated women and the rest of the world had just caught up with them.

I felt, I realized, extraordinarily at home. In Japan, outside the geisha community, everyone seemed to get up with the lark. Here, like me, they got up late. One would not dream of dropping in to see a geisha before noon. And unlike the punctual Japanese, they were never on time, as I had discovered when I was paying court to the mama-san. It was in many ways the looking-glass image of "real" Japan. All the usual rules were subverted. One should not take the comparison too far. Like Japan, it was a hierarchical, stratified society. But, within the small confines of the geisha communities, it was women, not men, who wielded power; and everyone hoped for girl children, not boys, so that they could carry on the line of geisha. It was a back-to-front world—which was of course the whole point. Men came to the "flower towns" looking for an escape from drab reality in a world of dreams.

So how had this dream world arisen? This was something I could only understand by looking into the past. Over the following months I sifted through texts to try and understand where the geisha had come from, what their role was in Japanese society, and why Japan had developed this parallel universe. I befriended geisha in Tokyo and in some of the hot spring resorts where Japanese go on holiday. I hung out with different classes and varieties of geisha. And I began to get some clues as to why Japanese men (some, anyway) might be angry at the very notion of my writing a book on geisha.

Geisha Past and Present

In this book I put together the pieces of the jigsaw puzzle. The first, fourth, sixth, and eighth chapters deal with the history of the geisha, their changing face and role through the centuries, and the many romantic tales, both fact and fiction, which have grown up around them. It is a secret history. In the standard histories of Japan, geisha are never mentioned; yet when I probed a little deeper, I found them there, playing a role in the great events of their day and consorting with the most powerful men of the country as friends, confidantes, mistresses, and sometimes wives. But they are always in the shadows, the women behind the decision makers.

Today they seem respectable enough; in fact there is a powerful geisha PR lobby driving home the point that geisha are not prostitutes with such insistence that even the most out-of-touch Westerner must have got the message by now. But in Victorian times and before, when geisha were in their heyday, they were the pinnacle of an outrageous alternative society. Like rock and roll stars today, they were the queens of a popular culture created by, with, and for the people, so subversive that the shogunate, the government of the day, spent much its time hopelessly attempting to repress it, or at least keep it within controllable bounds. Many of the writers who celebrated this culture found themselves in prison from time to time. The woodblock print artists whose work is so familiar to us today made a living portraying the courtesans, geisha, and kabuki actors who were the pin-ups of this alternative society.

As for the glamorous courtesans and rollicking male geisha who were like court jesters to the wealthy guests, the Japanese will tell you that both professions died out at least a century ago. I found differently . . .

And what of modern-day geisha? Very few Japanese have ever met one. In the evening the streets of Gion are crowded with Japanese tourists with cameras poised, waiting patiently like birdwatchers for a maiko to flit into view for a few seconds before darting into a nearby tea-house. Only the very wealthy or their guests will ever get to spend an evening in the company of maiko or geisha. Who are these women and why do they do what they do? In the rest of the book I look at the world of the geisha today, from the rites and rituals of geisha life and how a geisha does her makeup and kimono, to how she learns to charm at geisha parties. It is a journey in search of the last remnants of a dying tradition, to record some of these colorful personalities, their customs, their stories, their memories, their present and their past.

Inevitably I find myself looking at what it means to be a woman in Japan. What is the dividing line between geisha and prostitutes and between wives and geisha? And what of the men who spend their time with geisha? Almost all the people who recorded the geisha and their lives in stories, novels, and woodblock prints were men. In the few surviving writings and paintings by geisha, they portray themselves very differently, not as siren queens but down-to-earth women.

In Japan in the heyday of the geisha, relations between men and women operated very differently from the way in which we do things in the West. Until recently, all but the lowest classes had arranged marriages. The purpose of marriage was to create an alliance between families; to go against one's family and marry for love would have been quite unthinkable. It was also—hard though it is to imagine—considered shockingly improper to enjoy sex with one's wife. The function of conjugal relations was to produce children to perpetuate the family line. As for pleasure, men were expected to find that elsewhere.

I also look at the Japanese attitude to love and sex, untouched until recently by either the European notion of romantic love or Christian sexual morality. This is a culture in which hedonism, sensualism, and the art of the erotic, not at all the same as sex, were uninhibitedly developed in very sophisticated ways. In the floating world of the geisha, it was love, not sex or sensual pleasure, which was taboo.

chapter 1

japan before the geisha

High-class Courtesans
and the Culture of Desire

Because they fall
we love them—
the cherry blossoms.
In this floating world,
does anything endure?
      Ariwara no Narihira (823–880)[1]

The City of Purple Hills
and Crystal Streams

More than a thousand years ago, long before geisha were even thought of, Kyoto was the center of an extraordinarily effete, decadent, and promiscuous culture which transformed love into an art form and beauty into a cult. Centuries later, when pleasure quarters were built where men could transcend their everyday lives and imagine themselves noblemen of leisure, the courtesans and geisha modeled the dreams which they sold on the romantic culture of the Heian princes.

The Heian period lasted from 794 to 1195, the time of the Vikings, King Canute, and William the Conqueror. It began with the construction of a beautiful new capital in an auspicious location, a wide bowl-shaped valley surrounded by tree-clad hills, with sparkling rivers bordering it to each side. The official name was Heian-kyo, the Capital of Peace and Tranquility. Poets called it the City of Purple Hills and Crystal Streams; we know it as Kyoto.

There a city grew up of vermilion-painted palaces, slender-pillared temples, and spacious mansions of wood with wattled roofs. Noblemen and princes rumbled up and down the broad mud-paved boulevards in the shadow of the overhanging willows, in lavishly decorated oxcarts attended by retinues of liveried outriders. Under the rule of the emperor and his all-powerful ministers of state, the Fujiwara family, the country basked in three centuries of peace and prosperity. For the pampered aristocrats of the Heian court, it was a time of unending leisure which they filled with the pursuit of art and beauty. They spent their days moon-viewing, mixing incense, writing poems, and playing the game of love.

In this strange hothouse world, women lived their lives away from the sight of men, hidden in a kind of purdah in windowless unheated houses, shadowy by day and lit with oil lamps and tapers by night. When men came to visit they received them sitting behind latticed screens draped with silk curtains or opaque hangings. When they went out, they traveled concealed behind the closed window blinds of their ox-carriages, though they made sure that there was always an exquisite silk sleeve trailing outside to hint at the beauty within.

For within their secret world, the Heian noblewomen were articulate, literate, and highly educated. One, named Murasaki Shikibu, was the author of the world's first novel, *The Tale of Genji,* written around the year 1000, which recounts the romantic adventures of the charismatic Prince Genji. Several of the court women kept diaries in which they recorded their thoughts and feelings in extraordinary detail, leaving us very intimate accounts of what life was like for the aristocrats of those days.

This was probably one of the most lax societies the world has ever seen. Promiscuity was the norm. Following the Confucian precepts which governed society, marriage was a purely political affair arranged by the parents to create an advantageous alliance between families. Love and marriage had nothing to do with each other. A court lady was more likely to suffer censure for a lapse of taste in the colors of her robes than for her numerous lovers.

But what made the Heian period most extraordinary was the way in which art and the cult of beauty were bound up with love. For more than sexual desire or gut-wrenching passion, love was an art form, an opportunity to put brush to paper, to immortalize the moment in a small literary gem.

Having heard that a certain lady was very beautiful or, even more titillating, had beautiful handwriting, a nobleman would sit down to compose a *waka,* a thirty-one-syllable poem, and brush it, in his finest calligraphy, on delicately hued scented paper. When she received it, the lady would assess the handwriting and color of the paper as well as the wit and appropriateness of the poem before brushing a reply. The noble-man would be waiting with bated breath to see whether her hand-writing and poem lived up to expectations.

If the exchange of poems was satisfactory, he would eventually assay a visit. He would creep in at night and immediately, in the pitch darkness, remove his clothes, lift the silken counterpane, lie down on the hard straw mat next to the lady and without further ado consummate the relationship. Slipping away before dawn, he would then brush an eloquent morning-after poem, bewailing the rising of the sun or the crowing of the cock announcing the hour of farewell. The lady in her turn would brush a reply. Thus through poems they communicated their decision as to whether to continue the affair or not.

The most famous of all the Heian beauties was Ono no Komachi, a lady-in-waiting in the imperial court. So beautiful, proud, and passion-ate was she that she has never been forgotten. Her name has come down through the ages as Japan's all-time femme fatale.

Her story is recounted in Noh plays and legend. With her raven tresses that cascaded to the floor, a face like a blossom, and eyebrows painted into perfect crescent moons, she drove the noblemen of her day mad with desire. She would glide through the cedar-scented halls in her multilayered gauze and damask robes, oblivious to the thousands of love letters which lay discarded about her chambers. At night she slept in a room bright with tortoiseshell where golden flowers decorated the walls and strings of crystal beads hung in the doorway. When she passed the cup at banquets, people said it was as if the moon lay on her trailing sleeve.

But she was not just a pretty face. She was brilliant, accomplished, powerful, and tough-minded, a woman of burning passions which she wrote about in *waka* poems read and loved to this day.

Of the fickleness of men's love she wrote:

> *A thing which fades*
> *With no outward sign*
> *Is the flower*
> *Of the heart of man*
> *In this world!*[2]

Unlike the maidens of medieval Europe, waiting passively for a knight in shining armor to come courting, she herself burned with fiery passion:

> *This night of no moon*
> *There is no way to meet him.*
> *I rise in longing—*
> *My breast pounds, a leaping flame,*
> *My heart is consumed in fire.*[3]

She would only give herself to a man who could prove himself worthy of her. For the most lovelorn of all, a commander of the imperial guard named Fukakusa no Shi'i no Shosho, she devised the sternest of ordeals. He was to come to her house for a hundred nights and sleep outside on a bench used to support the shafts of her chariot before she would even consider his suit. Night after night he hitched up his stiff silk trousers and donned his tall lacquered hat or put on a wide-brimmed wicker hat and straw rain cape and ventured out into the elements. Evading the night watchmen and the barrier guards he walked through wind, rain, and snow, made a notch on the shaft bench, then waited through the night there, shivering. Ninety-nine days had passed and the joyful day, when he was to receive the reward for all his efforts, was dawning when he suddenly died, of heartbreak, perhaps, or exposure.

For such hard-heartedness, Komachi suffered the cruelest punishment of all—the loss of her beauty. Instead of dying young, like Cleopatra or Helen of Troy, and leaving a beautiful memory, she lived to be a hundred. After the death of Captain Shosho she was spurned and driven from court and ended up a tattered, crazed beggar woman. In folk legend and Noh plays she is portrayed as an ancient withered crone, hideously ugly, haunted by the unhappy spirits of the men who died for love of her.

Like the cherry blossoms, beauty is all too fleeting; and this is what gives her story its poignancy. The beauty of women can drive men to distraction and to their deaths but in the end men get their revenge: such women die old and alone. Komachi's tragic end made her all the more the perfect precursor of the geisha. Like her they too came to be regarded with ambivalence. They were sirens, so beautiful that men could not resist them—yet to yield and fall in love with one was to court disaster. At least in legend, if not in real life, Komachi had to be punished for her fearsome powers.

Shizuka's Last Dance

Even at the height of Heian promiscuity, when noblemen had no problem finding a companion for the night and flitted merrily from one aristocratic woman's chamber to another, there were also prostitutes who offered a different sort of pleasure. At one end of the scale were ordinary prostitutes who wandered the streets, waterways, hills, and woods and were referred to as "wandering women," "floating women," and "play women." At the other extreme were cultivated, refined professionals whom in English we might call courtesans. Some were of good family, fallen upon hard times; others were noted for their beauty, brilliance, or talent. Skilled musicians, dancers, and singers, they were often the invited guests and chosen companions of aristocrats. These high-class courtesans were the original precursors of the geisha.[4]

The most popular of the courtesans were the *shirabyoshi* dancing women (*shirabyoshi* literally means "white rhythm"). To heighten their allure, they cross-dressed in white male clothing and manly court caps. They carried swords like men and performed highly charged erotic songs and dances to music with a rhythmic beat. Like the supermodels and rock singers of today, they were stars and the chosen companions of the country's most powerful men.

The most celebrated of all was Shizuka Gozen, the concubine of the twelfth-century hero Yoshitsune. (Shizuka, alas, is probably legendary though the great warrior who was her lover is a very important historical figure, a doughty Richard the Lionheart of Japan; the two heroes, Japanese and Western, coincide in both period and story.) She was renowned throughout the country for her extraordinary beauty and also for the power of her dancing, so magical that once, when the country had been suffering from drought for a hundred days, the gods responded by sending rain as soon as she began to dance. This is not as extraordinary as it sounds. Dance began as a way of supplicating the gods in Japan and the women who worked in Shinto shrines often combined the roles of shamaness and prostitute. Centuries later when the first geisha appeared, they claimed the beautiful and spirited dancer as their ancestor.[5]

Shizuka's story began when her lover, Yoshitsune, was forced to flee Kyoto to escape his wicked half-brother, the shogun (generalissimo) Yoritomo. Besides warriors to defend him, he took with him twelve women with whom he was on intimate terms. But he soon realized that this enormous retinue was slowing him down and sent all the women back, including his favorite, Shizuka, who was pregnant with his child.

When she reached Kyoto, she was arrested and taken to Yoritomo's court. There she was interrogated as to Yoshitsune's whereabouts. But, being plucky as well as beautiful—characteristics which would come to distinguish the geisha too—she refused to give anything away. Far worse was to come. The cruel Yoritomo, discovering that she was pregnant, ordered that if the child was a boy, he should be killed immediately; he could not risk allowing any son of Yoshitsune's to live. The baby was barely out of Shizuka's womb when Yoritomo's retainers snatched him from her arms, took him down to the beach, and dashed his brains out against a rock.

Before letting her go, Yoritomo was determined to see this most famous of dancers perform. Caring nothing for her feelings, he sent an order for her to dance before him. Disdainfully she refused. Then his retainers persuaded her that she should perform a dance of supplication before the gods at Hachiman Shrine. Too late, she realized that she had been fooled. Yoritomo was watching, hidden behind a bamboo blind.

Shizuka's dance is still performed on the Japanese stage. Wearing an exquisite garment of Chinese damask over long white skirts which swirled around her feet like a train and a voluminous long-sleeved overgarment embroidered with diamonds, and with her floor-length hair swept into a loose knot on her head, she unfurled her crimson fan and stepped forward. First she performed one of the erotic *shirabyoshi* dances after which the dancers were named, singing and dancing with such grace and beauty that everyone who watched was bewitched. Then—when she was sure she had them in the palm of her hand—she burst full-throatedly into a defiant love song. Passionately she sang of Yoshitsune, her love and yearning for him, and her joy that he had successfully managed to evade his evil half-brother Yoritomo. Yoritomo was torn between rage at such effrontery and pleasure at the exquisite beauty of her voice. But she was, after all, a mere woman and therefore harmless, so he let her go unpunished.

She was still only eighteen. She returned to Kyoto where she cut off her floor-length tresses, shaved her head, and became a nun. A year later, or so the story goes, she died of grief. As for the historical Yoshitsune, he was tracked down and killed.

Japan's Great Cultural Renaissance

Living only for the moment, giving all our time to the pleasures of the moon, the snow, cherry blossoms, and maple leaves. Singing songs, drinking saké, caressing each other, just drifting, drifting. Never giving a care if we have no money, never sad in our hearts.

> Only like a plant moving on the river's current; that is what is
> called *ukiyo*—the Floating World.
>
> Ryoi Asai, c. 1661[6]

Had you arrived in Kyoto at the turn of the seventeenth century, you would have found yourself swept along with the mob to the sprawling entertainment district beside the River Kamo, stretching as far as the massive red gates of Yasaka Shrine at the foot of the Eastern Hills. One of the chief attractions was the burgeoning pleasure quarters packed with teahouses and taverns where women—who a century later would become known as geisha—sold tea or saké and might, for a consideration, entertain you with singing, dancing, or more, depending on the depth of your purse. Here and there on open-air stages, under wooden roofs, groups of women performed lively dances to the plink plonk of the shamisen or the tootle of the flute while their audiences lounged on red felt rugs or low platforms, tucking into picnics.

Kyoto was the official capital of the country and, along with the bustling mercantile city of Osaka, the center of commerce and culture. Artists of the time painted people in festive robes dancing through the streets between red-painted temples and tile-roofed wooden houses, and crowding to see performances of dance, music, and drumming. Outside the wattle fencing surrounding the stages were stalls selling food. Inside, women in rich kimonos, men with wicker hats or samurai swords, even a couple of Portuguese with big collars, bulbous noses, and tall hats, stood watching the shows.

You could gawk at puppets, wrestling, jugglers, or sword swallowers, laugh at the clowns and jesters, admire the rare animals in cages, try your skill at target practice, shoot darts in the blowpipe parlor, or while away the day in singing and dancing. There you would have felt sorely tempted to fritter away the rest of your life in fun. There was everything a person could want, enough to distract and delight him for the rest of his days. It was an entertainment mecca, a nonstop medieval carnival such as Chaucer might have enjoyed.

On the other side of the world, a century had passed since the heyday of the Italian Renaissance and the glorious rule of the Virgin Queen, Elizabeth I, in Britain. In Japan, after more than four hundred years of warfare and upheaval, there was peace again such as had not been seen since the halcyon days of the pleasure-loving Heian aristocrats. The country had changed beyond all recognition. As the medieval knights—the samurai—fought their bloody civil wars, Kyoto had been burned to ashes time and time again. Now all that was over. The different warring states that made up Japan had been unified, leaving the people free to turn their attention to becoming prosperous and developing the arts of peace. It was the beginning of an extraordinary Japanese Renaissance.

The man who brought all this about was the great general Ieyasu Tokugawa, who defeated the last of his rival warlords in the Battle of Sekigahara in October 1600 and declared himself shogun and ruler of all Japan. The emperor had always been merely the titular ruler of the country. He spent most of his time isolated in his splendid palace in Kyoto, performing religious rituals, and had no real power. It was Shogun Ieyasu who was the true ruler. He chose as the seat of his military administration the little fishing village of Edo, an area of marshland and rivers a few days' walk to the east of Kyoto, where he had established his castle a decade earlier. Edo gradually grew in size and importance. Eventually it was to become the great city of Tokyo.

Determined that the country would never again descend into civil war, the shoguns—Ieyasu and his successors—set about fencing in the population with rigid systems of control. Among other measures, they sealed off the country from the outside world to ensure that no subversive ideas entered to disturb the delicate balance. Foreigners and in particular Catholics were not allowed in and Japanese were not allowed to leave. Anyone breaking these rules was liable to execution. Only one small window was left open—the remote southern port of Nagasaki, where Chinese junks brought their goods and a few Protestant Dutch merchants were allowed to trade.

For the next two and a half centuries the Japanese were to develop a unique culture and lifestyle, largely free from outside influences. Western explorers were extending the bounds of the world they knew; in 1610 Henry Hudson discovered Hudson Bay, in 1620 the Pilgrim Fathers reached New England and millions of slaves were being shipped from Africa to the Old and the New Worlds. The Dutch were a power all over the globe and had laid claim to an area which they called New

Amsterdam, later to be known as New York. But the doors of Japan remained firmly closed.

To create a well-ordered society in which there would be no room for the slightest possibility of rebellion or upheaval, the shogunate adopted neo-Confucianism, with its rigid codes of behavior and emphasis on hierarchy and respect for authority, as the official basis of government and the underlying ethical code for society. The system remained in force until the end of the Tokugawa period in 1853, after which in theory it began to change. But many of the attitudes and social structures which it engendered remain in place to this day.

The shoguns divided society into rigid classes, with a different set of laws governing each. Sumptuary laws were issued decreeing what each class could and could not wear, what they should eat, how they should wear their hair, where they could and could not live, whom they could marry, and how they should decorate their houses.

At the top of the hierarchy were the daimyo, provincial princes who governed their own domains but had to pledge fealty to the shogun. Then came the samurai, the military class who had grown in numbers mightily during the years of warfare and were now the army, police, and administrators of the new system. Below the samurai came the farmers, who ranked high because they were responsible for producing the rice by which everyone lived, though in fact they had miserable lives. They were followed by the artisans, who were also producers; they were craftsmen and builders.

Right at the bottom came tradesmen and merchants who, so the argument went, produced nothing. They just passed goods around from the producers to everyone else, skimming off a profit along the way, and were thus considered worthless parasites. In reality, of course, they were absolutely essential to the life of the country, ensuring that goods were shuttled from the provinces, where they were produced, to be sold in the cities.

In practice the main division was between the samurai and the rest, lumped together as "townsmen." But the trouble with relegating merchants to the very bottom was that the samurai desperately needed and wanted the goods which the merchants sold and quickly spent their miserable stipends on them. Over the centuries their stipends never increased at all; they were rigidly prescribed. So the merchants started lending money, first to the samurai, then the daimyo, and eventually to the shogun himself, and thus became richer and richer.

There were a couple of classes so low that they did not even feature in the Tokugawa ranking system. One was the *hinin* (nonhumans), most of whom were beggars or did the work that no one else wanted to do. The other encompassed popular entertainers—everyone from grand courtesans, dancers, tea-serving wenches, saké servers, and itinerant prostitutes to actors, roving minstrels, musicians, jugglers, and jesters. They were all lumped together under the term *kawaramono*—riverbed folk—and (unless, like the courtesans, they were lucky enough to have a patron) they lived in ghettos in the dry riverbeds and along the river banks, frontier areas of the city which were outside government control, considered unsuitable for permanent habitation because of flooding. This was the class from which the geisha were to emerge.

Like everything else in the highly regulated Confucian society of seventeenth-century Japan, prostitution needed to be organized. The best way to manage it was to control it, to herd as many prostitutes as possible into one place and to make prostitution legal there but illegal anywhere else. Along with the kabuki theater, the pleasure quarters were classified as the "bad places" where the lower orders, and anyone else who wanted to, could go to let off steam and exercise their baser instincts. But, "bad" though they were, they fulfilled a recognized need. Ironically the geisha and the whole culture of eroticism arose directly out of the rigid strictures of Confucianism; the walled cities of pleasure which were to become the heart of the counterculture in Japan were created with whole-hearted government approval.

Confucianism required unquestioning obedience to authority. Within the state, this was the shogun, acting in the name of the emperor. Within the household, it was the father, who was to be accorded as much loyalty and respect as one would give the ruler of the country. The basic unit of society was not the individual but the family, which had to be preserved and protected at all costs. A woman had to obey her father, then, after she was married, her husband, and finally, if her husband predeceased her, her son.

Marriage was a political matter, nothing to do with love. It was an alliance between families which was arranged by the head of the household with the help of a go-between, far too important a matter to be left to the will of the individuals concerned. Rather than marrying the man, a woman married into the household. She became a *yome,* which means "daughter-in-law" as well as "bride," and moved into her husband's house with her in-laws, where she was more like a glorified domestic servant than our concept of a wife.

As for conjugal sex, the only function was to produce a male heir who would ensure the continuance of the household and carry out the ritual respects due to the ancestors. Apart from that, sexual gratification was not supposed to take place within marriage. In other words, a husband was not supposed to love his wife, enjoy sex with her, or give her sexual pleasure. That was the theory; though in reality many a Japanese mother provided her daughter with a "pillow book" of sexual techniques to try and lure her husband away from the sirens of the pleasure quarters and the manifold other temptations available to him.

Just so long as a man did his duty by his wife, supported her financially and produced an heir, he was at liberty to amuse himself in any way he pleased. As François Caron, who was in Japan with the Dutch East India Company in 1639, observed, "One Man hath but one Wife, though as many Concubines as he can keep; and if that Wife do not please him, he may put her away, provided he dismiss her in a civil and honorable way. Any Man may lie with a Whore, or common Woman, although he be married, with impunitie; but the Wife may not so much as speak in private with another Man, without hazarding her life."[7]

Besides enjoying oneself with the wife and concubines, there was no disgrace in visiting the "bad places." And the options were not limited to the pleasure quarters or the female sex. In fact, a man who chose to stay home with his wife and children would have seemed a bit of a wet-blanket goody goody, probably tight-fisted, and certainly far from a stylish man about town.

The Lusty Lady of Izumo

One of the most urgent tasks for the new shogunate was to clamp down on vice, which had increased enormously over the years of civil war. Kyoto had become a center of prostitution, with women who had lost their menfolk, itinerant nuns, and unemployed shrine maidens wandering the streets. There were also thousands of prostitutes servicing travelers along the rivers and roads, at ports, and in front of shrines and temples where pilgrims gathered. The problem came to a head not long after Ieyasu Tokugawa established peace.

The cause of all the trouble was a woman named Izumo no Okuni (Okuni of Izumo). Okuni claimed to be a shrine maiden and shamaness from the Grand Shrine at Izumo (from where she took her name) though this may have just been an invention to give her an air of mystery. She was, in any case, a dazzling dancer and by definition a prostitute; in those days, the two were one and the same.

Around 1603, when peace had barely been established, she set up an open-air stage in the dry riverbed of the Kamo and, with her troupe of wandering female entertainers, began to dance. Those who saw her were electrified. After two centuries of civil war, people were hungry for pleasure, diversion, and beautiful women in silk kimonos. It was from Okuni and her dancing that the geisha, with their irresistible combination of charm, entertainment, and eroticism, were to develop.

As word spread, crowds descended on the riverbed to watch Okuni perform. Artists of the time portrayed her dancing wildly, accompanied by singers, a flute-player, and people beating hand drums before an eager audience of top-knotted samurai and robed women and children, sheltered by huge red parasols, with the townsfolk jam-packed in front of the stage.

Some of her dances were adapted from ancient folk dances. One of these was the Buddhist prayer dance, for which she dressed in priest's robes, sporting a conical black hat and baggy black trousers and carrying a bell which she struck with a small hammer. Sometimes she dressed as a Shinto priest and at other times she mimicked a Christian one, wearing a large golden rosary.

But the most thrilling part of her show was when she played a man. Audiences cheered, applauded, and roared with laughter when she sauntered out wearing brocade trousers and an animal skin jacket. With a painted mustache like a dashing young man about town, she would mime chatting up a teahouse woman, wooing a courtesan, or having an assignation in a bathhouse. Okuni's dancing was not just brilliant but cheerfully erotic. It was so extraordinary that a new word had to be coined: *kabuki,* from the verb *kabuku,* meaning "to frolic" or "to be wild and outrageous." Okuni's sexy dancing was the seed of the kabuki theater and also of the floating world of the courtesans and geisha.

Okuni's fame spread all over the country. In 1607 she and her all-women troupe went on tour to Edo and gave a public performance at the shogun's castle there. Soon there were imitators—troupes of prostitutes and courtesans performing erotic dances and bedroom farces throughout the great cities. It was showbiz; the actresses were stars. But, while the court ladies and townswomen imitated their stylish ways, men were more interested in their bodies. A contemporary wrote, "Men threw away their wealth, some forgot their fathers and mothers, others did not care if the mothers of their children were jealous . . ."

There was nothing wrong with eroticism. But the shogunate could not risk anything that threatened public order. When men started fighting over the actresses, it was time to put a stop to it. In 1628, after a major brawl, the authorities banned women from performing in public. It was a law that was extremely difficult to enforce. It had to be passed again in 1629, 1630, 1640, 1645, 1646, and 1647. Finally the manager of the last offending theater was thrown into prison and women disappeared from the public stage, not to reappear for another 250 years.

Banned from public performance, some of the women dancers took up work as prostitutes, licensed or unlicensed. Others found positions in samurai households where they gave private performances or set themselves up as teachers of music and dance. These were the sort of women who a century later were to become known as geisha.[8]

The authorities had banned women's kabuki. But they had said nothing about kabuki performed by young men, which now became hugely popular. The young men incorporated acrobatics and juggling into their kabuki and the most beautiful took on female roles.

Alas for the efforts of the authorities, these beautiful young men too were prostitutes. Those who played women dressed the part off stage as well as on. They lived in little shacks near the riverbanks, notably in the area of Kyoto called Miyagawa-cho, now one of the geisha districts, and used their performances to attract customers. Most of them were under fifteen, the age of adulthood, which probably made them all the more attractive.

For Buddhist priests who had abjured the company of women it was perfectly acceptable thus to work off their frustrations with a clean conscience. The youths also appealed to samurai, among whom homosexuality was considered the purest form of love. In any case, in this society—free of Christianity's guilt-inducing notions of sin—love was simply love. Homosexual and heterosexual love were seen as different sides of the same coin. Both, as far as the authorities were concerned, were equally liable to lead to public disorder. Eventually in 1652, after the death of a shogun who had himself been partial to young men, this variety of kabuki was also banned and replaced by kabuki played by adult males, as it is today. Thereafter kabuki and the women's world of courtesans and geisha together made up the heart of the demimonde.

Pleasure for Sale:
The Shimabara Licensed Quarter

Japan's first pleasure quarter opened in Kyoto even before Ieyasu Tokugawa's great victory of 1600. In 1589, when Tokugawa's predecessor, the enlightened warlord Hideyoshi Toyotomi, was governing the country from his castle in Osaka, one of his favorites, a stable hand called Saburoemon Hara, asked permission to open a brothel. Hideyoshi granted him a license, and he built a small walled-in quarter with a single gate, not far on foot, horseback, or by palanquin from the emperor's palace. He called it Yanagimachi (Willow Town). There he set up brothels and teahouses and installed some high-class, educated courtesans to lure the sophisticated gentlemen of Kyoto.

It was an immediate success. Hideyoshi himself used to sneak in, in disguise, with his retainers. It was, however, altogether too close to the imperial palace for propriety and in 1602 was moved to a site further south. In 1641 the quarter was finally established a decent distance from the center of the city where it would not corrupt upstanding citizens. Thereafter business continued until it burned down in 1854. But it reached the apogee of its prosperity and fame in the seventeenth and early eighteenth centuries, when, in the West, Louis XIV, the Sun King, was establishing his glittering court at Versailles and in Britain the pretty orange-seller, Nell Gwynn, was bewitching the Stuart king, Charles II, with her charms.

Thanks to the peace which the shogunate had brought about, the country was quickly becoming prosperous. An end of warfare meant that all hands could be turned to production, developing arts, crafts, and trade. Seeking a share of the growing pool of wealth, people flocked to the rapidly expanding cities.

This was the height of the Japanese Renaissance, the glittering Genroku period. By then, money lenders and merchants had built up stupendous fortunes. Samurai, trying to subsist on their stipends, were forbidden to get a job; not only was there no upward mobility, there was no downward mobility either. There was nothing they could do but borrow from the money lenders, who got richer and richer. Every now and then edicts were issued forbidding merchants from, for example, wearing silk, living in a three-story house, and decorating their rooms with gold and silver leaf or furnishing them with gold lacquer objects; edicts had to be issued, of course, because that was precisely what they were doing. These supposedly low-class townsmen lavished their money on luxuries, filling their storehouses with fabulously expensive gold screens, ceramics, lacquerware, tea bowls, books, prints, and sumptuous kimono. All this big spending further stimulated the economy by providing a market for the artisans.

But no matter how rich the merchants became, they were prohibited from using their wealth to improve their status by, for example, marrying into a samurai family or moving into the samurai section of town. And the wealthier they became, the more likely it was that the government would confiscate everything they had. Merchants did not pay taxes, as that would have given them rights; instead, every now and then, the shogunate found a pretext to seize their riches. Therefore it made ample sense to squander as much of one's fortune as possible, as quickly as possible, on pleasure—and where better to do so than in the newly burgeoning pleasure quarters!

Something had gone badly wrong in the shoguns' plans. The idea had been to sweep vice under the carpet, to restrict the perpetrators of vice—the prostitutes and the kabuki actors, their companions in sin—to specific areas of the capital and thus control both them and their vulgar customers, the nouveau-riche merchants. But instead the pleasure quarters rapidly turned into the most glamorous part of town. Everyone from samurai to the imperial princes and even the emperor himself sneaked off for surreptitious visits.

As well as sex, romance, and sensual pleasure, Shimabara offered all that a sophisticated man about town might demand: elegance, culture, and brilliant conversation with beautiful women in an atmosphere of refinement. It was a place where merchants could entertain clients and show off their glamorous connections, basking in the company of these not-quite-reputable stars. As for what happened afterward, that was practically irrelevant. The show was the thing.

In 1661 a writer called Ryoi Asai coined a word for this new way of living: *ukiyo* (the floating world) from which came the term *ukiyo-e* (pictures of the floating world) for the woodblock prints which depicted the courtesans, prostitutes, and later, geisha who were its denizens. In the past, the word *ukiyo* had been a Buddhist term, referring to the transience of all things. In Ryoi's *Tales of the Floating World,* it took on a new slant. Life was indeed transient; so what better way to spend one's time than in the pursuit of pleasure, like a gourd bobbing lightly along the stream of life!

For men it was a topsy-turvy world of pleasure which was the reverse in every way from the world of work and family outside its gates. There, it was said, a man would forget what time of day it was, what period of history, and even his own wife. There the outcast courtesans and prostitutes could play at being queens and the low-grade merchants kings. As for the samurai, who were supposedly at the top of the tree, they were dismissed as bumpkins.

For the women, however, it was no dream. It was where they lived and worked. Even if they wanted to leave, their wings were clipped. Gorgeous though they were, the inhabitants of the pleasure quarters were caged birds. They had been brought to the quarter as small children and had grown up entirely in this hothouse world of women. They knew nothing else. For all their finery and glamour, they were virtual slaves, indentured to the brothel owners.

Almost all were from the lower classes, the beautiful children of impoverished rural families or debt-ridden townsfolk. There were professional procurers or pimps, called *zegen,* who scoured the countryside and poorer sections of the city. When they found a suitable child, they would offer the parents a set sum of money. Buying or selling of persons was illegal so the child would be bound with a contract for a fixed period of time, usually ten years.

For the parents, sending a child off to the pleasure quarters was nothing out of the ordinary; it is still done to this day in Asia. Apart from the much-needed money and the brutal necessity of reducing the number of mouths to be fed, they probably felt they were giving their daughter a chance in life. Going to Kyoto to eat fine food, wear fine clothes, meet fine people, and be educated offered far more hope than staying in the countryside hoeing the soil for the rest of her life. As for the child, according to the Confucian code it was her filial duty to put the well-being of her family ahead of her own. Girls who were sold to the pleasure quarters were considered virtuous and admirable for having sacrificed themselves for their family.

Most were recruited when they were six or seven and had only the haziest memories of life outside the walls of the pleasure quarter. While peasants were lucky if they had millet, the children in Shimabara ate white rice, wore beautiful kimonos, and learned to walk, talk, and comport themselves in the exaggeratedly feminine style of the quarter. Shimabara had its own dialect, as did the other pleasure quarters, with distinctive slang that was charmingly polite yet playfully seductive. Any child who managed to escape could thus be immediately identified by the way she spoke and sent back again. For visitors it made the pleasure quarters feel all the more like a dream world, an exotic foreign land.

The children were the property of the brothel owner. Before they even arrived, they had already incurred an enormous debt: the outlay involved in buying them from their parents. Their food and kimono were provided by the brothel; but every grain of rice and every bolt of silk only served to increase the burden of debt. By the time they were old enough to start working, their debt was so huge that they had no choice but to work day and night in a desperate attempt to repay it.

Initially the children worked as maids. When they were older, if they showed promise they became *kamuro* (child attendants to a courtesan). The courtesan taught them how to behave and ensured that they were trained in accomplishments such as calligraphy, tea ceremony, and music. There were many little secrets to be absorbed: how to lure men, how to wind them around their little fingers with tears or protestations of undying love, how to write love letters, how to hold men off long enough to drive them mad with desire, how to pleasure them in the bedchamber, and how to fake an orgasm while conserving one's energy for the next customer. The key rule was to play at love but never, never to allow oneself to feel it. That way lay disaster.

At thirteen or fourteen, when the child reached sexual maturity, there was a grand celebration accompanied by a rite of passage which the girl had to accept with gritted teeth—*mizuage,* literally "raising or offering up the waters"—ritual deflowerment, conducted by a patron who had paid mightily for the privilege. If she was uncommonly lovely she might be designated a *koshi,* the second rank of courtesan, though there were many that slipped through the net and ended up as lower-grade prostitutes, sitting patiently behind the latticed windows of the teahouses waiting to be chosen by a customer.

At the very pinnacle of the hierarchy of prostitutes and courtesans were the *tayu,* the aristocrats of the courtesan world. Some were the concubines and courtesans of the imperial princes; unlike the lower ranks of courtesans, *tayu* were permitted inside the palace. And in their leisure time the princes went on horseback or by palanquin to amuse themselves at the famous Shimabara pleasure quarters where the *tayu* lived.

If a man wanted to enjoy the company of a *tayu,* the first step was to go to an *ageya,* a house of assignation (the precursor of the teahouses of the geisha districts) to apply for a meeting. If he was a sophisticate, he would ask for one of the *tayu* by name; some were so popular that it might take months before a day became free in their calendar. The owner of the *ageya* would write a letter to the bordello where the courtesan lived, roll it up, and give it to a messenger. While the customer was waiting, he would enjoy the services of jesters and dancing girls and ply them with food and drink, all of which, of course, would be added to his bill.

Hours later, the *tayu* would sweep in, dressed in layer upon layer of gorgeous kimonos and accompanied by a flotilla of child attendants and dancing girls, having progressed at snail's pace along the boulevard with her entourage. They would while away the evening playing music, dancing, exchanging poems, and enjoying the tea ceremony and incense ceremony—exactly as if they were ladies and gentlemen of the Heian court. Sex did not automatically follow. After all, it would lower the courtesan's worth if she were too easily available. A proprietor who owned a beautiful *tayu* would want to increase the value of his or her investment by making her as exclusive as possible.

If the man wanted to spend the night with the courtesan, he would have to engage in a long and very expensive courtship. The earliest that one could hope to experience her luxurious silk bedding was at the third visit. And even then, if the *tayu* was not satisfied with the man's performance, she could decline to sleep with him. If she did agree to spend the night with him, the cost was 90 silver nuggets *(momme)* which equaled one and a half gold nuggets *(ryo),* in modern currency about $675. It was costly but, for a wealthy man, the only sort of person whom a *tayu* would consider, hardly prohibitive.[9]

The *koshi,* the second rank courtesans, charged sixty silver nuggets, and the *sancha* (teahouse waitresses-*cum*-courtesans) charged thirty. At the Shimabara even the lowest class of prostitutes, the *hashi,* whom one could buy for just one silver nugget, were said to be elegant.

But no matter how famous the courtesans became, they were still slaves of debt, constrained to work out their ten-year contract. In fact the system ensured that, no matter how hard they worked, their debts only increased. There were always new costs being incurred—the purchasing of the splendid kimonos necessary to carry on their trade, the costs of bedding and of clothing and supporting their retinue of retainers, the tips that had to be paid to the bordello staff. They had just three days off a year. If they missed a day's work for any reason at all they had to pay the bordello out of their own pocket the sum they would have earned. Most carried on working until they were twenty-seven, the usual retirement age. Those who were successful would have plenty of supplicants begging to marry them after that.

They probably accepted the hardships with stoicism. That was the way it was in the floating world and, in any case, any other life would have had its hardships too. Within the narrow confines of their gilded cage they were queens. The one chance of escape—if they wanted it—was to find someone prepared to buy out their contract and make them his wife or mistress. As the old saying went, the courtesan's favorite lie was "I love you," the customer's "I will marry you."

The names and rankings changed over the centuries but everyone agreed that the greatest courtesans of all time were the *tayu* of seventeenth-century Shimabara.

The Courtesan and the Swordsman

In the early days of the Shimabara quarter, there were seven celebrated *tayu* courtesans in Kyoto. Of these, Yoshino was the most adored. Many legends have gathered around her, not least that she was the lover of Miyamoto Musashi, the greatest swordsman of all time and author of *The Book of Five Rings* (a bible for practitioners of the martial arts and more recently for businessmen). He learned his secrets, so the story goes, from the gentle but insightful Yoshino.

Yoshino was entertaining him and his friends in the pleasure quarter one snowy night when he slipped quietly out of the room. She was the only one to notice him leave. He returned a few minutes later. But there was a splash of red on the hem of his kimono.

"What is that?" asked one of his friends.

"Just a peony petal," said Yoshino and quickly wiped it away with a napkin.

When the party came to an end, she suggested lightly that he had better stay there with her. With her unerring instinct she had guessed that he had been engaged in a duel to the death in the few minutes he had been away. The retainers of the two men whom he had killed, several dozen of them, were waiting right outside to ambush him and exact revenge.

Sitting in her chamber he was silent, tense in anticipation of the hopeless battle that lay ahead. Suddenly Yoshino picked up her *biwa,* a priceless lute, took a knife, and smashed the curved sound box to pieces. From the ruined instrument she picked out the crosspiece, a single piece of wood, and showed it to him.

This, she explained, was the heart of the instrument; all the sound came from this. If the crosspiece were as taut and unyielding as he was at that moment, a single stroke of the plectrum would break it. But if he could be as flexible and responsive as it was, no one could defeat him. Inspired by her words, he bounded out into the snow and, with a few nonchalant slashes of his sword, decimated the dozens of men gathered outside. For the rest of his sword-wielding career, he never forgot her or her advice.

The historical Yoshino was born on the third day of the third month 1606. She was sold to the pleasure quarters at the age of six and at fourteen was so beautiful and accomplished that she was promoted to the rank of *tayu,* a rare and extraordinary honor. So famous and so hugely desired was she that she had no need ever to bestow her favors on anyone. Her wealthy and adoring patrons made sure that her income was high enough for her to be able to pay all her annual expenses in advance. But no matter how much they paid her, she kept them at a distance, hopelessly yearning for her.

One day she was called to entertain at a gathering of Kyoto's most influential literary coterie, presided over by the emperor's fourth son. There she met Joeki Haiya, a merchant's son. Not only was he handsome, refined, and accomplished enough to satisfy the most demanding courtesan, he was an adept of the tea ceremony, which he hosted with wonderful finesse, and also extremely rich. At the time he was twenty-two, she twenty-six. He fell hopelessly in love, so much so that he laid out the enormous fortune necessary to buy out her contract, for—beautiful, accomplished, and celebrated though she was—she was still the property of the bordello keeper. Having bought her freedom, he married her.

Thus far is history. The rest may or may not be legend. Joeki's adoptive father, goes the story, was furious that the boy had brought the family into disrepute and disowned him. After all, Yoshino might be a superstar but until she married she had been a glorified prostitute who made her living by selling her body (or so he thought). Reduced to poverty, the lovebirds retired to a humble house on the outskirts of Kyoto. Joeki began to sell off his much-loved collection of tea ceremony utensils to support them.

Then one day Joeki's father, far from home, was caught in a rainstorm and sought shelter under the eaves of an unprepossessing house. Through the window he heard a gentle, refined voice inviting him to rest inside. He walked across the stepping stones of a humble but perfectly arranged garden and into a house where everything, though poor, was of the most exquisite taste. On a wall was a single piece of calligraphy by the most accomplished master of the day.

The lady of the house appeared, dressed in a plain, humble kimono which could only enhance her radiant beauty. Dignified and gracious, she knelt and performed a tea ceremony for him, whipping up a bowl of foaming green tea. On returning home he recounted the tale of his adventure to friends and discovered that this vision was none other than Yoshino. He summoned his son immediately, was reconciled with him, and took the couple back into his family.

Yoshino died in 1643 at the age of thirty-eight (very young in modern terms but not so extraordinary in those days). Joeki grieved for her for the rest of his life. Without her, he declared, the magnificent city of Kyoto, with all its luxury and culture, was nothing but a desert.

Music of a Bygone Age

Once the most glittering of pleasure quarters, today Shimabara has become a shabby backwater. But there are a couple of splendid old buildings with blackened beams and tatami-matted rooms, where five or six women still preserve the *tayu* traditions. There in a huge, ancient house called Wachigaiya, I came face to face with one.

She was a tiny fairy-like creature, barely visible beneath her voluminous layered kimonos. Her face was chalky, her eyebrows and eyes etched in black and her underlip an intense peony red. Her hair was swept into loops and coils, as bulky as a Restoration wig. On it she supported an enormously ornate headdress studded with tortoiseshell and silver hairpins and decorated with silk flowers and foliage, with dangling mother-of-pearl ornaments and strings of coral weighted with gold-leaf blossoms.

She was wrapped in layer upon layer of priceless antique kimonos. At her throat was a thick collar of beige brocade embroidered with a swirling pattern of irises. On top of that came a red kimono with a quilted hem which swept the floor and swung heavily as she walked, and above that an exquisite robe of thick black silk glistened with lustrous gold flowers, swirling around her feet like a train. The obi, a swathe of orange silk brocade with a gold-thread design of chrysanthemums and maple leaves, was tied in the front in an enormous knot which hung in great folds from her waist to her knees. This was a symbol of her availability. In theory it might be untied—if you happened to be rich and fortunate enough to be permitted to do so.

Underneath it all, she had a cheeky, elfin face with a tiny nose and pointed chin. How long had she been a *tayu*, I asked, then gasped when she opened her small mouth to answer. In the chalky-white face with the blood-red lips, her teeth were painted black. It was macabre, like looking into a black hole.

Four years was the answer. She was twenty-four and she was interested in the particular styles of dance and music which the *tayu* performed, quite different from the dance and music of the geisha tradition. She was fascinated, she said, by the history and traditions of the *tayu* and the stories of the great *tayu* of old. She loved the world of darkness and shadow in which the *tayu* moved. It was, she said, more *shibui* than the geisha tradition. The word *shibui,* which literally translates as "astringent" or "sober," evokes a mood of old gold, glimmering shadows, and rust.

Dusk had fallen. In the banqueting hall guests were waiting, cross-legged on the floor. The women among them knelt demurely. Huge smoking candles flickered, set in tall golden candlesticks. Dimly visible in the gloom of an alcove was an ancient scroll bearing a poem brushed with exquisite skill.

Then the *tayu* appeared, framed in the doorway like a visitation from another age. She was transformed, she was a shamaness. Aloof, withdrawn, self-contained, she did not speak, smile, or glance at the guests. She was to be looked at, not to look. As she swept gracefully into the room, deftly swinging the heavy quilted train of the kimono, more layers became visible, rippling at the sleeve and hem.

Solemnly she knelt, lifted a shallow red-lacquered bowl brimming with saké and put it to her lips. Then she picked up a *kokyu,* an instrument shaped like a small shamisen with a square base and long narrow neck, and rested it on her knees. Taking a bow strung so loosely that it looked as if it could not possibly produce any sound, she scraped it across the strings to coax out a thin scratchy melody, turning the instrument so that the bow touched each of the three strings.

It was an extraordinary, archaic sound. It lifted the hairs on the back of your neck and took you back across the centuries to a time when, one could imagine, rakes and dandies dissipated fortunes in places such as this. Lastly, rising to her feet, she danced, mesmerizingly slow and stately, while the guests and I, sitting in the shadows, watched, entranced.

But the most unforgettable thing was that under the layers and layers of brocade and silk, her tiny feet were bare. It was the most erotic sight, it sent a shiver up the spine. They peeked from beneath the heavy finery, the only reminder that underneath the painted face, the priceless headdress, the three layers of under-kimono and four layers of over-kimono, there was a real woman.

It must have been even more poignant in the old days, if anyone then ever stopped to think about it. For in those days, for all their sumptuous finery, their robes embroidered with gorgeous landscapes and their velvet and damask bedding, the courtesans did not own their own bodies. They were chattels, to be bought and sold.

The Harlot Queens
of the Nightless City

> *Closing time is midnight—*
> *So why do I now hear*
> *The wooden clappers*
> *Strike out four times?*
> *In Yoshiwara, even the*
> *Wooden rhythm sticks are liars.*
>
> Geisha song[10]

When Saburoemon Hara was petitioning to start a brothel in the great city of Kyoto, Edo was nothing but a few fishermen's shacks in a marshy area where three rivers met. But once Shogun Ieyasu established it as his capital it became a boomtown such as the world had never seen before. It was here, in the rough northeast of the country, in the shadow of the shogun's castle, that a pleasure quarter was to develop which would put all the others in the shade. This was where the culture of love was to be taken to its zenith and the geisha were to flower.

It was a gold rush. People flocked from all over the country to help in the building of the new city and make their fortunes. Mansions, palaces, temples, shrines, shops, stalls, and houses sprang up, while alleys, roads, and a maze of canals that made the city an eastern Venice spiraled out from the walls of the shogun's castle to the newly reclaimed land beside the river. In 1500 Edo had a population of 1,000; in the early 1600s it was an urban center of 150,000. By the end of the seventeenth century it was the largest city in the world with a population of well over one million. London, the largest European city, had yet to reach a million.

Edo was a man's city, a frontier town akin to those of America's Wild West, with just as many bars, brothels, and brawls. More than half the population were samurai, retainers of the daimyo (the ex-warlords who governed the provinces). This was a direct result of the shogun's policy of *sankin kotai* (alternate attendance), which required all the daimyo to maintain a mansion in Edo as well as their provincial seat. While they had to shuttle back and forth, their families lived permanently in Edo, effectively hostages, supported by a huge staff of vassal samurai. Most of the samurai were unmarried; they could not afford to support a family on their stipends. To add to this multitude of men there were thousands of merchants and tradesmen from Kyoto, Osaka, and points west, who arrived to set up businesses and sent money to their wives and children back home. As the great comic novelist Saikaku Ihara wrote toward the end of the century, it was "a City of Bachelors."

All these frustrated men provided fertile soil for prostitution. Among the flood of people hoping to make fortunes or at least stay afloat in the new city were a goodly number of harlots, not to mention procurers and brothel-keepers who came from all over the country. Even before anyone had been given a license to open a pleasure quarter, professional brothel-keepers from Kyoto who had spotted an irresistible opportunity were erecting a red-light district with streets and beautiful wooden houses in a broad grassland dense with rushes near the coast. Just as in later years, when the geisha areas became cultural centers, the district offered far more than sex. There was also plentiful entertainment: kabuki, shrine dancing, temple dancing, the spider dance, the lion dance, wrestling, singing, and twanging *joruri* music. "How these conspiring courtesans allure men without resorting to force is beyond our comprehension," wrote a commentator of the time disapprovingly.[11]

Following the initiative of Hara, who had founded Shimabara, a wealthy brothel-owner named Jinemon Shoji petitioned the shogun for a license to establish an official pleasure quarter. Like Shimabara, the Yoshiwara was built, rebuilt, moved, and burned down in a fire before it was finally established in 1656 in a reed plain *(yoshi wara)* a decent hour's journey from the city.

By the end of the century it was far larger than the country's other famous pleasure quarters. Shimabara women were said to be the most beautiful; Shinmachi, where the playboy merchants of Osaka went to enjoy themselves, had the most sumptuous buildings and luxurious facilities; the women of Maruyama in Nagasaki wore the most gorgeous kimonos; but the Yoshiwara girls outdid them all with their *hari* (attitude or style). At its height there were more than three thousand courtesans in the Yoshiwara, though only a few held the rank of *tayu*.

For the people of Edo, the Yoshiwara offered nonstop drama. The vast majority, who could never even dream of being able to afford an evening with a courtesan, could still follow their exploits in print. For the pleasure quarters together with the kabuki theater were the heart of a cultural renaissance, both democratic and subversive, produced by, for, and about the townsfolk and treated with great suspicion by the shogunate who made periodic attempts to clamp down on it. The courtesans and their clientele were the prime subject matter of woodblock prints, kabuki plays, and the courtesan critiques and *tayu* biographies which poured off the newly developed printing presses. Like the lives of the rich and famous today, they offered endless fascination and vicarious excitement.

The stories of the time are full of grand guignol—passion, love, debauchery, men ruined for love, suicides, deaths—and also of ribald humor. Like the great *tayu* of Kyoto, the courtesans of the Yoshiwara stood the usual customer/merchandise relationship on its head. They were at liberty to turn down any client, no matter how wealthy or aristocratic. Many of the sizzling stories of the day, much appreciated by the townsfolk, concern courtesans who rejected lovesick nobles and fell in love with handsome but low-born and impoverished clerks.

Much as the lower orders loved such bodice-ripping melodramas, the real lives of the courtesans tended to be a lot more down to earth. Besides the elegant, high-class courtesans of the official pleasure quarter, there were also many unlicensed and distinctly lower-class prostitutes operating illegally. Around the mid-1600s, many of these were to be found in bathhouses. These were a little like the Turkish baths of today, with large reception areas where customers could lounge, drink tea, and be entertained after bathing. As far as the Yoshiwara brothel-keepers were concerned, this was unwarranted competition. They frequently petitioned the shogunate to have it stamped out.

Katsuyama was a real-life prostitute who appeared at a bathhouse called Tanzen in 1646. She was a beauty with a warm, open face and a cheeky, larger-than-life personality. But what the customers loved most was when she dressed up as a man. There had been nothing like it since Izumo no Okuni took to the stage dressed as a man back in 1603 and stunned the populace with her wild *kabuku* dancing. Wearing a wicker hat, man's kimono, and two swords like a samurai, Katsuyama would bring the house down with the Tanzen-bushi dance, named after the bathhouse, strutting and swaggering in jaunty macho fashion. As with all such dances, there was an erotic coda.

Katsuyama became so popular that she outshone all the *tayu* of the Yoshiwara. In 1653, after a brawl between a bunch of townsfolk and some rival samurai, the authorities closed down the bathhouse. Katsuyama was head-hunted by one of the top Yoshiwara bordellos, which gave her instant promotion to *tayu*. When she made her first grand procession down the main boulevard of the quarter to an assignation with a client, the great courtesans were so curious about this upstart that they all turned out to watch. They were so impressed with the cocky way in which she kicked out her feet in the "figure of eight" walk and with her distinctive topknot that the "Katsuyama gait" and the "Katsuyama knot" continued to be in vogue for a century afterward.

The whole thing was a game. Like any game, you had to play it to the best of your ability and you had to stick to the rules; but in the long run it was not to be taken too seriously. And whatever went on in the licentious night-time dreamworld of the Yoshiwara was always forgotten the next day. It never infected the world outside those enchanted walls. That tradition carried over into the world of the geisha. Mystery was of the essence.

It was all showbiz. But in the floating world, nothing could continue unchanged for long. By the eighteenth century, the pleasure quarter culture had been thriving for over a hundred years. The courtesans, with their stilted conversation and layer upon layer of starchy clothing, were beginning to seem a little passé. It was time for something new.

Gradually the number of women worthy to be designated *tayu* began to decline. The term itself, which had been used exclusively in Shimabara, disappeared as the focus of culture and life shifted to Edo. The last recorded *tayu* was in 1761. (The *tayu* of Wachigaiya, sadly, are not a continuation of the line but actresses, playing out a charade, a recreation of a lost era.)

It was then that a new breed of woman first began to step out not just in the pleasure quarters but in the town: a woman who was not a caged bird, who dressed with understated sophistication, not showy glitter, and who sold not her body but her arts.

chapter 2

the world of the geisha

Love, Passion, and Jealousy

In the floating world where all things change
Love never changes by promising never to change.
 Geisha song[1]

Love and Death

 Love was the currency of the fantasy world in which the geisha operated, yet for a geisha to fall in love was a disaster. In the past, at least,
the geisha's profession was fueled by desire; just as today, where rock and
roll stars roll their hips suggestively, groupies line up to service them,
and actresses wear more and more revealing dresses to the Oscars, the
entertainment industry was predicated on it. But it was a perilous game:
to flirt with men, to snuggle up to them, to stir their desire so that they
would call for you again but—no matter how intimate you appeared to

be—never to lose your head, let alone your heart. The edge of danger was one of the things that gave the game its excitement.

To play at love was one thing, really to fall in love quite another—and in the supercharged world of the geisha it was always a danger. Usually the courtesan or geisha would fall in love with someone young, handsome, and poor who was not even a customer. If they fell in love with a customer, that would be equally disastrous, for customers were inevitably married. Once the pair were overcome by desire and could no longer endure the limitations imposed by society on their meetings, they were doomed. Unlike such love affairs in the West, marriage was almost never the answer.

Often the only solution was death. In fact to die together came to seem so hugely romantic that many couples yearned to express their love for each other in this way, like Romeo and Juliet. The great dramatist Chikamatsu Monzaemon (1653–1724), often described as the Shakespeare of Japan, created a whole genre of kabuki plays about double suicide, of which the most famous was *Love Suicides at Sonezaki,* inspired by a real-life incident in 1703.

The stage version of the story goes as follows: the beautiful nineteen-year-old courtesan Ohatsu is in love with Tokubei, a handsome twenty-five-year-old clerk who is far too poor to be able to buy her out of bondage. His uncle has arranged a marriage for him with a wealthy relative but Tokubei informs him that he cannot go through with it. He therefore needs to return the dowry which has already been paid to him. But he has already lent the money to the wicked Kuheiji, an oil merchant whom he imagines to be a friend of his. When Tokubei demands the money back, Kuheiji denies all knowledge of the loan. Kuheiji then swaggers off to the brothel to make his suit to Ohatsu; he too wants to buy her. Hiding beneath the verandah, Tokubei overhears his suit. The lovers are ruined. The only recourse is to commit suicide.

Ohatsu puts on a white kimono, signifying death (corpses in Japan are dressed in white), with a black cloak above it so that they will not be seen. Taking with them a rosary, the pair flee the brothel and set off for the woods of Sonezaki Shrine. As the bell tolls the coming of dawn, they pray, embrace each other for the last time, then bind themselves tightly to a tree so as to look beautiful even in death. Weeping, Tokubei takes out his dagger and cuts her throat, then, with a razor, slashes his own. By their deaths, these two humble people have become ennobled. "They have become models of true love," declares the narrator in the final words of the play.[2]

Chikamatsu's plays were so successful that they inspired a boom in copycat love suicides. By 1722 there was such an epidemic that the government banned plays about double suicide and took stern measures against such suicides themselves, displaying the perpetrators, dead or alive, for three days and condemning survivors to work for the untouchables, the most ignominious punishment imaginable.

But to this day love suicide is still a recognized phenomenon in Japan. Each year some young couples, prevented from marrying by parental pressure, choose this way to be together. In Japanese eyes, far from being macabre, it is profoundly romantic. On a recent visit to Japan, some friends asked me how many love suicides there were a year in Britain. They were completely incredulous when I told them there were none.

The most celebrated love suicide of modern times was the novelist Osamu Dazai (1909–1948), a fin-de-siècle character who lived not at the end of a century but at the end of an era, as Japan was slipping inexorably toward apocalyptic war. A writer of intensely passionate, sometimes sardonic novels chronicling the dying gasps of the crumbling Japanese aristocracy, he was an attractive, hard drinking, devil-may-care kind of man, obsessed with dying a beautiful death.

While still a student, he met a geisha named Hatsuyo Oyama, moved her in with him, and took her down to Tokyo where he was to study French literature at the Imperial University. But his grandmother, the stern old matriarch of their wealthy and very conservative northern family, was fiercely opposed to any alliance with a geisha. She disinherited him.

Almost out of pique Dazai made a suicide pact with another woman whom he had picked up on a drinking spree. It was 1930 and he was twenty-one. They went down to the coast at Kamakura, just outside Tokyo, and flung themselves into the sea. As luck would have it the girl drowned but Dazai survived. His brother had to rush down to Tokyo to hush things up.

Later he tried to commit suicide with Hatsuyo, his geisha lover, after she had had an affair with one of his friends while he was in hospital trying to conquer his addiction to painkillers. He himself had incessant affairs; but the notion of his lover/wife having an affair was more than he could tolerate. The two went off to a hot spring resort in the mountains and took an overdose of barbiturates together. This time both lived, and Dazai went on to write a succession of brilliant novels.

After the war he was acclaimed as Japan's greatest postwar novelist and awarded several literary prizes. His debauched lifestyle continued. He had a wife and child and a mistress and child and was working on a novel called *Goodbye,* a comic tale of how a man rids himself of a succession of unwanted women. He had also begun a new relationship with a woman named Tomie Yamazaki. On June 13, 1948, the pair drowned themselves together in the Tamagawa Reservoir. It was a fitting end, the death he had been looking for so long. He was just a few days short of his fortieth birthday.[3]

Of Love and Kissing

There are many different words for love in Japanese, none of which means quite the same as the English word—though it is important to remember that what we, modern English speakers, mean by "love" is probably not at all the same as what the ancient Greeks, the Romans, or the medieval troubadours of courtly love meant by it or, for that matter, the modern-day French, Italians, or anyone else. Love is an invention, culturally conditioned; notions of love vary place by place, era by era, and culture by culture.

Unlike the chivalrous knights of the European Middle Ages who devoted themselves to unattainable ladies, suffered torments of undeclared passion, and yearned after women whom they saw as goddesses, put on pedestals, and worshipped, Japanese men fell in love with real women, not bloodless ideals. They did not go to war with a scented glove tucked into their armor. It was possible to have sex without love—in fact, that was by far the safest course. But no one ever considered the possibility of love without sex. In fact the closest they ever came to the European notion of courtly love was probably the samurai's idealized love of beautiful boys. According to the *Hagakure,* an eighteenth-century treatise on samurai ethics, this was a form of love which was purest when it remained undeclared.

Love never resulted in marriage—which meant that there was no culture of wooing, courting, dating, and finally falling to one's knees one moonlit night and slipping the ring shyly onto the finger. Thus a 1915 visitor could write, "The fact is, of course, that Cupid has a very bad time in this country; it is an unknown land to him. Soft eyes and coy glances, fair spring days and moonlight nights in autumn, wanderings in country lanes and by the sea, hand-squeezing, sighing, sweet confidences, and all the other 'ministers of love' have no place here."[4]

In fact by then Japanese intellectuals knew all about the Western concept of love. They called it *rabu,* the Japanese phoneticization of the English word, to differentiate the noble emotion of platonic love from base physical passion. It had an extra luster because it was an exotic foreign emotion conveyed in a foreign word, rather like talking about *amour* or *amore* instead of just plain love. In the late nineteenth century and early twentieth century there were many angst-ridden Japanese novels written celebrating *rabu*.

The novelist Kafu Nagai, who spent his whole life among geisha, prostitutes, and bar girls and went to the grave with a geisha's name tattooed on his body, wrote that the most transcendent moment of his life was when he exchanged a few words with a young American woman on Staten Island. They talked of opera, the irrelevance of marriage, and the poetry of the night sky, then parted with a gentle handshake.

"I felt strangely forlorn," wrote Kafu the great sensualist, "at the thought that never again as long as I lived would such a beautiful thing happen to me."[5] It was an experience of *rabu,* pure and unadulterated by the gross physical passion which permeated all his other relationships.

It is still awkward to say in Japanese "I love you," partly because, like the equally reticent British, Japanese do not usually express such emotions in words. The most common phrase is *suki desu* which literally means only "I like you"—though, as always in Japan, the meaning is communicated more through intonation and gut feeling than through the words themselves. The phrase "to fall in love" is rendered by a rather clumsy direct translation of the English words. Under "love," an English-Japanese conversation dictionary published as recently as 1969 comments, "Marriage in Japan is generally arranged by the parents and is seldom the result of mutual love. The Japanese language therefore is poor in expressions of affection and those which exist are apt to be taken in a bad sense."[6]

Likewise the most commonly used word for kiss is the adopted *kissu,* not surprising for a society where kissing was until very recently considered a shockingly private and erotic activity. Even in the woodblock prints depicting the floating world of the courtesans and geisha, kissing is almost never shown. After all, it was probably not very appealing to press one's mouth up against a face covered in white lead-based paint, added to which a courtesan or a geisha would be reluctant to smudge her makeup. In fact the erotic touching of lips was one of the most esoteric of the geishas' arsenal of sexual techniques.

Long before the word *kissu* was coined, in 1878, Junichiro Oda, one of the first translators of English literature into Japanese, came across the outlandish phrase "I should sleep well if I could get one kiss from those coral lips" in Edward Bulwer-Lytton's *Ernest Maltravers*; to Japanese of the time it was virtually incomprehensible and distinctly pornographic. Showing great ingenuity, he rendered it ". . . if I could get one lick of your red lips." His readers probably thought the concept as well as the words quite hilarious.[7]

Kissing, in fact, was not part of normal human interaction. It was considered so indecent that when there was a proposal for August Rodin's statue *The Kiss* to be exhibited in Tokyo in the 1930s, there was public outrage. The police banned it. There was a suggestion that the sculpture should be shown with the heads wrapped in a cloth so that no one would see the offensive kissing; the naked bodies were not a problem. In the end the Rodin was not shown until after the Second World War, which was also when the first screen kiss occurred in a Japanese film.

I bathed my snow skin
In pure Tamagawa River.
Our quarrel is loosened slowly,
And he loosens my hair.
I am all uncombed.
I will not remember him,
I will not altogether forget him,
I will wait for Spring.

Geisha song[8]

To fall in love with a geisha was to play with fire—as Hideo, a youthful curator at a Tokyo modern art museum, discovered. He was in a hole-in-the-wall drinking house a couple of years ago in Shibuya, a bustling, fashionable, youthful Tokyo neighborhood, when he met a bewitching young woman. She was twenty-three, he not yet thirty. She was wearing rather gaudy clothes, too bright, too tight, and too revealing; at first he took her for a prostitute or a bar girl. But her face enthralled him. For the quiet studious young man she was a vision from another world. It was only after they had become lovers that she revealed she was indeed from another world: she was a geisha.

He showed me photographs of a laughing girl with a mane of tumbling black hair and a dazzlingly lovely face. She might have been a model; she had one of those perfectly proportioned faces with porcelain skin, a delicate nose, and eyes and mouth a little larger than life. He also had pictures of her as a geisha, kneeling demurely in a kimono, her face a bland white mask.

"I preferred her real face," he said. "I never saw her geisha life or met her geisha friends. I once went to see her when she gave a public dance performance, but that was it. She kept me well away from that side of her life."

She had grown up in the poorest, slummiest part of Osaka, a wildflower springing up on a dung heap. When she was fourteen her father walked out, leaving her behind with her overworked hairdresser mother. At seventeen she took the train to Tokyo and found a job as a hostess in a sleazy bar.

Then she met a professional gambler. He rented a luxury apartment in an expensive area of Tokyo for her, gave her an allowance and bought her all the clothes she wanted, then moved in himself.

She had always daydreamed about being a geisha; she was drawn by the beauty and brightness of the geisha life. But she had never before imagined that it might be possible. To join a geisha house, take classes, and buy the requisite number of kimonos cost a fortune, far more than a girl like her could ever afford. But the gambler had money and, more important, the right connections. He took her to meet the proprietress of a geisha house in one of the five Tokyo flower towns and she was accepted. Thereafter she lived with him and worked as a member of the geisha house.

Then she met Hideo. Compared to the customers at the teahouses where she entertained, he was a boy, not much older than she was. He was smooth-skinned and bespectacled, earnest and serious, part of a fresher, cleaner, more real world than she had ever seen before. He talked intensely about art, aesthetics, music, and the meaning of life. Whatever he said was sincere. He did not flirt or play games like the customers did.

And he had no money. He had only himself to offer. He could not even take her out on a date, let alone support her or buy her expensive kimonos. On the rare occasions when they went out for a meal, she paid. For the first time in her life, here was a man that she could love for himself, not because of what she could get from him.

Their love affair had to be secret. She was not supposed to spend time with anyone who was not a customer, let alone sleep with him. He was getting for nothing what other men paid a fortune for, if they got it at all.

"She was so bright and full of joy," said the young man wistfully. "She really made me feel alive. I'd been feeling low when I met her. She'd come over and we'd go out drinking. It was as if the sun had come out."

Then, a year after she met Hideo, a customer who had seen her at teahouse parties took a fancy to her. Following the proper procedure, he approached the teahouse proprietress and said that he would like to become her *danna,* a word that in the geisha world means patron-*cum-*

lover, almost like a husband. He was the chairman of an enormous corporation, one of the most powerful and wealthy businessmen in Japan. To become the mistress of a man like this was a once-in-a-lifetime opportunity.

There was only one problem. She loved Hideo and she knew that while he would tolerate the professional gambler whom he considered no more than a meal ticket, he would hate it if she had a "real" *danna*. If she became the property of such a man, she would no longer be free to carry on any clandestine relationships; and in any case Hideo would never agree to play second fiddle.

Hideo knew nothing of all this. She did not discuss it with him. Then one Sunday she was invited to the chairman's country villa. She could not decide what to do. If she went, Hideo would know immediately that something was afoot. If she did not, she might never again have such an opportunity. But she was a girl from the Osaka slums. She had learned the hard way that the only important thing in life was survival.

That weekend she told Hideo that she was going, just for the day, to the customer's villa.

"I thought, 'I see,' " said Hideo. " 'So that's the way it's going.' "

The next Sunday and the Sunday after that, she went to the chairman's villa. Finally she accepted his offer to become her *danna;* it was too good to refuse.

"I was too poor for her," Hideo said regretfully. "Of course I suffered after she had gone. It was unbearable. But I'm proud that I had an affair with her. I don't regret it, not in the slightest. It was the best thing that ever happened to me. It was the happiest year of my life."

Women in a Men's World

Now, as a general rule, where passionate love is the theme in Japanese literature of the best class, it is not that sort of love which leads to the establishment of family relations. It is quite another sort of love,—a sort of love about which the Oriental is not prudish at all,—the mayoi, or infatuation of passion, inspired by merely physical attraction; and its heroines are not the daughters of refined families, but mostly hetarae, or professional dancing girls.

Lafcadio Hearn[9]

In theory modern Japanese men, born after the war, had little interest in geisha. But, to my surprise, the most unlikely people, when I told them I was researching the geisha, proved to have connections in the flower and willow world which they were eager to show off. One was a rather louche television producer I knew, in his forties, who one day whisked me off to Kagurazaka, literally "Slope of the Music of the Gods," in the publishing district north of the Imperial Palace in Tokyo. One of his directors came with us; the producer made sure I realized that the geisha connection was his, not the director's.

The first teahouses in Kagurazaka appeared 150 years ago, around the time that the American commodore Matthew Perry was steaming into Tokyo Bay with his black ships, breaching Japan's closed society. Its geisha (there were sixty-three when I was there) were noted for their elegance and classy dancing, the producer told me as we clambered up the steep little street, brilliant with neon signs. Along the road were bars, restaurants, and pavement carts selling roasted sweet potatoes and grilled octopus. Red paper lanterns swung invitingly outside closed doors.

Opposite the huge vermilion gates of a shrine we ducked into a shadowy cobbled lane. Around a dark corner, where outsiders would not stumble upon it, was a small wooden house with reed blinds swaying in front of the windows. We stopped to admire the intricate weaving of the blinds, then slipped under the linen curtain at the gate and followed stepping stones through a narrow mossy garden to a sliding door.

Inside was a room just big enough for eight customers to sit squashed on high stools along two sides of the bar. The master of the house, a beaming, burly man in a bright red collarless shirt, greeted us. He and Kurota-san, my host, it transpired, were old college chums— which explained why a modern media executive like Mr. Kurota chose to frequent this particular bar in this particular area. He sat us down, plied us with beer and saké, and set about preparing a nonstop succession of succulent dishes of fish, vegetables, and rice.

The real boss was ensconced at a table in the corner—his eighty-five-year-old mother, tiny, trim, and straight-backed, immaculate in a pale moss-colored kimono and an obi the color of dark moss into which was tucked a fob watch which she consulted from time to time. Her black hair was tied back in a bun, revealing a pinched, sharp-featured face with pale, finely lined parchment skin. In her time she had been one of the most celebrated geisha in Kagurazaka and was still a power in the geisha union, Kurota told me, sotto voce. Behind her, taking pride of place on the wall, was a painting of Mount Fuji rising out of gold-tinted clouds with a personal inscription by a famous artist of half a century ago.

"He was one of my lovers," sniffed the old geisha. "He painted it for me."

Another group of four businessmen crowded in, filling the tiny bar. Beyond were a couple of tatami rooms, the sliding doors removed from their grooves to make one big open-plan space, where two parties of rowdy businessmen were gathered, enjoying a noisy night out. As the saké flowed, the voices and laughter grew deafening.

Kurota and his friend, loosening their ties as their faces flushed, were quizzing me about the Beatles as they picked at morsels of trout, boiled green soya beans, and tiny beautifully cut vegetables. They were in gray suits with uninspired haircuts though, as media men, they were allowed a degree of wackiness not granted to more buttoned-up executives. In any case, they were off duty, and off duty, once they have consumed a little saké, Japanese men are adept at throwing aside barriers.

"I'm not going to ask your age," began Kurota with a cheeky sideways glance. "But which musical era do you remember best? The Beatles? The Rolling Stones?"

"Oasis," I lied. "Blur, Suede, Primal Scream—they were around when I was young."

The master joined in. He had a comical, weathered face. He had gone into the fashion business, then ran a restaurant, and finally came home to help his mother with her bar.

"I wish I knew who his father was," Kurota confided under cover of the noise. "Must have been someone famous." Famous or not, the master was a joker.

"Do you know what *uzura* [quail] is in English?" he chuckled as he served us a dish of raw grated yam topped with seaweed and raw quail's egg. "It's the name of the American ex–vice president—Dan Quayle!"

Everyone laughed uproariously.

"Where's your wife?" I asked Kurota. Here I was in the great modern city of Tokyo with two well-traveled cosmopolitan television producers. Yet, apart from the old geisha, I was the only woman in the whole place. It was rather rude to ask such a direct question; but enough saké had been drunk and I thought I could get away with it.

"At home, sleeping," said Kurota, unfazed. "She was a magazine editor until we got married. Then she said, 'I can't be bothered to work anymore.' That's the way it is with Japanese wives. She stays home, has children, and brings them up. Her world is very narrow—the PTA [Parent Teachers Association] and the parents of our children's friends; that's about it. I go out and enjoy myself, then get home late and wake her up and she gets angry. She says, 'Why did you wake me up?' and goes back to sleep. In the West, people go to the pub for a drink, then go home, get changed, and go out with their wives. But we Japanese can't do that, our homes are too far away."

"That's why we have geisha," said his friend, butting in. "Ordinary girls are good at having babies and bringing up children. But geisha are good at chatting. You see this old geisha here . . ."

The old geisha was engaged in some outrageous conversation with the four businessmen, fluttering her fan coquettishly while her tongue rattled wickedly. The men, flushed and shiny-faced, returned her banter, guffawing loudly.

"An ordinary old lady would be very cozy," Kurota's friend went on. "But the world she knows is very small and the things she can talk about are very few. Geisha know how to please gentlemen, how to make them have a good time. But they wouldn't make good wives."

The day after my memorable evening with Mr. Kurota and his friend, I dropped into his offices to thank him for his hospitality. I started chatting about how much I had enjoyed the meal, the company, the old geisha, and the master with his clowning and jokes. But Mr. Kurota had changed. The affable, chummy character of the previous night, who had ribbed me mercilessly about my age and the Beatles, had disappeared. Brusque and businesslike, he changed the subject. Shortly afterward he growled that he had a meeting and left.

Too late, I realized that I had committed an unforgivable faux pas. Whatever had happened in the night-time world of the geisha happened only there. Whatever one said, whatever one did was forgotten the next day. There were no memories and no repercussions. There was no crossover into the real world.

Two Faces of Womanhood

A practical guide to doing business in Japan, published as recently as 1987, offers advice to the Western executive who is invited to a geisha party. The Japanese host would naturally, out of courtesy, invite his wife too if she is traveling with him. What is the executive to do?

The proper response, advises the author, is to make sure that your wife is otherwise engaged. Buy her a ticket to kabuki or the ballet, then "tell your Japanese contact how sorry your wife is not to be able to accept his kind invitation. He will accept your excuse graciously, with a secret sigh of relief!" He reassures the worried Western wife that nothing untoward goes on at a geisha party. "You are not sending your husband off to a den of iniquity."[10]

Until Westerners turned up in Japan 150-odd years ago, Japanese society operated in a way that seemed perfectly logical and perfectly satisfactory to its members but from an Anglo-Saxon point of view was inconceivably alien—though Mediterranean peoples might have had less trouble coping with it. Marriage, love, sex, and relationships were all conceived of in a way utterly different from in the West.

Initially, given the superior strength of the West, the Japanese made token efforts to appear to do things our way. But it was not until after the Occupation, when the Americans made a radical attempt to impose Western ways on Japan, that any real change began. Most of the men who frequented geisha houses were young before the Second World War and had grown up with prewar assumptions and attitudes. And even men like Kurota and his friend, born well after the war had ended, still lived their lives largely according to the old patterns.

Japanese wives always joked that when their husbands came home from work in the evening, instead of a sugary sweet "Hello, Darling" and a lingering kiss, as in American movies, they would bark "Tea!" followed not long after by "Bath!" It was not that the wives hankered after heart-on-the-sleeve displays of affection. Far from it. The joke was the contrast between the two radically different styles of behavior.

Once, when I was fresh to Japan and naive about such things, I asked a Japanese man of my acquaintance, a lecturer at a highly esteemed university, how to say "darling" in Japanese.

"What do you mean?" he asked.

"Well, when you call your wife, what do you say?"

He grinned at me, then bellowed "Oi!" like a sergeant major on a parade ground.

Some years later I was supplementing my income by teaching English to a class of businessmen in Tokyo. Racking my brains for something to discuss one evening, I asked them to list the attributes of the ideal girlfriend. Predictably "beauty" was top of the list, followed by "intelligence," "sense of humor," etc. Then we turned to the ideal wife. I was expecting a similar list but to my surprise it was turned on its head. "Healthy body" came top, followed by "good child-bearer," "good with children," and "good at housekeeping." "Beautiful," "intelligent," and "sense of humor" were right at the bottom.

"What's wrong with a beautiful wife?" I inquired, puzzled.

"If you had a beautiful, sexy wife, you'd be in trouble," volunteered one. "You'd be chasing off other men all the time." In their eyes wives and girlfriends were entirely different species.

One young man to whom I taught English in London some years ago took it even further. He was a high-flier, a handsome twenty-nine-year-old executive in a major Japanese trading company who had been seconded to the London office. We used to meet in grand London restaurants and converse in English. The snag was that his favorite topic of conversation was his exploits with prostitutes. English whores were dirty and diseased, he told me; Japanese colleagues who had been around for a while always advised newcomers to steer well clear. The approved alternative, it transpired, was to take regular holidays in Spain.

He chose to disclose this in a Soho restaurant where the tables were uncomfortably close together, making it virtually impossible not to be overheard. He was just back from his first Spanish holiday.

"How was it?" I asked, all innocence.

"Ah, the señoritas! So lovely! So wonderful!" he cried ecstatically. Despite my pleas that we change the subject or at least switch to Japanese for this particular part of the conversation, he spent the rest of the meal regaling me with his sexual adventures.

"You're a good-looking young man," I said. "Why don't you get a girlfriend? Then you could have all the sex you wanted without having to go to prostitutes."

His argument was perfectly logical.

"If I had a girlfriend, she'd be hassling me all the time to get married," he explained. "I'm very busy with my career. I don't have time for that sort of thing. Prostitutes are much easier. You get enjoyment, you pay your money, and that's it. After you get married, that's when you have a girlfriend. Then they can't hassle you."

The most unbridgeable cultural gap was that he did not see anything wrong, shameful, or even embarrassing about going to brothels and paying for sex. It was just one of those things that men did, not much different from going down to the pub with the lads.

Even in modern Japan, a Japanese man took it for granted that he had two different spaces in which to operate. Both contained women with whom he had relationships. In the world of home there was the wife, in charge of the household, the children's education, and the purse strings. He gave her his salary, and she gave him money with which to go out and have fun. The other world, the world of the evening, was populated by very different sorts of women—geisha, hostesses, entertainers, some of whom he had also known for years.

Between them, all these women made sure that he was taken care of from morning to night. Wife, concubine, mistress, geisha, and hostess were all expert at mothering a man, smoothing away his problems, stroking his ego, and ensuring that he always thought he was the boss. He was wrong, of course, to think so. All these women—wives, mistresses, and geisha—were adept at wrapping him around their little fingers and he was supporting all of them.

They also knew each other. There were times when the two worlds met. When a man died, the geisha whom he had supported were often in evidence, pillars of strength, helping the wife take care of the funeral arrangements.

Across the River Kamo in Kyoto, a few minutes' walk from the geisha areas, there was a narrow backstreet lined with warehouses from which emanated the powerful odor of vegetables pickling in rice bran. The owner, an urbane fifty-year-old who had studied for his MBA in the United States, was a scion of an old Kyoto family which had owned the pickling plant for generations.

When he was a child in the fifties, he told me, there were always geisha and maiko around the house. They were like aunts who came to help his mother when she had important guests to entertain. She would put envelopes of money and small gifts into the little boy's hand and say, "Give this to the *geiko-san*." (*Geiko,* literally "arts child," is the Kyoto term for geisha.) He knew many of the top geisha of Kyoto. Some were like aunts to him, others he had grown up with.

It was normal. The wife had her role, the geisha had theirs. His father had supported geisha and his mother had not been jealous; though, he confessed, he sometimes heard huge rows in other houses.

"In those days," he said, "a wife knew that as her husband became more powerful, he would go and 'play' in the geisha quarters. That was a sign of his success. My mother would tell my father, 'Off you go! *Asobinasai!* Go and play!' "

Jealousy

It is very clear that we do not marry for love. If a man is known to have broken this rule, we look upon him as a mean fellow, and sadly lacking in morality. His own mother and father would be ashamed of him. Public sentiment places love for a woman very low in the scale of morals . . . We place love and brutal attachment on the same plane.

Naomi Tamura (1904)[11]

I was forever hearing that wives saw their husbands more as children than as partners and were happy if they strayed, just so long as it was no more than that. Nevertheless, there was a whole tradition of stories in Japanese literature dealing with the fearful power of jealousy. It is considered a force so terrifying that to this day when Japanese women get married, part of the traditional bride's costume is the "horn hider," a stiff white headdress which engulfs her head like an enormous cocoon. Supposedly it conceals the "demon horns of jealousy" and immunizes the new husband against them. When the marriage code was first set down in the early years of the Meiji period, the late nineteenth century, one of the seven grounds on which it was ruled that a man could divorce his wife was jealousy. (The others were sterility, adultery, disobedience to parents-in-law, larceny, severe disease, and talking too much.)

One day I was sitting with a couple of women. One was an elderly ex-geisha, the other the wife of a powerful businessman who herself came from the kind of family where, in the old days, geisha would have been a part of life. The two had known each other for many years. They were gossiping about the way attitudes had changed over the decades.

"Relationships have changed a lot," began the wife. "There's not the same feeling of responsibility."

"That's right," said the geisha, shaking her head. In her mid-seventies, she had a thin little face with a pointed chin and big eyes. She was dressed in a plain kimono with her hair pulled back into a tight gray bun. "In the Meiji period, if a man had a geisha girlfriend, his friends would make sure she was all right after his death. But by Taisho [1912–1925], things were different.

"I remember hearing about a Shimbashi geisha who was the mistress of a very successful man. She was like a second wife to him. But although they were together for a long time, she never had any children. Then his wife died. He took the geisha into his household as his new wife but his children—the children of the first wife—wouldn't accept her. When he died too, his son threw her out of the house! It was shocking. The ironic thing was, the son carried on just like his father. He had a Shimbashi mistress too; he even had a child by her. His behavior was the mirror image of his father's but he still didn't take care of his father's geisha. Everyone was appalled."

"I remember years ago, when I first got married, my father-in-law had a geisha," said the wife. "His wife was so jealous. Poor thing! She used to prepare the most exquisite meals every night, just like a top-class restaurant, and she was always dressed really beautifully. But no matter how hard she tried, he would say he just wanted tea and rice, then rush off to the teahouse to eat. I felt so sorry for her."

"Then there was that husband who took his geisha with him everywhere like his wife," reminisced the geisha. "The wife was disfigured, I think she was scarred or handicapped; anyway, she couldn't appear in public. The geisha was beautiful and the wife agreed that she should be her husband's public consort. But when he died, the wife kicked her out immediately and took everything. It was terrible, she was like a demon. The geisha was destitute. I remember his friends were all discussing what to do and how to take care of her."

It was not surprising that wives should sometimes be jealous—they were human, after all. But despite the pain it might cause them, most accepted the Faustian pact. As the wife, they occupied a position of great respect in society. In Japan no one was "just" a housewife. Taking care of the house and rearing the children were seen as jobs essential for the well-being of society. Wives knew that within the household they were all powerful. If they wanted to buy a new car with the housekeeping money, there was no need to discuss it with their husband. With the husband as the breadwinner and the wife taking care of the house, it was a very efficient division of labor.

When they married, they expected to lead a life very separate from their husband's and many preferred it like that. As the old saying goes, the ideal husband is "healthy and not around." They also knew that while they could not expect love or fidelity, they were assured of financial security. To this day divorce rates in Japan are still far lower than in the West.[12]

Instead of trying to fulfill her husband's every fantasy so that he would never need to look elsewhere—to be the perfect wife, the perfect mother, a lady in public, and a whore in the bedroom, as a Western wife might—Japanese wives accepted that one woman was usually not enough to fulfill a man's needs. Just as there were two worlds, so there were two sorts of women to populate them. Wives and geisha were complementary, two sides of the same coin, two faces of womanhood.

Born and bred in Kyoto, Reiko had had geisha around her since childhood; they were part of the scenery as far as she was concerned. As the daughter of a Buddhist priest and the wife of another, she knew everyone, like a vicar's wife in the West. She was an insider, as much a part of traditional society as the geisha were.

Over chilled barley tea she asked me how I was getting on with my research, then launched into her own idiosyncratic impressions of the geisha world.

"You know who their main customers are, don't you?" she asked with a mischievous smile. "I'll tell you. There are something like three thousand temples in Kyoto. Some of them are small ones like ours, where the priest lives there all the time. But the bigger ones have a revolving system of abbots. The abbots are appointed for four or five years. They come up from the countryside where they live; they usually have a small temple of their own there. The wife and children stay in the countryside, taking care of the temple, and the abbot is here on his own. After a while—you can imagine!—he gets lonely. So off he goes to Gion; or he calls for a geisha to come over to the temple."

"What about contraception?" I inquired tentatively. It was not a question I had ever dared put to a geisha. But Reiko was so cheerfully uninhibited that I decided I could relax, put all my carefully learned politeness aside and ask whatever I wanted.

"Geisha use condoms, like everyone else," she replied. "But we're not Christians so we're not so bothered about being single mothers. In the past there used to be a lot of single mothers. These days geisha tend to retire and marry when they get pregnant."

Extraordinary though it might seem, the pill was only licensed for contraceptive use in Japan in June 1999. Until then it was banned as being potentially dangerous to health. As a result Japan was, as Mother Teresa of Calcutta described it, "an abortionists' paradise." There were any number of male doctors who profited from this situation, not to mention the priests who presided over temples dedicated to the souls of aborted or miscarried fetuses. One survey revealed that 23 percent of married women had had at least one abortion. The problem was less acute for married couples; women often joked that the main form of contraception among married couples was that after having produced the regulation two children, they stopped having sex. The main people who had to worry about contraception were those providing extra-marital sex.

It did not pass unnoticed that the Japanese government licensed Viagra in February 1999, after a mere six months' debate and before licensing the pill; there was no problem, it seemed, with a drug which gave men control over their sexuality though there was with a drug which did the same for women.[13]

But what of the wives, I asked. How did they feel when their husbands went off to the pleasure quarters? Were they not jealous, as a Western wife would be?

In the past, said Reiko, women had taken it for granted that they were inferior and subordinate to men. You brought up even your own son with great care, giving him as much deference as you would your husband and using only kind, respectful words when you spoke to him. In those days, women were taught to assume that if their husband was rich, he would go off to have fun in Gion. It was a high-status activity, something to be proud of, certainly not to complain about. If a man brought home a geisha as his concubine, everything would be fine just so long as the geisha remembered the protocol. Even if the husband slept with the pretty young newcomer and not with the withered old wife, nevertheless the wife was still number one. The geisha always had to remember her place and bow very low when their paths crossed. At the husband's funeral, no matter how close they had been, she would still take her allotted place low in the ranks.

"Sometimes everyone got on better if there was a nice young wife living there too," said Reiko. "It kept the husband happy and made everything more harmonious. But if the number one and the number two wives both had children, that sometimes created problems."

Then she had an inspiration. The best way to understand all this, she said, was to meet one of her old schoolmates who had been the top maiko of her day.

Mrs. Sato was startlingly youthful, little changed from the heart-stoppingly beautiful maiko in the photographs which she brought out to show me. She might have been in her thirties rather than her early fifties. Her face was a delicate heart shape, her skin silky smooth without a trace of a line, and her eyes large, limpid, and set wide apart. Her nose was small and straight and her pretty, laughing mouth neither too large nor too small, just as the ancient canons of beauty dictated. She had the easy confidence of a woman who has been worshipped and admired as an acknowledged beauty for years. When she was growing up, her family ran a teahouse in Gion, so naturally she became a maiko.

"My husband was a customer, one of my *danna-san*," she told me. "That was how I met him. I remember he really wanted to marry me. He used to say, 'Leave this life. Let's get married.' I'm not going to tell you what his job is or everyone will know who he is. Let's just say he's in property.

"He was the top *danna* of Gion. He was twenty years older than me, but that doesn't mean he was old; I was only twenty or so at the time. We were lovers for three years. We've been married thirty years now. I must say, these days I get fed up with having him around the house night after night. I wish he'd go out and 'play'!"

In Japan, said the irrepressible Reiko, butting in, the wife's job is to take care of the husband. He might love and adore you and want to make you happy—but that is only when you are courting. Everything changes the moment the ring is on your finger. Once you are married, you suddenly discover that you are not a lover anymore but a mother.

"We're managers!" she cried. "You get married, you have a baby straight away and after that your hands are full. You're taking care of the baby, your husband—he's another baby—and all the family finances. It's a real nuisance having the husband around the house; he just gets in the way. It makes life much easier for everyone if husbands go off and 'play.'

"Mine certainly did," she added. "Probably still does. I certainly don't think he's the perfect husband."

I had put down my fork and was listening aghast at the outrageous turn the conversation had taken. Of course in theory Japanese wives took their husbands' infidelity for granted, but I had never before heard anyone speak so directly about it.

I was well aware that husbands and wives in Japan often led completely separate lives. When I lived in small-town Japan I had had many very close women friends; but I never seemed to meet their husbands. Couples never did things together as they do in the West. Even in the evening when I went for dinner, the husband was never around.

After I had remarked on this over the course of a year and a half, some of my women friends made a special effort and invited me around to meet their husbands. Then I realized what the problem was. In most cases the couple had absolutely nothing in common apart from the children and the roof over their heads. I wondered how on earth they had ended up together. Some, of course, would have had a marriage arranged by their parents; some, I suspected, simply got married because it was time and the person in question was around and available. The women and the young girls whom I knew never seemed to expect love or to hold out for it, as a Western woman would. Proverbially what a woman looked for in a man were the three *takai*, the three "highs": to be tall, to have a high salary, and to be the graduate of a top university. Love came a poor second if it made a showing at all.

The prime relationship in most women's lives, as far as I could see, was not with their husbands but their children. As if to make up for the lack of romantic love in their lives, women overwhelmed their children with love. As for the husbands, their prime relationship seemed to be with their workmates. They worked together all day and in the evening went out together to party or "play." Often they spent weekends playing golf together.

If a wife was lucky, she would never see her husband at all. He would stagger home drunk last thing at night, fall into bed, and be off to work at the crack of dawn next morning. Some nights he might phone up and say he was working late and was going to spend the night in the city. The wife carefully avoided thinking too much about it. It made it very easy for a Japanese man if he wanted to have an affair.

But I had never before heard a Japanese woman say straight out that she wished her husband would go off and "play" with other women.

Reiko and Mrs. Sato were half joking, I suspected. They were also so-phisticated Kyoto-ites. They came from old Kyoto families. Reiko had lived for generations side by side with the flower and willow world, the one place where the romantic was allowed to blossom in Japan, while Mrs. Sato had grown up within it. Their attitudes were perhaps more rooted in the past than those of most modern Japanese women.

"My husband had a Taiwanese lover a while ago," said Reiko. "I got really jealous. But then one day I met her. I liked her, she was sweet. After that I didn't mind. Even if men play around, we still feel confident just so long as they introduce the girlfriend to us. Once you've met her, then you can relax and feel secure."

"It was like that with my husband's first wife," said Mrs. Sato. "I knew her quite well when I was still a geisha. The three of us went out for dinner several times."

"Didn't you feel guilty?" I asked, amazed at these revelations.

"Not in the slightest," said Mrs. Sato, smiling sweetly. "She was a lot older than me. There was no reason to feel bad."

"I don't get angry if my husband plays around," said Reiko. "That's fine. The only thing is, I have to be the most important. If the other woman gets to be more important to him, that's when I'd get an-gry. That was proper behavior in the old days. The wife had to be num-ber one. Wives don't have lovers, of course," she added, as if that was perfectly obvious.

"We don't have time," said Mrs. Sato. "We're busy all day long, every day—bringing up the children, cooking perfect meals three times a day . . ."

"The day my husband goes out to 'play,' that's when I can finally relax," laughed Reiko. "I can always tell. When he gets back, he's ultra nice to me. He gives me presents or flowers. He's quiet and well be-haved. A husband is like a child; I'm like his mother. If he does some-thing stupid, I tell him off."

The key thing, they agreed, was to keep the home harmonious and peaceful. If one's husband was frustrated then he would be in a bad tem-per and infect everyone else with his bad temper and the whole family would be miserable. But if he went off to "play," if he had a girlfriend or went to visit a geisha, he would be in a good mood for days afterward.

Not only that, he would be contrite and sheepish. There would be harmony in the home.

"If my husband is happy, then I'm happy too," concluded Reiko. "If my husband is stressed then I get stressed too and we have a row. If he spends time with another woman, he'll be in a good mood when he gets home. Then we're all in a good mood."

Later when Mrs. Sato had gone off to powder her exquisite nose, Reiko confided that her husband was one of the biggest landowners in Kyoto. He owned woods, he owned mountains—in fact, he owned most of Kyoto. I would not have expected less of someone who had been the most famous and beautiful maiko in the entire city.

chapter 3

inside the pleasure quarters

The *Maiko* of Kyoto

Waiting anxiously for you,
Unable to sleep, but falling into a doze—
Are those words of love
Floating to my pillow,
Or is this too a dream . . . ?
My eyes open and here is my tear-drenched sleeve.
Perhaps it was a sudden rain.
    Geisha song[1]

Present and Past

Once I had become an accepted part of the geisha world in Kyoto, I took to spending my days and evenings in geisha houses and teahouses with maiko, geisha, and the "mothers" of the houses—*okami-san*—or chatting to the motley collection of individuals who populated the geisha world. Elderly barmen reminisced about their favorite maiko of decades past and showed off their collections of signed photographs, scented business cards, fans, and the towels which maiko handed out to mark rites of passage in their careers. Men who boasted of being regular customers dropped the names of maiko they were friendly with and talked of taking them bowling on their days off. Shopkeepers along Shijo Street whose families had served the geisha community for generations regaled me with stories of past and present maiko. And whenever I had a spare moment I pored over books on geisha history or read novels written in the days when any love story had a geisha as the heroine and ended not "and then they got married and lived happily ever after" but "and then they committed love suicide."

It was difficult not to be aware of the enormous gulf between the way maiko and geisha had lived even in the recent past and their present-day lives. The turning point, as everyone always told me, was Showa 33 (1958), the year that prostitution had been made illegal. Yet some of what gave the geisha their special flavor still remained. In the past love had been the forbidden fruit, made all the more romantic because it was illicit. But today too the geisha were somehow beyond the pale—respectable yet not respectable. On the one hand, they were the symbol of Kyoto; posters of maiko inscribed "Welcome to Kyoto!" greeted travelers as they arrived at the central railway station. People on the edges of the geisha world would happily describe their customs and rituals and boast about the geisha they knew. But when I asked if they would let their own daughter become a geisha, they always looked askance and mumbled, "Well, it's a difficult question."

It was impossible also not to be aware of the devastating decline in numbers. Old people—both geisha and shopkeepers—remembered the days when the whole area between the River Kamo and the Eastern Hills, from north of Fourth Bridge down to Fifth Bridge, had been a special world. Every dwelling had been a teahouse or geisha house and every shop had served the geisha community. In the 1920s, at the height of the geisha era, there had been 80,000 geisha throughout the country. In Gion alone there were 2,500 geisha and 106 maiko.

When the teahouses reopened after the war, around 1948, there were still 1,200 geisha and 160 maiko in Kyoto. In those days the flower and willow world was a thriving industry, governed by protocol and ritual, with geisha clattering on their wooden clogs from teahouse to teahouse every day to pay their respects to the teahouse mothers and sometimes entertaining from the morning of one day to the small hours of the next. But by 1999 there were just 195 geisha and 55 maiko left, of whom 90 geisha and 22 maiko were in Gion.

I wondered if I was seeing the end of a way of life or if the geisha would somehow survive. What did it mean to be a geisha today? Could they still be called "geisha" when so much of what had made them geisha had disappeared? In modern Japan, they were no longer the heart of the entertainment industry nor, as they had been, sirens and idols, the most desired women of their generation. What role could they play when they had become almost an anachronism?

The kabuki actors, once their fellow leaders of the demimonde, equally disreputable "riverbed folk," had turned respectable. Stuck in an unchanging Edo-period time warp, they now put on costume dramas for the populace to enjoy. But even if the geisha had wanted to follow this course, it was not open to them. The essence of the flower and willow world was its secrecy. It was open only to a few well-heeled initiates. If the geisha became popular entertainers, their seductive mystery would be lost. But if they did not, how could they survive?

And what of the geishas' past? Was it a distant memory? In fact, as I discovered early on, it was still very much alive.

"When I think about the old days I always remember them as dark," said my friend Mr. Kato as we sat with his parents in their printing shop one day. "The buildings were lower, the ceilings were lower— everything was low and dark. When I think of the street then, it was all blacks and browns and reds. Those slatted screens that hang in front of the windows so no one can see in—they were all dark brown."

There were, he said, plenty of daughters of geisha in his class at primary school. Sometimes there would be rumors, so-and-so's father is the owner of such-and-such construction company, so-and-so's father is a doctor or a dentist or an actor. In the rest of Japan people might have thought it was strange; but here in the geisha districts one-parent families were normal. The children certainly never suffered prejudice, in fact no one thought twice about it. The only trouble was, they were spoiled.

The beginnings of Gion, the entertainment district on the banks of the River Kamo in early-seventeenth-century Kyoto. Musicians and dancers perform for the audience while pleasure seekers arrive by palanquin. (Fenollosa-Weld Collection, 1911, Museum of Fine Arts, Boston)

The ninth-century femme fatale, Ono no Komachi. Woodblock print by Eizan Kikukawa (1787–1867). (V & A Picture Library)

A tayu courtesan of Shimabara. Woodblock print by Kunisada Utagawa (1786–1864). (V & A Picture Library)

A geisha in front of the Great Gate of the Yoshiwara. Woodblock print by Kunisada Utagawa. (V & A Picture Library)

A bustling Edo street, Saruwaka-cho, from *One Hundred Famous Views of Edo,* by Hiroshige Ando (1797–1858). (Nagoya TV)

Geisha entertaining young rakes at the fashionable Shikian restaurant on Nakasu island in the 1780s. Woodblock print by Shumman Kubo (1757–1820) (right-hand panel). (British Museum)

Oishi Kuranosuke plays blindman's buff with the geisha of Ichiriki-tei, the famous Gion teahouse, to fool his enemies, who are watching from the garden. (Nagoya TV)

Otatsu of the Ryogoku (Fukagawa) district of Edo. As a Fukagawa geisha, she is
the epitome of chic. She steps out, barefoot in her wooden sandals and wearing a loose,
square-cut haori jacket. Woodblock print by Eiri Chokyosai (active 1789–1800).
(MUSÉE DES ARTS ASIATIQUES, PARIS)

Sadayakko on towering clogs, hair bristling with hairpins, painted by William Nicholson (1872–1949). (VICTOR ARWAS, LONDON COLLECTION)

Taka the Literary Geisha (on right). (THE ISODA FAMILY)

A courtesan in full regalia and her child attendant, posing for an unknown
late-nineteenth-century photographer.

Turn-of-the-century geisha enjoying a meal. One has propped her shamisen against the wall behind her to the right. (VICTOR ARWAS, LONDON COLLECTION)

Geisha in a rickshaw, posing with the runner for a late-nineteenth-century photographer. (VICTOR ARWAS, LONDON COLLECTION)

Prostitutes on the lookout for customers in a poorer section of the Yoshiwara after the Second World War. (CORBIS IMAGES)

John Wayne (1907–1979) and actress Eiko Ando on a break from filming John Huston's *The Barbarian and the Geisha* (1958), the story of the first American consul, Townsend Harris, and his concubine, Okichi. (CORBIS IMAGES)

Every now and then you'd hear them saying, "Uncle's coming today!" You knew that whenever their father turned up, they got whatever they wanted.

"But there was also a girl from the country. Her parents must have received a 'preparation fee'."

" 'Preparation fee'? " I queried.

"For having made her and brought her up until then," he explained as if it was the most normal thing in the world. "They had sent her off to a geisha house to be raised. I felt sorry for her. I remember she was always crying in class. She was the only maid in the house. When she got back from school she had to clean and help the maiko and geisha with their kimonos and makeup. She was busy all the time; she didn't have any friends. She got two days off a month, the seventh and the twentieth. That was twenty-five years ago. There were quite a few like her at school with me, but she was the only one in my class. I don't know what became of her. She probably ran away. She's certainly not around now."

"Granddad used to mess around with geisha," rumbled Mr. Kato's father unexpectedly. We all settled into deferential silence. "My mother, my real mother, that is—I had three or four 'mothers'—used to have a geisha house. She'd been a geisha herself."

"Grandma was a geisha? You never told us that before!" gasped Mr. Kato and his mother in unison.

"Granddad ran a Chinese restaurant," Mr. Kato senior went on imperturbably. "In the war there was no food here so he used to go out to the country to get supplies. My last 'mother' was the owner of the inn where he stayed. She was the mistress—the 'number two wife'—of someone important. In those days guys had children all over the place. That was normal. No one ever asked who anyone else's parents were. You didn't go round asking that kind of thing." Young Mr. Kato and his mother were murmuring and tut-tutting together at these revelations.

In Mr. Kato senior's time—before the Occupation, the imposition of universal compulsory education to the age of fifteen, and the 1958 law ending licensed prostitution—*zegen,* somewhere between talent-spotters and pimps, used to go out and scour the poorer parts of the countryside for pretty young girls whom they would take back to Kyoto to be trained. In those days maids might arrive in Kyoto at the age of six or seven and, after a period of servitude and training, became maiko at eleven. That was why they wore four-inch-high clogs, to add to their height, for they were not yet fully grown. Modern-day maiko teetering down the street on their clogs sometimes towered above their clients.

There had been many other changes. In prewar days, the majority of the maiko in Kyoto were from geisha families; their mothers, grandmothers, and sometimes great-grandmothers had been geisha. The girls from the countryside were on the bottom rung of the ladder. But in modern times, many daughters of geisha wanted to take up another career or marry a "normal" man and have a "normal" life. At least one elderly ex-geisha I spoke to begged me not to refer to her by her real name, because none of her family, not even her son and daughter, now grandparents themselves and highly respected members of society, had any idea that she had been a geisha.

Modern maiko, conversely, were mainly not from Kyoto and, even if they were, were not from a geisha background. The first criterion was that they had to be pretty; like modeling, this was a career where social background counted for nothing and a pretty face was all. They also had to be fit and healthy, for the maiko training involved hard work and long hours. But the biggest difference was that they had all become maiko out of choice. Some had seen maiko, perhaps on television, perhaps on a school trip to Kyoto, and had been starstruck by these fairytale creatures. Others had studied traditional Japanese dancing and wanted to pursue the art more deeply. In most cases their parents had been horrified at the idea; but the girls wanted so badly to become maiko that they reluctantly gave their consent. It was the exact reverse of the bad old days, when children had been sold by their parents out of desperate poverty.

As far as the old ladies of the geisha community were concerned, the result had been a disturbing drop in standards. Before the war the daughters of geisha began their dancing classes at the age of six years, six months, and six days. In those days it had been a serious profession and children started young, like students of the Bolshoi Ballet. Modern-day maiko did not even begin their training until they were fourteen or fifteen—by which time they had had so much so-called education that, instead of listening obediently and repeating again and again, as was expected, they were prone to question every instruction they were given.

As an elegant seventy-year-old, the fourth generation of a family of geisha, told me with a disdainful lift of the eyebrows, "In the old days at least you could expect girls to have basic manners." Now, she huffed, they knew nothing: how to put on a kimono, how to walk in one, how to kneel and rise elegantly with one knee just an inch or two above the other, or how to open the sliding paper fusuma doors with a discreet motion of the hand, fingers and thumb held straight and pressed together. Some had never sat on tatami before and didn't even know how to use chopsticks. "You have to teach them everything!" she concluded with an extravagant sigh.

The Maiko's Robing Ceremony

Most of what goes on in the geisha world happens behind closed doors. It is a little like Hollywood. Every now and then you might spot a geisha or maiko on the street as she flits from teahouse to teahouse or, if you are the guest of someone very wealthy, meet one entertaining at a geisha party. But you only ever see the public face, immaculately made up, eternally composed and gracious. As for the private life of the geisha, that is an entirely different matter, utterly closed to outsiders.

So when I was invited to sit in on the backstage preparations for the debut of a maiko called Kanosome, it was an enormous privilege. The debut—*misedashi,* literally "store opening"—is one of the most momentous rites of passage in the geisha's career, when she steps out for the first time at the age of fifteen as a fully-fledged maiko on the geisha stage. It would also be an opportunity to witness the putting on of the mask, the moment of transformation when the fresh-faced teenager becomes a denizen of another world.

It was the rainy season in Kyoto by the time Kanosome's debut came up. Standing on the rickety balcony of the small room where I lived, I looked in dismay at the rain pounding on the roofs, sluicing through the gutters and sweeping in great sheets along the street. The

River Kamo, usually a calm little stream with paths along both banks populated by joggers and courting couples, had turned into a savage brown torrent. Mammoth waves, big enough to surf on, surged along with frightening speed.

Nothing, however, would prevent me from going out. Huddled under an umbrella I splashed past the dark shuttered and screened wooden houses of Gion and along the covered pavement of Shijo Street. Dripping, I found the house, slid open the door, and went inside.

Upstairs, Kanosome was kneeling on the floor, her cotton yukata folded down so that her shoulders were bare. The room had the orderly chaos of a theater dressing room with kimonos hanging around the walls and bowls, brushes, and tubs of makeup spread across the floor. At fifteen, she had the face of a classic Japanese beauty such as one sees in woodblock prints, a perfect melon-seed shape with a slightly protruding lower jaw, large wide-apart eyes, well-shaped eyebrows, and a mouth neither too big nor too small. Without makeup she was just a nervous, excited teenager. Despite the waxed medieval hairstyle with its red ribbons, tortoiseshell combs, and decorations, one could imagine her in jeans or school uniform, riding her bicycle, satchel on her back.

Patient, obedient, she sat motionless on her knees while Masami, the senior geisha of the house, massaged her shoulders, then took a knob of soft white wax and rubbed it thoroughly into her face. One of the most popular geisha in the city, Masami was normally to be seen in white face, kimono, and wig. She was lively, entertaining, and beautiful, with a wide face and full laughing mouth. But that day she had a different role to play. In simple pony tail and jeans, she applied herself very seriously to the magical business of transmuting the girl before her into a work of art.

Taking a tub of white makeup, Masami put some into a dish, mixed in a trace of pink, then carefully applied a layer to Kanosome's face with a wide flat goat's hair brush, leaving a clean line of unpainted skin at the hairline. It was an extraordinary transformation, as if the girl had put on one of the beautiful but expressionless masks which actors wear in the classical Japanese Noh theater. She had lost the idiosyncratic features of a teenager and become an icon from another age.

In the old days, the makeup was white lead and had a disastrous effect on the skin. Women quickly aged and their skin became yellow-tinged and prematurely wrinkled from having it applied every day. Sometimes young geisha died from the poisoning. Nowadays maiko and geisha use a gentler makeup, produced by Kanebo, the Japanese cosmetics manufacturer—though modern women, as well as geisha, still swear by nightingale droppings, sold by the bottle in organic cosmetic shops in Japan, to cleanse the skin and give it a pearl-like pallor. To get the luminous white of the face, Masami explained, she mixed a little pink into the white; true white would give a sallow tint on Japanese skin. But for the throat and shoulders, she used pure white to set off the brilliant red of the collar.

Next Masami puffed on a layer of white powder, patting until Kanosome's face was as smooth as alabaster and as pristine as an artist's canvas. She filled in the eye sockets and the sides of the nose with pink, then brushed a layer of white around the girl's neck and shoulders, puffing powder over the top.

Kanosome's family and a couple of her school friends had traveled from the city outside Tokyo where they lived to witness this rite of passage. They crowded into the room, whispering nervously. Squashed in a row along one wall, they sat formally on their heels. Her parents looked ridiculously young to have such a grown-up child. Her father, in a brown suit, shuffled to his feet, took out a video camera, and started filming. It was like a wedding except that there was no groom. They were seeing their child for the last time. It was a hugely emotional occasion, even more so than it would have been for Western parents. For in Japan girls usually live at home with their parents until they marry, then move straight from their parents' home to their husband's.

Taking a narrow brush Masami shaded in the eyebrows in feathery strokes, painting them very straight like moths' wings, then outlined the eyes in red, extending the line out at the corners. Finally she painted in a line of black around the eyes.

"The trick is to get the face the same every time," she said. "When they first try and do it themselves, it's a mess. Our other maiko has a different face every day."

"She'll never be able to do this herself!" tut-tutted Kanosome's small round grandmother.

"Sshh!" whispered Kanosome, motionless as an artist's canvas.

Then Masami took a silver template and placed it against the girl's back, adjusting the position at the nape of her neck. With a large flat brush she painted the back in white, up behind the ears and down to the center. She removed the template, revealing a titillating three-pronged tongue of bare skin. Usually a maiko would paint her own face, using two mirrors to paint her back and leaving a two-pronged V of unpainted flesh which supposedly hints at a woman's private parts.

Two *otokoshi* bustled in, middle-aged women in skirts and white gloves. There have been *otokoshi,* literally "male staff" or "boys," ever since there were geisha. They were the geishas' assistants. They helped them dress, carried their shamisen boxes as they went back and forth from geisha house to teahouse, and were often their confidants, privy to the tastiest items of gossip. But these days there were only five of the original male "boys" left, all rather old. Their job had largely been usurped by women.

Chatting and laughing, the *otokoshi* helped Kanosome into her under-kimonos, first a filmy red petticoat, then a white cotton under-blouse with a red collar and long red sleeves, then a floor-length red petticoat, tying them all in place with silk ribbons. Then they laid a brocade collar, embroidered in red, white, and silver, around her neck. Kanosome stood like a tailor's dummy while the women tugged, readjusted, and tied.

Hanging on the wall was a sumptuous black kimono with a stream in white and pale turquoise swirling across the hem and shoulders. Blossoms and leaves floated along it and there was a stylized bridge across it. There are appropriate kimonos for each season and each event. This was a formal kimono used only for ceremonial occasions. It was made of a light almost transparent silk gauze with a very loose weave called *ro,* worn in summer.

Helping Kanosome into the garment, the women tugged the collar and back of the kimono right down to the middle of her back to expose the familiar breathtaking expanse of white skin and the three-pronged tongue of unpainted flesh at the nape of her neck. Tying it in place with ribbons, they took the obi, a weighty band of sumptuous gold brocade and wrapped it round and round her. Then they inserted a cushion to pad the back and tied it all with silken strings so that the two long ends dangled to the floor. They were heaving and tugging so vigorously they had to stop for breath and wipe the sweat from their brows.

For the final touch, Masami took a small stick of intensely red safflower paste, moistened a thin brush, and carefully painted a tiny petal of red in the center of Kanosome's lower lip. The upper lip she left white; it is only after a year that the maiko begins to paint her upper lip. Then, after tucking two silver dangling combs into the girl's coiffure, she handed her a mascara brush and mirror. To everyone's horror, a black dot appeared on the immaculate white of the face. Masami touched up her handiwork, laughing cheerfully. After all, under all the paint, Kanosome was still a child.

"What a pretty maiko . . ." said Kanosome's mother in uncertain tones.

The teenager had disappeared. In her place was a beautiful painted doll, all lips and eyes etched on the pure white canvas of her face.

"It's your own daughter," smiled the *okasan,* the proprietress of the house, elegant in a dark blue kimono. *Okasan* means "mother"; from now on Kanosome would address her by this title. The two mothers could not have been more different. The *okasan* of the house was slim, elegant, and rather icy, like a nightclub hostess; whereas Kanosome's real mother was plump, comfortable, and homely. She was giving up one for the other.

Preparations completed, we swept off to the teahouse, owned by the *okasan,* where Kanosome was to celebrate the beginning of her professional career as a maiko. The narrow entrance was decorated wall to wall with enormous colorful paintings of the gods of good luck with "Kanosome" brushed in huge black characters on each. Here the family bade her good-bye, watching rather wistfully as she stepped into her high wooden clogs and out into the night.

"Oki-ni, oki-ni," she piped, using the Kyoto word for "thank you." It must have sounded disturbingly affected to her parents' Tokyo ears. Somehow her demeanor had changed along with her appearance. What on earth had happened to their little girl? She was not even talking the same language as they were anymore.

Bowing, she set off with her new mother, clattering down the road, her obi swinging heavily behind her. The two would parade through the neighborhood so that Kanosome could be formally introduced to all the teahouse owners. Usually it was a grand parade, the maiko's moment of glory when, like a Hollywood starlet, trailing a pack of photographers and the odd TV cameraman, she showed herself in all her finery to her public. But the rain had kept the photographers away.

"You must be proud of her," said Kanosome's grandmother to the young father, filming their retreating backs with his video camera.

"Hmm," he said slowly. The bland Japanese mask, conveying the illusion that everything is eternally fine, slipped just for an instant. He looked down sadly. "Well," he said finally. "She really wanted to do it."

At the far end of the alley two small figures were silhouetted for a moment, sheltering under a huge oiled paper umbrella, before vanishing from sight around the corner.

First Steps in the Geisha World

Harumi was in her second year as a maiko when I met her, even though she was only fifteen. She had wanted to become a maiko so badly that she had left home when she was thirteen to move into Haruta geisha house, and had finished her schooling at the same time as she was beginning her maiko training. I used to see her clip-clopping past my house in her maiko regalia. With her heart-shaped face, large limpid eyes, tiny retroussé nose, and mouth like a bow, she was as perfect as a china doll and the epitome of maiko prettiness.

I bumped into her when I sat in on classes at the Kaburenjo, the "dance and music practice place" which housed a theater, classrooms, and the offices of the district geisha union. (Despite Mr. Kimura's intransigence, I had finally managed to gain entry.) Fresh-faced without her makeup, in a plain indigo-and-white cotton summer kimono, she had a simple red ribbon in her waxed hair. She shone in the drumming class where she played the *tsuzumi,* a small rather beautiful hour-glass shaped drum of gold-painted lacquered wood with a skin made from the hide of a young horse. Looking straight ahead impassively in the prescribed fashion, she rested it on her right shoulder, held it in place with her left hand and beat out a rhythm with the fingers of her right, breaking into a childish giggle when she made a mistake.

There was something irresistibly attractive about maiko with their combination of little-girl cuteness and teenage vulnerability beneath their archaic coiffures. But they were the most difficult of all to meet; regarded as children, they were fiercely protected by the geisha house mothers. It was also difficult to be invited inside a geisha house. After all, these were private homes, where the geisha and maiko lived. Even when I visited a teahouse, theoretically open for business, I never got further than the home bar, the equivalent of a Victorian parlor, at least for the first few weeks.

I was curious to venture a little deeper inside this world. Who were these little girls I saw flitting about the streets like butterflies? Why had they chosen this anachronistic lifestyle when so many other options were open to them? What were their day-to-day lives like? Did they have regrets about what they had given up? But the doors always seemed to be closed and I dared not knock too insistently. It was not until I had become a familiar face in the geisha world that one day a geisha, who had befriended me at the local coffee shop, suggested casually that I should meet her neighbor. Thus it was that I ended up sliding open the door of the Haruta geisha house where Harumi lived.

The Haruta house was a big rambling chaotic house with a yapping lapdog and a constant stream of visitors. Haruta-san herself, the "mother" of the house, was a large, expansive, open-hearted woman who had had, as she told me, a tough life.

She had been born fifty-two years before in the rural impoverished island of Kyushu, the love-child of a geisha and a wealthy landowner. Her father took her into his household but from the start she was relentlessly bullied by his seven other children. When she was ten she ran away to look for her mother.

But the mother, who had long since married and had other children, was far from pleased to see her. She told the child that she had not even wanted to have her. She had fallen downstairs to try to induce a miscarriage when she was pregnant with her. She beat her, treated her like a housemaid, and refused to let her go to school, then sold her to a hospital where she was forced to wash filthy rags from morning to night. After four years of utter misery, young Haruta found some pills and swallowed three hundred, hoping to kill herself. She was found, revived, and taken back to Kyushu by her mother's sister. But at fourteen, she was barely educated; she had missed four years of schooling. And there was no work to be found in Kyushu. Her life still seemed hopeless.

There was nothing for it but to go back to Osaka and look for work in the "water trade," the Japanese term for the sex industry. She found a job in a "cabaret," a low-grade bar not far removed from a brothel. There she became friendly with a woman who was the girl-friend of a Kyoto textile merchant. She persuaded Haruta-san to try the life of a geisha. With the merchant as her guarantor, Haruta ended up in a geisha house in Kyoto. Once again she was at the bottom of the heap, tormented and bullied. But nothing could be as bad as what she had al-ready gone through. She persevered and in the end inherited the name, the house, and the business.

The geisha world had been her salvation. When I met her she was the comfortable mother hen to a brood of maiko and geisha, including a couple of children of her own, happily established in Kyoto's world of women.

"I'm very kind to the maiko and geisha," she confided. "That's not to say I'm not stern. They have to learn to behave properly. But I would never, never treat anyone the way I was treated."

Harumi, the youngest maiko in the house, took me upstairs to show me the room she shared with Haruka, her "older sister." Japanese rooms are usually cramped and tatty but theirs was large, spacious, and airy with fresh tatami matting on the floor, smelling of rice straw. From the open window you could see the tiled roofs of the neighboring houses and the narrow street outside. The room was full of little-girl clutter— piles of stuffed animals, toys, dolls, a bookcase full of books, magazines, and comics and a large mirror which ran the length of one wall, like in a theater dressing room, with drawers underneath it filled with brushes and tubs of unguents and makeup. There were photographs of pop stars, famous geisha, and several pictures of the Hollywood star Leonardo di Caprio pinned along the top. Filling the wall above it was an enormous poster of Masahiro Nakai of the fabulously popular singing group SMAP, heartthrob to millions of Japanese teenage girls.

Despite her little-girl looks, Harumi was unusually grown up and confident for her age. Maiko often are, perhaps because they leave home so young. She sat on her heels, cuddling the house cat, a tawny-eyed tortoiseshell, and chatted cheerfully in her piping voice, using the quaint, rather stilted Kyoto dialect and geisha forms of words. In her spare time she loved music and films, she told me. She had seen the film *Titanic* on video four times and adored the star, Leonardo di Caprio. Or she went shopping with a schoolmate who had become a maiko at the same time as she had.

"Ever since I was ten I've yearned to be a maiko," she piped, smiling prettily. "I would see them sometimes on television and once when we came to Kyoto on a school visit, walking along the street. They looked so beautiful in their kimonos! I dreamed and dreamed of looking like them. I've always loved to wear a kimono."

Her father, a carpenter, was strongly opposed to the notion of any child of his taking up such a profession. It would also mean that she would have to give up her formal education long before high school. But her mother, a taxi driver, thought it was a good idea.

"She thought it would be good for me to learn good manners, like going to finishing school. It would help me when I got married."

In the past, children sold into the geisha districts often had to work as maids for years. They lived in the geisha house, being treated like dogsbodies but getting the chance to have the patina of the geisha world rub off on them. For Harumi her period as a *shikomi* (literally "in training") or *tamago* ("egg") lasted just six months. Like the child-maids in the old days, she did a little cleaning, ran errands, and helped the maiko and geisha dress. As in any traditional Japanese apprenticeship, the real purpose was for her to absorb the atmosphere of the house, get a feel for how things were done, and get used to the notion of discipline.

But the most difficult thing to get used to was wearing traditional Japanese clothing. Instead of running around in jeans or a skirt, like any modern Japanese child, suddenly she was spending her days in a *yukata*, an ankle-length kimono-like garment that wrapped her knees like a bandage. She also had to hobble around on wooden clogs or dainty slippers so short her heels hung off the back. Her hair, which she tied back in a ponytail, grew wild and shaggy as she coaxed it to become long enough to sculpt into the maiko's coiffure. And whenever she made the tiniest mistake, someone would be sure to snap at her.

"Everyone corrects you," she remembered. "Every person I spoke to told me off every single time I made a mistake. It was so hard to bear!"

The first thing she had to learn was to speak Kyoto dialect and use the archaic geisha vocabulary. It was like losing all trace of her former self, even the way she talked, which marked which area of the country she came from and what class she was. She also began to learn the gracious ways of the geisha world. Bowing, greeting, speaking in a high-pitched, girlish voice had to become second nature for her. For a start, she had to memorize the names, ranks, and position in the hierarchy of everyone in her geisha district. As she flitted down the narrow lanes, she was eternally bowing and greeting each person that she met with *"Ohayo san dosu."* This means "Good morning," but the words and tone are infinitely softer than the standard Japanese "Ohayo gozaimasu."

Every maiko told me the same thing: the worst aspect of the new life was not the dance and music classes, not leaving home and living apart from one's family, but "human relations"—learning to fit into the geisha community. They had to learn, as I myself had, to put up with being at the very bottom of the geisha hierarchy and to accept without ever answering back the harsh words and endless sniping of the vinegar-tongued "older sisters," some of whom were in their seventies and eighties. As they said in the geisha world, if someone told you that grass was black, ordinarily you would say, "Don't be so stupid, of course it isn't, it's green!" But a would-be maiko had to learn to agree very quietly that it was indeed black, a wonderful shade of black; in fact she couldn't imagine why she had never noticed before.

Throughout the training period the matriarchs—the "mothers" and the "older sisters"—kept a close eye on Harumi's progress and on her developing skills in language, manners, and the all-important "human relations." They also got together with the teachers to discuss her aptitude for the various arts. During the mornings she attended normal school, finishing off her standard education, and in the afternoons went to the classrooms in the Kaburenjo to take her first classes in dancing, singing, and playing the drum, flute, and shamisen.

Then came a dance test to assess her progress as a *shikomi*. It was the first time Harumi had ever performed in public. Worse still, she had to dance before an audience of the most formidable old ladies of the community. "I was so nervous," she remembered with a giggle, "having to dance all alone before such important people!"

That first hurdle overcome, Harumi was ready for the next— *minarai,* "learning by observation." Now, for the first time, she would have the thrilling experience she had been dreaming of for so long. She would put on the mask, she would see the alabaster face which henceforth she would present to the world.

But she was still not yet a maiko. To indicate the lower rank, her obi was only half the length of a maiko's obi, stretching not from neckline to ground but only to the back of her knees. Woven into it was the crest of the Haruta house.

"I was so nervous when I went to *o-zashiki* for the first time," she said in her little-girl falsetto, stroking the cat and tickling it under the chin. (*O* is an honorific, *zashiki* literally means the tatami room where the party takes place.) "I wondered what I should say to the customers. The older sisters helped me. They told me I must pay attention to the customers' saké cups and fill them quickly so they were never empty. I was so nervous I just sat still, I dared not say a word. The customers told me I looked like a doll! The hairstyle felt so strange. My head was heavy, I could hardly keep it balanced. The kimono felt so heavy too. It was hard just to walk. And when I had to walk in *okobo,* I thought I would fall! Now I'm used to them. Now I can run in them."

She showed me the bolster-shaped lacquered wooden pillow, rounded on the bottom and padded on the top, on which she had to rest her neck to prevent her hair getting mussed. It looked like a medieval torture device. In the past house mothers used to spread brown flaky rice husks under the pillow. If a girl's head slipped even for a second during the night, the brown flakes would stick to her hair, providing incontrovertible evidence. She would be scolded or worse until she had learned.

"I hate the pillow worst," she said. "I can't sleep properly. I have to sleep on my side, I can't sleep on my back. Then I have to wake up to turn over and change sides."

For Harumi, *minarai* lasted a month, the standard length of time for modern maiko; in the past it might have been a year or more. Every night as she slept her head rolled off the high wooden pillow and ruined her hair. Every day she struggled to paint her face, trying to get the surface alabaster smooth and the features perfectly symmetrical; and every day the face turned out different. Whenever she got something wrong, Haruka, the senior maiko, or Haruta, the house mother, snapped at her.

Finally, dressed in her *minarai* kimono, she would set off for the teahouse, the *minarai-jaya* where her training in proper party behavior took place. All evening she attended at parties, watching and listening, learning how to sit, how to behave, how to chat, how to keep the conversation light and entertaining, and assiduously filling saké cups and changing ashtrays. There was little verbal instruction. In the Japanese way, she was expected to watch carefully and learn by observation, absorbing every detail of this new world.

chapter 4

male geisha and dancing girls
of the eighteenth century

Wine and women
Balm for the soul,
This floating world is
Women and wine.
  Geisha song[1]

Shichiko the Male Geisha

The first time I met Shichiko he looked like a very conservative Japanese man. He wore the traditional outfit of baggy trousers and a cotton jacket, all in moss green, immaculately pressed, and carried a fan which he tapped prissily on the table whenever he wanted to make a point. But then I happened to glance at his feet. He was wearing *tabi*, toed linen socks which Japanese men traditionally wear indoors. *Tabi* are always white—except for Shichiko's. His were an intense shade of royal blue covered with dragonflies. And, despite all his attempts to look serious and solemn, a smile or even a laugh kept breaking out across his horsy jut-jawed face.

Shichiko had come to tell me about *taikomochi,* of which he was one. *Taikomochi,* he explained, were the first geisha—and they were men. They played the same music as the females, they danced and, instead of being up on stage like kabuki actors, they were down there chatting with the customers, in every way just like their female counterparts. But, historically, male geisha had been around long before.

The word *taikomochi* means drum-bearer, in reference to the small hand drum which some of them carried. Back in the seventeenth century, the pleasure quarters supported not only courtesans and prostitutes but an enormous population of brothel-keepers, owners of houses of assignation, cooks, maids, bouncers, cleaners, and assorted hangers-on. The *taikomochi* were the party masters who kept the fun and games going. They were the ones for whom the term *gei-sha* ("artiste," "entertainer" or, literally, "arts person") was coined. Like court jesters, they sang, pranced, and told jokes and stories. When a bunch of men went out drinking, they would call a *taikomochi* to entertain them. *Taikomochi* and saké went together.

"Are taikomochi gay?" I inquired rather boldly.

"Nah," said Shichiko firmly. "You want to have fun that way, you go to Shinjuku [Tokyo's famous gay district]. You don't mess about with *taikomochi.*"

This was a little disingenuous. Of course, no one ever talked about that sort of thing anymore. Nevertheless, at least until the end of the war, it was taken for granted that any traditional actor's job involved the selling of sexual favors.

But *taikomochi* had almost died out. At present, Shichiko told me, there were only five or six left in the whole of Japan. They worked almost exclusively in Asakusa in Tokyo's East End, which was where I had met him.

Some weeks later I went to watch him perform. It was at one of the regular dance displays which geisha give; though, this being downtown Tokyo, the atmosphere was very different from a Kyoto dance meeting. The room was crowded with elderly shop-owners and bigwigs, squashed together on cushions on the tatami floor. The plump, prosperous women wore matronly kimonos, while the men were in gray suits. The band—five old women on shamisen and five women singers—struck up and the geisha came out in ones, twos, and threes to show off their skills.

Then Shichiko burst on stage in a maroon men's kimono, announcing, "We're male geisha—but we don't wear white paint!" Balancing a folded scarf comically on his head to imitate a geisha's wig, he undulated along, pigeon-toed, eyes cast coyly down, then knelt in front of an imaginary mirror and mimed applying makeup, boasting in a fluting falsetto, "I've got an important *danna* who takes care of me." I had, I thought, worked out what *taikomochi* were all about. They were stand-up comics, doing mime and impersonations to the accompaniment of shamisen and song.

But then things began to go quite a bit further. In a corner of the stage was a large white folding screen.

"Gay? No, sir, not me," said Shichiko, back in his own persona now, addressing an imaginary customer—*danna*—behind the screen. "Absolutely not. I don't do that kind of thing. I've called a geisha for you. She'll be here any minute."

By now he had advanced until he was half hidden behind the screen. Suddenly there was a hand on his ear, grabbing at him and tugging him while he struggled fiercely to escape. (It was, of course, his own hand, though it looked as if it belonged to the fictitious *danna*.) A hand wrapped around his face, then his sleeve was tugged, then his kimono, until he was dragged out of sight behind the screen. He burst out again.

"*Danna*, wait," he protested. "Stop, stop! I'm not the geisha."

Again he was dragged bodily behind the screen by the imaginary *danna*, again he escaped. Finally he groaned, in tones of exaggerated resignation, "Okay, *danna*, okay. But just once, okay? From the back?" With that he pulled up his kimono skirts, revealing a pair of blue baggy trousers. He turned to look behind the screen, pointing derisively, scoffing, "What's that? Is that all? Is that yours?"

Then he turned so that his rear end was concealed behind the screen and proceeded to mime being penetrated extremely realistically with yelps of pain, rolling his eyes in comic anguish. Finally he made great play of wiping himself clean with tissues, an essential conclusion to the sex act in Japan. He even gave the floor a swab.

I was utterly shocked. Particularly considering the conservative nature of the audience, this struck me as being outrageous in the extreme. But I was the only one. No one else was shocked in the slightest. The shop-owners and their matronly wives laughed heartily and clapped enthusiastically as if it were a familiar everyday skit, skillfully carried out. The geisha returned to the stage for the second part of their performance. I later discovered that the "gay sketch" is indeed a set piece and a standard part of the *taikomochi* repertoire (there are other, considerably more outrageous sketches)—a classic, in fact.

Later, when I met Shichiko again, I asked him about it. "It's just a joke," he said, impatient at my tedious Western literal-mindedness. "It's a symbol of how far we'll go to please our customers, if you like. We treat the customers like kings. Whatever they ask, we can't say no." It was just a game, not real life; and in games anything goes.

Jesters in the Pleasure Quarters

Right from the founding of the pleasure quarters in the seventeenth century, there were jesters prancing about, playing tricks, doing risqué sketches, and singing ribald or melancholy songs to the accompaniment of the shamisen. They kept the mood upbeat and the jokes coming. The canny old brothel-keeper Jinemon Shoji, the founder of the Yoshiwara in the great city of Edo, was particularly fond of one of these talented young men and allowed him to wear his crest. He is said to have been the first to dub them geisha.

There were jesters of all levels of distinction, from serious musicians and accomplished dancers to *nodaiko* (talentless *taikomochi*), useless hangers-on who boosted the numbers in a merchant's retinue so that he could appear important and who lived off tips and scraps from his table. Talented or talentless, they were an important and popular feature of the quarters and their numbers increased steadily over the years.

The instrument that marked out the geisha, male or female, was the shamisen. A three-stringed banjo-like instrument, introduced from the tropical kingdom of Okinawa in the mid-sixteenth century, the body was of red sandalwood, mulberry, or quince wood. Originally it was made with snake skin stretched taut as a drum over the sound box. Snake skin being hard to find in the colder climate of Japan, it was replaced with dog or cat skin which is used to this day. Traditionally the best shamisens are made from the immaculate soft white pelt of a young female virgin kitten which has yet to be mounted and has therefore not been scratched by a tomcat. Played with a large plectrum of wood or ivory, the instrument makes a melancholy sound, perfect to accompany plaintive love songs. The shamisen became the definitive instrument of the pleasure quarters; it was said that its sound could stir erotic yearnings where none had existed before.

Initially the courtesans too entertained with the shamisen. But after a while it became such a commonplace skill that the higher ranks began to leave it to the lower orders. Instead of entertaining their clients by singing and dancing, the top courtesans would sit regally in their sumptuous robes surrounded by their entourage of child attendants and junior courtesans. Male geisha and younger courtesans took over the job of performing. Around the end of the seventeenth century male geisha began to specialize. Musicians and dancers kept the name "geisha"; clowns and professional fools were *taikomochi* or jesters.

Some of the jesters traveled around with troupes of dancing girls, some worked in teahouses, entertaining customers during the interminable wait for the courtesan to arrive, and some joined the entourages of wealthy merchants. Some, like Shakespeare's fools, were the best friends of powerful men, dispensing advice and flattery along with songs and buffoonery. Others were distinctly tricky.

Kiseki Ejima (1667–1736) was the most famous chronicler of the demimonde of his day. The son of a wealthy Kyoto shopkeeper, his early years were a rake's progress through the pleasure quarters. Having squandered the family fortune on high living, he reluctantly took up writing. His acidic and entertaining novels, with titles such as *The Courtesans' Amorous Shamisen* and *Courtesans Forbidden to Lose their Tempers,* were bestsellers.[2]

Male geisha often feature in his tales of life among the demimonde. In one of his stories, the *taikomochi* reflect on the hardships of their life:

"We jesters have to drink when we'd rather not," they sigh. "We have to praise the tiresome little songs of our patrons, hear ourselves called fools by real blockheads, force a smile if we're offended, and tell a roomful of people what even a woman would keep secret. No, there's nothing so bitter as to entertain for a living. If you happen to please, you may be hired five times and get only one bu [$100 in today's money] or two at most. In this wide world, is there no country where it rains hard cash?"[3]

The Fashionable
Pleasure Quarter of Gion

From the start, it was a hopeless task to try and keep pleasure restricted to the pleasure quarters. For young gallants, there were plenty of places other than the quarters, with their stilted conversation and overdressed courtesans, where they could go to enjoy an evening of witty repartee culminating, with luck, in sex. The most fashionable of these was Kyoto's glittering and sophisticated quarter of Gion, soon to become famous for its geisha.

Gion was not walled in; neither was it officially sanctioned. Unlike Shimabara and Yoshiwara, it was not the result of an administrative decision to keep prostitution in one place. Instead it had been created by free enterprise, operating in response to demand, which made it all the more vibrant and lively.

While the *keisei,* "castle-topplers," of the nightless cities were spinning ever more complex webs of romance to ensnare the wealthy and privileged, there were less arcane and more affordable alternatives springing up outside the gates. Wherever people gathered there was a never-ending supply of unlicensed prostitutes. At coaching inns along the post roads linking city to city, at inns and taverns in the post towns, at the bustling points where the highways entered the cities, at bathhouses and in hot spring resorts—wherever there were men in search of pleasure, there were women to serve their needs.

As in medieval Europe, people tended to gather at places of worship—temples and shrines. They would go to pray and then stay on to have fun and take refreshment. As it was for Chaucer's pilgrims, visiting a holy place or going on pilgrimage was the closest anyone in those days ever got to going on holiday. There was certainly no requirement to be solemn or earnest about it. Under the peaceful and prosperous rule of the Tokugawa shoguns, entrepreneurs began to build stalls and shops in and around the shrine precincts to serve the needs of pilgrims.

Gion grew up around Yasaka Shrine, on the opposite side of town from Shimabara. Dedicated to a local deity who took particular care of cotton merchants, the temple was one of the most famous and popular in the country. When nouveau-riche travelers arrived from rough and ready Edo to the east to sample the sophisticated delights of Kyoto, they would lighten their purses there first.

Screen paintings of the time show a sprawling complex of large and small shrine buildings with delicate vermilion pillars supporting sweeping cypress shingle roofs, with a squat red pagoda behind. Visitors would arrive on foot or by sedan chair, passing through the enormous *torii,* the red-painted wooden gateway, shaped like one of the monolithic Stonehenge portals, which marked the entrance. The grounds were the scene of much merriment. Paintings show pilgrims dancing exuberantly in circles, flourishing fans, accompanied by drummers and shamisen players and groups of people playing shuttlecock, while women conducted tea ceremonies among the trees and palanquin-bearers snoozed. Flanking the main gate of the shrine were tile-roofed stalls where smiling women in kimonos, their long hair looped into loose coils, brewed tea and steamed round white *dango* (skewered rice flour dumplings).

These were the first teahouses. Gradually they took to serving stronger beverages and more substantial food and the women began to sing and dance for their customers. They also provided other, more personal services, though this was strictly illegal. But the name "teahouse" *(ochaya)* remained.

There was never any lack of candidates among local women to be *cha-tate onna,* tea-brewing women. Apart from women of the town, there were also shrine maidens, who officiated at Shinto ceremonies and petitioned the gods. Such maidens had to be virgins. Once they had lost their virginity, they were ritually impure and quickly found themselves unemployed. The obvious course for an ex–shrine maiden was to betake herself to one of the burgeoning teahouses in search of work.

Under the shoguns nothing could get far without official permission. Teahouses, like brothels, smacked of the salacious and had to be licensed. The first teahouses in Gion appeared in 1665 but it was not until 1712 that the authorities sanctioned their establishment and officially designated the area a teahouse quarter. Teahouses now began to mushroom throughout the entertainment zone that stretched between Yasaka Shrine and the River Kamo. The whole area was given over to pleasure with side shows, street dancing, acrobats, and peddlers along the lantern-lit streets and games, music, and singing within the teahouses.

Besides Gion the authorities also licensed two other teahouse quarters, both of which would later become famous geisha districts. One was Pontocho, a straggle of teahouses alongside the River Kamo, on the bank opposite Gion. There, in summer, merchants and samurai lounged on platforms set above the river, drinking saké, flirting with the waitresses, and enjoying wonderful views of the tree-covered Eastern Hills. The other was Kamishichiken, up in the northwest of the city at the entrance to another great shrine, Kitano Tenmangu. More than a century earlier, in 1587—at the height of Elizabeth I's reign in Britain—the then-ruler, Hideyoshi Toyotomi, had presided there over the biggest tea ceremony of all time, inviting the entire population of the city to celebrate his decisive defeat of the last of his great rival warlords.

Kamishichiken was rather exclusive; it drew its patrons largely from the silk merchants who lived in the same area. But Gion, the most famous and fashionable, welcomed any men wealthy and stylish enough to know how to enjoy themselves there, be they Osaka merchants, Edo parvenus, or Kyoto playboys.

The Dancing Girls of Edo

While the tea-brewing ladies and dancing girls of Gion rapidly turned into courtesans every bit as accomplished and seductive as the caged birds of the licensed quarters, Edo, the "City of Bachelors," was developing its own breed of freelance prostitutes. And it was in Edo, in a rather disreputable section of town called Fukagawa, where prostitutes and courtesans did business out of small wooden houses along the side of the River Sumida, that the first woman to call herself a "geisha" appeared. It was around 1750. Her name was Kikuya and she was a prostitute who had made a reputation for herself with her shamisen-playing and singing and decided to make entertaining her full-time profession.

Fukagawa (Deep River) was to become the most renowned of the unlicensed pleasure quarters, famous for the stylish bravado of its women. Back in 1683, three decades before the first licenses were issued for teahouses, it was already thriving. That year a poet and author named Mosui Toda (1629–1706) wrote a guidebook to the Edo of his day entitled *A Sprig of Purple*. In this he described a shrine to the god Hachiman in a place called Eitai Island, shortly to become known as Fukagawa.

Like Yasaka Shrine in Kyoto, this was an important place of worship in a rather remote part of town. In fact it was so out of the way that it might have had to close for lack of business were it not for the fact that the authorities "took mercy and tempered the stringency of the law" against unlicensed prostitution. By Mosui's time the approaches to the shrine were occupied entirely by teahouses, each employing "ten women of remarkable beauty" who were more than happy to "comfort the pilgrims." As a result, the area bloomed and became prosperous.[4]

There were illegal red-light districts all over Edo but Fukagawa had the most, seven in all, known as the *oka basho* (hill places). It was a kind of suburb, conveniently outside the jurisdiction of the city magistrates, lined with wharves and warehouses belonging to the wealthy timber merchants who also had villas there. A famous big-spender named Bunzaemon Kinokuniya had a mansion there and, when he was not busy taking over the entire Yoshiwara for the night, he often enjoyed sampling the local talent.

Some time in the 1680s—the last decadent years of the Stuarts in the West—some daimyo and upper-crust samurai began hosting parties at which dancing girls—*odori-ko*—were hired to perform before the guests. For the lower orders this offered a great opportunity to obtain gainful employment for one's daughter or, with luck, settle her in a position in a good household. So townsfolk started sending their daughters off for dancing classes.

A few decades on, the dancing girls had expanded their repertoire.

By then Edo—and in particular the outlying district of Fukagawa—was overflowing with young women who called themselves *odori-ko* but were really prostitutes. Every now and then the authorities would swoop down on unlicensed areas, round up working girls, and send them off to the licensed quarters, where they would be forced to work for three years without pay. Some were out of their teens, too old to be *odori-ko,* which literally means "dancing child." These older *odori-ko* began to call themselves "geisha," after the male geisha of the pleasure quarters.[5]

The first female geisha, Kikuya, must have been one of these—and she must have been a star, for her name has been remembered through the centuries, though nothing is known of her beyond her reputation as a brilliantly accomplished singer and dancer. Around the same time that she was strutting her stuff around the teahouses of Fukagawa, across the country in Kyoto, in the walled city of Shimabara, the first female drum-bearer sauntered in to a party. She was referred to as a *geiko,* "arts child," which is still the word used for geisha in Kyoto. Soon geisha were all the rage. Tea-brewing women, dancing girls, and drum-bearers took to calling themselves "geisha," insisting that they were not mere prostitutes but artistes. A new profession was born.

The female geisha were an instant success. Unlike the courtesans and prostitutes of the pleasure quarters, they were independent, smart women who made a living by their skills and their wit and who were not bound by traditions that forced them to behave in certain ways. They did not have to engage in endless formality and could take sexual partners as and when they pleased. They were women of the world. And although the geisha quarters were clustered in particular parts of town, they were not walled in. The women could come and go freely. They were not caged birds.

While Shimabara quickly embraced the new trend, the Yoshiwara held out against it for a decade. At last, finding their business threatened by the popularity of this new breed of woman, the brothel-keepers there started to hire freelance female geisha to compete with the dancing girls, geisha, and *geiko* outside the gates. These geisha worked as entertainers, like the male geisha, in the Yoshiwara, on one condition: they were not allowed to steal the courtesans' clients by sleeping with them. The geisha of the "hill places" had no such restrictions.

The first geisha in the Yoshiwara was recorded in 1761. Called Kasen of the Ogiya house, she was a prostitute who had earned her freedom and set up in business as an entertainer. Thereafter the number of female geisha swelled until they completely overwhelmed the male geisha. In 1770 there were 16 female geisha in the Yoshiwara and 31 men; in 1775, 33 female geisha but still 31 men; and by 1800 there were 143 females as against 45 men. By that time the word "geisha" primarily meant a woman, not a man. As the last of the grand *tayu* courtesans disappeared, the geisha moved center stage.[6]

Times were changing. The peak of prosperity had passed, the Genroku period—when one commentator wrote of the pleasure quarters that "their splendor was by day like Paradise and by night like the Palace of the Dragon King"—was over.[7] The great economic slowdown of the 1750s was under way. Inflation was rampant, the population boom of the early years of the Tokugawa peace had slowed and, crippled by corruption and incompetence, the shogunate was incapable of improving matters.

Two classes, in particular, suffered: the peasants, who were largely dependent on a single crop—rice; and the samurai, who received their fixed stipends in rice, which then had to be handed over to the merchants in exchange for pitiful amounts of cash. While the townsmen hoarded rice, the samurai declined into genteel poverty. The economic malaise was made all the more oppressive by a calamitous barrage of natural disasters. Fire leveled the flimsy wooden structures of Edo again and again. There were storms, earthquakes, volcanic eruptions, tidal waves, and a string of bad harvests leading to devastating famines in which half a million peasants died. The mood of the country grew darker.

The townsfolk, however, were not suffering at all. In fact, they were growing ever wealthier. Many profited from the misery by lending money and selling their goods at extortionate rates. Sporadically the shogunate tried to clamp down on ostentatious spending. There were regular edicts that "Townsmen and servants may not wear silk," "Townsmen may not wear cloth mantles," "Townsmen may not live extravagantly," and "Townsmen may not give lavish entertainments." Those who were too obviously prosperous also ran the risk of having their riches confiscated and redistributed into the shogun's coffers. In any case, affluence was no longer a novelty. Many merchant families had enjoyed prosperity for several generations and no longer needed to flaunt it.

The result was a new aesthetic of restraint. Townsfolk, nervous of having their fortunes impounded, took to wearing sober robes with a sumptuous lining, only visible when they flung off their jacket, and spent their money on tiny but inordinately expensive items such as intricately carved *netsuke* toggles of wood or ivory, tobacco pouches, and the like. They lived in homes with austere external walls concealing a sumptuous interior, like the beautiful Sumiya teahouse which stands to this day in Shimabara. By the mid-1700s, the courtesans of the pleasure quarters, in their showy kimonos, were beginning to seem rather passé. They continued to have their aficionados. But modern young men about town were starting to prefer the more understated attractions of the geisha.

While the courtesans tied their obi in front, geisha tied theirs chastely at the back like ordinary townswomen. Instead of flamboyant multilayered kimonos, they sported plain monochrome ones with the narrow white collar of the under-kimono visible at the throat. Their coiffure was relatively simple, decorated with two or three hairpins and a single comb, rather than an armory of tortoiseshell pins, combs, ribbons, and dangling decorations like the courtesans wore. Some of the understatement which gave the geisha their special flavor was the result of official ordinances. They were forbidden to wear elaborate kimonos even if they wanted to.

By now no one could deny that the geisha were a profession in their own right. The brothel-keepers of the Yoshiwara were becoming more and more worried by their success and popularity. In 1779 a man called Shoroku, the proprietor of the Daikokuya, one of the oldest establishments in the quarter, proposed setting up an inspection station, a *kemban,* to regulate and control them. With the backing of the other brothel-keepers, he promptly retired and appointed himself comptroller. Installed at the Great Gate of the Yoshiwara, he sold 100 permits to geisha. He had a staff of two inspectors and dozens of clerks who processed all requests that geisha be sent to entertain.

The *kemban* took 30 to 50 percent of the geishas' fees. They also kept an eye out to ensure that the geisha did not engage in prostitution and interfere with the business of the Yoshiwara. Wherever a geisha went, she was accompanied by a man who carried her shamisen. It was also his job to keep an eye on her and make sure she did not try to run away. As for Shoroku, he ended up a very rich man with an enviable collection of fine art and antiques.

Shoroku established rules of conduct to distinguish geisha from courtesans and prostitutes and ensure that they did not steal their customers. Geisha were to be recruited from among the less beautiful women. They were to wear a severe kimono and simple hairstyle. They were to work in twos or threes, never alone, so as to discourage propositioning, and they were not to sit too close to guests. If a prostitute accused a geisha of interfering with her customers, there would be an inquiry. A geisha found contravening the regulations was liable to lose her license for several days or even permanently.

Such constraints only applied to those who wished to work in the pleasure quarters. There was never any doubt that the geisha of Fukagawa, stylish and talented as they were, slept with whomever they liked, whenever they liked. But prostitutes were prostitutes and geisha were geisha. If a geisha chose to enter into a relationship with a client, that was legally classified as misconduct, not prostitution. And such activities were the free choice of the geisha. Prostitution was never something they were forced to engage in.[8]

The Stylish Geisha of Fukagawa

The geisha of Tatsumi goes walking,
Bare white feet in black lacquered clogs.
In her haori jacket, she's the pride of Great Edo.
Ah, the Hachiman bell is ringing.

Geisha song[9]

The Fukagawa geisha—also known as Tatsumi geisha, as in the song—were particularly famous for their sex appeal. Above their plain, understated kimonos they wore a *haori,* a loose, square-cut jacket with huge sleeves originally worn by men. This gave them a raffish air reminiscent of the kabuki actors who played women's roles and who, on leaving the theater, would toss a jacket on over their women's costume. The geisha never wore *tabi* (toed linen socks). Even in the dead of winter, they always went barefoot, their red-painted toenails framed against the black of their lacquer clogs peeping out from under the hem of their kimonos. The word for this casual, effortless chic was *iki,* which the Fukagawa geisha—more than any other—embodied.

In those days Fukagawa was by the sea, though nowadays, after centuries of landfill, the sea has been pushed a long way away. Young blades who wanted to enjoy the company of geisha would take a roofed houseboat down the river and along the seashore. There were temptations even before they disembarked. There were boats owned by cut-price prostitutes known, in the slang of the time, as *funa-manju* (boat dumplings), ready to offer their services then and there on board. On land there were *kekoro* (literally "kicks") and *maruta* (logs) ready to waylay them, and right at the bottom *yotaka* (nighthawks) who carried out their work in the open air; as to exactly what these colloquialisms referred to, that has been lost in the mists of time and will have to be left to the imagination. In Fukagawa the lowest grade of prostitutes were called *ahiru* (ducks), perhaps because they lived near the water; Ahiru became the name of the quarter there.

As the young man reached the Fukagawa area, he would be beguiled by the strumming of shamisen and the sound of singing from the restaurants and teahouses along the waterfront. The geisha were fine musicians who had spent years studying their art. Even though they might choose to augment their income with prostitution, they had a skill with which they could support themselves for the rest of their lives. In comparison with the chic, independent geisha, the courtesans of the pleasure quarters seemed stuck in a time warp.

The young man who wanted to win himself one of these stylish modern women had to be a very cool character himself. While the ideal woman was *iki,* the equivalent for men was to be a *tsu*—a sophisticate, a connoisseur. The word arose around 1770 and quickly became an enormous fad. Being a *tsu* meant knowing one's way around the demimonde, knowing the rules of the game so thoroughly that one was completely at ease. Every self-respecting Edo man wanted to be thought a *tsu,* certainly not a *yabo* ("boor," the opposite) or a *hanka-tsu* (a half-baked *tsu,* a charlatan).

As it happened, the typical *yabo* was likely to be a samurai, an uncouth provincial type who had no idea how to dress stylishly and talked in stiff outmoded language. A *tsu,* in contrast, had no need to be rich or to have high social status. If he looked good and had savoir faire, he was welcome. Thus the countercultural values of the demimonde, which focused obsessively on style, dress, and appearance, seeped through to permeate society at large.

One of the most brilliant figures of the time was a man called Kyoden Santo (1761–1816). A poet and comic novelist, he was also a famous artist who worked under the name Masanobu Kitao and practically lived in the Yoshiwara. Both his wives were second-rank Yoshiwara courtesans. At twenty-four, he published a book called *Romantic Embroilments Born in Edo* (1785). Told cartoon-style in drawings, with the dialogue and narrative festooning every available space, this is the story of Enjiro, the spoiled son of wealthy parents.

Enjiro fancies himself as a great lover *(iro-otoko),* and wants the whole world to know it. But sadly, being ugly, this is rather difficult for him to achieve. The best way to become truly famous is by committing love suicide with a courtesan. So he buys the freedom of a woman called Ukina, paying a lot of money to have a window in her brothel broken. The two scramble down a ladder, feigning elopement, though the brothel staff ruins the effect by cheerfully waving them off. Still, he sets off into the woods with her, having arranged for friends to arrive and stop them before they actually commit the act.

Unfortunately at this stage two robbers turn up, waving swords and wearing the Japanese equivalent of balaclavas, sinister black scarves tied around their faces revealing only their eyes. They set upon the helpless pair and offer to help them die. "We didn't mean to kill ourselves when we set off to commit suicide," groans Enjiro.

In the end the robbers make off with their clothes, leaving them naked but for their loincloths and an umbrella. Enjiro has become famous, though not in the way he intended.

Kyoden's story caused great hilarity and was hugely successful, with the scene of the pair walking along miserably, practically naked, re-produced on innumerable woodblock prints and paper fans. Clearly there were plenty of Enjiros to be found around Edo and in the pleasure quarters.[10]

The licensed and the unlicensed districts, the two worlds within and without the walls, frequently mingled. Whenever there was a clamp-down on illegal prostitution, the unfortunate women were shipped off and dumped in the nearest licensed quarter. Given that the walled cities were never allowed to expand a single yard, there must have been terrible overcrowding and considerable squalor. Moreover, each influx of un-trained, unqualified prostitutes dragged standards in the quarters down another notch.

Every now and then there was a devastating fire. In the hundred years following the first appearance of the geisha in 1760, the Yoshiwara burned to the ground ten times and there were several other fires which destroyed sections. When this happened, the brothel-keepers were per-mitted to relocate temporarily to one of the unlicensed areas until the walled city was rebuilt. The unlicensed quarters were by now so much more lively, popular, and accessible than the licensed that it was a great opportunity to advertise their wares and increase their profits.

One such upheaval took place in 1787, when some brothel-keepers set up temporary houses in a fashionable riverfront zone called Nakasu Island after a fire. The area had been known as Three Forks in the hey-day of the Yoshiwara, when a courtesan named Takao was murdered there by her disappointed suitor. After the shogunate instigated a pro-gram of landfill, it developed into the most sophisticated and exciting entertainment district in the country, packed with famous and exclusive restaurants and teahouses, with resident geisha to take care of guests.

At its height there were 18 restaurants, some of which catered only to the deputies of the provincial lords, 93 teahouses, 14 boathouses, and at least 27 geisha, not to mention brothels, theaters, and assorted food stalls. The most famous restaurant of all, depicted in many wood-block prints, was the Shikian (Four Seasons Hermitage). Nakasu was an eighteenth-century equivalent of London's Soho, within easy reach of the city center, with fun for ordinary folk too, where people could go for the day to enjoy sideshows, jugglers, freak shows, mimes, and street theater.

For the women of the Yoshiwara who were transported to this lively environment, there was a far greater degree of freedom than usual. Here no one worried about formalities like the first and second meetings, where clients and courtesans exchanged cups of saké. Instead they could jump straight to consummation, which was supposed to be withheld until the third meeting. Likewise, there were fewer staff around who needed to be tipped, which made it easier on the customers. Conditions were so crowded inside the small temporary brothels that sometimes a girl's feet touched someone else's head and everyone could hear the noisy carousing of the drunken customers and the courtesans' insincere declarations of eternal love to each and every one of them.

Morality was not the only thing which was slipping. For while privileged debauchees sang, danced, and frittered away their time in the company of geisha and courtesans on Nakasu Island, the poor were starving to death. In 1787, after seven years of bad harvests and famine, rioting peasants broke into the shops and storehouses of the wealthy rice merchants, first in Osaka, then in Edo and Kyoto, wrecking, destroying, and making off with sacks of hoarded rice.

Despite the economic woes of the rest of the country, it was still a golden age for pleasure. At the Yoshiwara and the other government-recognized licensed quarters (of which there were about two hundred throughout the country), the partying never stopped. For the man about town there was unlimited choice. He could trawl the unlicensed quarters with their edge of illegality, enjoy himself at the less risky licensed quarters, and take his pick among courtesans, geisha, and straightforward prostitutes.

The Yoshiwara was still unquestionably the most famous pleasure quarter in Japan. Artists depicted its beautiful, languid women in woodblock prints which rolled off the presses to be snapped up by an eager populace. Guidebooks, like the fanzines of modern times, listed their attributes and special skills. Ambitious young men, eager to be recognized as *tsu* sophisticates, studied the manuals describing the latest fashions, desperately checking that they had the right undergarment, silver pipe, and tobacco pouch, could drop the right names, and could spot the most celebrated courtesans and geisha.

They did not realize that their elaborately hedonistic lifestyle would soon be threatened. For cataclysmic events were about to overtake the precious world of Edo, the Yoshiwara, and Tokugawa Japan. And the women who would dominate the brave new world which was to follow would be the geisha, not the courtesans.

inside the pleasure quarters

Becoming a Geisha

I know she is light and faithless,
But she has come back half-repentant
And very pale and very sad.
A butterfly needs somewhere to rest
At evening.

　　Geisha song[1]

❧

The Professor of Hairstyling

Whenever I had a spare moment I dropped into Professor Ishihara's hairdressing salon to the north of Shijo Street, in the oldest part of Gion (his Japanese title is Ishihara Sensei, "Teacher Ishihara"). He knew everything one could ever want to know about geisha, maiko, their history, and their hair. His wife, I had heard, was from a family that ran a teahouse, though that was the one thing that he would never talk about.

A laid-back, humorous, dapper man always dressed in an elegant pin-striped suit, he had penned three books on the history of maiko and *tayu* hairstyles and was working on a fourth. He was the only person left in Japan who knew how to create the ornate hairstyles of the *tayu* courtesans.

"In Edo times you could tell everything about a person just by looking at their hair," he told me one day. "In those days there was a different hairstyle for each class of person. You could tell from someone's hairstyle what class they were, what kind of work they did, and what part of the country they came from. The geisha world is the only place where that still goes on. There are different hairstyles for each stage of the geisha's career, different hairstyles for geisha in different parts of Japan, and different sorts of kimono.

"This," he explained, showing me a picture of an ornate hairstyle, decorated with ribbons, ornaments, and silk flowers, with a bagel-shaped rolled knot of hair worn high on the head, "is *ware-shinobu*. It's the maiko's first hairstyle. It means that she is young and cute.

"And this"—turning the page to show me a less heavily decorated hairstyle with the knot lower down—"is the maiko's second hairstyle, *ofuku*. It means that she is to be congratulated, she is no longer a virgin. Maiko used to start wearing their hair like this when they were thirteen."

"Thirteen?" I was aghast. It was hard to get to grips with the idea that the old geisha I knew had lost their virginity—in other words, been deflowered whether they liked it or not—at the tender age of thirteen.

"They all had it," he said carelessly. "They all had *mizuage*. If you listen to the old grannies at the teahouses, they'll tell you, 'We were children, we didn't know anything, what could we do?' In those days Kyoto was full of rich silk traders and kimono merchants. The *danna* would pay for *mizuage,* buy the girl a house, and pay her an allowance. The wives? They were like employees, they just thought it was normal. Nowadays they'd ask for a divorce! For three hundred years it was perfectly normal for men to pay and for women to give sex. All that's stopped now, of course. Ever since 1958 it's been completely different.

It's much more serious now. The maiko all concentrate on their dancing. The *ofuku* hairstyle just means she's more senior."

Once you became a senior maiko, he said, there was no further to go. You wore your hair in the *ofuku* style, though there were a couple of other styles worn for special occasions: *yakko-shimada,* a sweeping elegant style worn for the New Year celebrations, decorated with sprigs of dried rice for fertility and good luck; and the *katsuyama,* named after the seventeenth-century bathhouse attendant who became a great courtesan famous for her splendid topknot. The maiko's last hairstyle, which was very ornate indeed, was the *sakko,* which she wore for her last month before graduating to become a geisha.

The door opened and a young woman came in, piping in a fluting falsetto, *"Ohayo dosu! Sensei, o tanomo shimasu!"*—"Good morning! Professor, could you please . . . ?" In the mornings maiko were always pale and subdued after the previous night's parties. Without further ado, this one, in an everyday cotton *yukata* and with her long hair loose and shaggy, sat down, picked up a teen magazine, and started leafing through it.

One way to spot an ex-maiko is the perfectly round little bald patch on the crown of her head. Having been tugged and pulled by the hairdresser week after week for five years, the hair never grows back. Watching Professor Ishihara at work, it was easy to see how this could happen. He was like an artist struggling to create beauty out of his chosen material—hair.

With curling irons heated over a portable charcoal brazier, he stretched the hair until it was smooth, shiny, and perfectly straight. Then, combing in globs of white pomade and oiling his comb with *bintsuke* oil (the same oil used to keep sumo wrestlers' topknots rigid), he parted and sectioned it. Beginning with the hair at the crown of the head, he tugged it firmly into a ponytail, tied in a roll of handmade paper to give bulk, and swept it forward to form the central knot of the entire edifice. He sculpted the hair at the back of the head up and over it, coiling it into a stiff loop, with a thin frame of lacquered wood to hold it in place. The front of the hair meanwhile was rollered. Then he set to work on the two side pieces, stretching them round, with plenty of *bintsuke* oil, and tying them with string to the central knot so that they formed two wings, one on either side of the face. He slipped a thin lacquered wooden band like a hairband through the two wings to hold them firmly in place and tucked a wad of artificial hair inside each.

Then he took a hairpiece, a ponytail of coarse black hair from the Tibetan yak, and tied it onto the central ponytail of the maiko's own hair. He combed the whole lot together, folded it forward, looped it back, opened it out and—lo and behold!—there was a bagel-shaped knot. Finally he teased the front of the hair into an arch and attached it too to the central knot. He added a hairpin to conceal the center of the bagel, some pieces of stiff black paper to keep the shape of the wings precise, and a couple of crinkly red ribbons. The whole masterful creation took about forty minutes and the end result was a sleek, shiny coiffure with not a single hair out of place, firm enough to survive a week's working, playing, and sleeping.

"Oki-ni," said the maiko, transformed from a shaggy-haired young woman into a creature bearing such an immaculate pompadour that a man would be terrified to touch her in case he mussed it. Bowing and smiling, she slipped out of the shop.

Joining the Geisha Family

For Harumi, the first serious decision of her career was whether she should go through with *misedashi,* the three-day debut to become a maiko, or whether she should leave. Until that point the costs the house mother had incurred in training and housing her were not exorbitant. But the debut itself was expensive; and thereafter the costs of classes, kimonos, makeup, and regular trips to the hairdresser, not to mention pocket money and other living expenses, would amount to a huge sum. If she wanted to drop out, this was the moment to do so. Otherwise she would be committed to the maiko life for the next five years. It was a big decision for a child of fourteen to make.

Many of her friends had already discovered that it was not the glamorous life they were expecting and had dropped out. As Haruta, the house mother, put it, "The flower and willow world runs according to strict rules, like Japan in the old days. At home, children are free. Here they are not free. I tell them, try it for a year, but most of them give up within three months. They're children, they don't understand properly."

"It is much tougher than I expected," said Harumi. "From the outside maiko look so pretty. But when you have entered this world, you discover what a hard life it is. Ten of us started at the same time. Six have left. I feel lonely without them."

For Harumi there was never any question. If she had been planning to leave, she would have left long before. Besides, she had already been enchanted by her first taste of stepping out, painted and dressed as the epitome of feminine beauty. Despite all the discipline and hard work, it was still every girl's dream, an eternity of dressing up.

Before her debut, there was an important rite of passage to be undergone. In order to be initiated as a full member of the geisha family, Harumi needed to be adopted by an "older sister," a senior maiko or a geisha who would be her mentor, teach her the basics of the geisha lifestyle, keep an eye on her progress with dancing and music, and, most important, shoulder the responsibility if she made a mistake. For a maiko it is a weighty deterrent against breaking the rules if she knows that it is her "older sister" rather than herself who will take the blame.

She would also be given a professional name; until then, she had been called by the name she had been born with. Like a surname, which shows one's link to the family of one's birth, her professional name would show which geisha family she belonged to and in particular her relationship with her "older sister." The older sister of Haru-mi—whose name means "Spring Beauty"—is Haru-ka, "Spring Flower," the senior maiko of the Haru-ta, "Spring Field," house.

Women who were maiko thirty or forty years ago can remember petitioning a particularly famous maiko or geisha and begging to be taken on as her younger sister. Those who succeeded in being adopted by a ravishingly beautiful geisha or one of the top dancers could be sure that they would be introduced at the best teahouses, where they could bask in her reflected glory. For an ambitious maiko, this is still the way to ensure a brilliant career. Similarly, geisha might watch out for promising maiko, either particularly lovely or particularly talented at dancing, and take them under their wing.

Most maiko, however, are content to leave the choice of older sister to their house mother. Haruta, the mother of Haruta geisha house, told me, "You need someone who has common sense. It's like bringing up a child. She has to be strict with her, like a parent. Sometimes I choose a maiko, sometimes a geisha; but I always choose from the girls I've reared myself at the Haruta house."

The moment of transition was marked by a ceremony which took place on an auspicious day chosen by a fortune teller au fait with the omens. Called *san-san-kudo,* "three times three, nine times," it is exactly the same as the most solemn and binding part of the Japanese wedding ceremony, a bit like the exchange of rings in the West. It was almost as if Harumi was marrying into the geisha community, in the same way as a nun marries into the church. Like a nun, henceforth if Harumi wished to marry she would have to give up her geisha vocation.

Dressed in all her finery, her hair tricked out with combs, ribbons, hairpins, ornaments, and silk flowers, her face painted to doll-like perfection, wearing a formal black kimono, she knelt solemnly beside Haruka in a tatami room in the geisha house. First Haruka took a small red-lacquered saucer brimming with saké and drank it in three sips, then passed it to the maid to refill. Next Harumi drank from the same cup. Then the ceremony was repeated with a middle-size saucer, then a large one—three saké cups, three sips from each.

The following day was the beginning of Harumi's debut. For three days she was the star of the entire district. Every waking second she was on display as she paraded the streets trailed by photographers, meeting everyone, sliding open teahouse doors, bowing again and again, piping, "Tanomo, okasan, oki-ni . . . ," "Asking your favor, mother, thank you . . ." The house mothers gave her gifts of money in envelopes which the dresser or Haruta—whoever happened to be with her—tucked away in a capacious sleeve. Each contained 10,000 to 20,000 yen, $100 to $200. Multiplied by the number of houses in the district, it came to a sizable amount of money, though it was still only a small contribution toward the exorbitant costs of the *misedashi.* In the evening there was party after party and most of the customers too gave her sizable tips. By the end of all the meeting, greeting, and partying she was completely exhausted.

Living in the same house, Haruka really was like an older sister to Harumi. At eighteen, she had nearly completed her maiko training. She kept an eye on Harumi's progress, helping her master the minute rules and customs which determine every second of life in the geisha districts. A few days earlier, there had been a small concert at the Kaburenjo where the maiko displayed their musical skills, particularly in drumming. It was an important occasion for Harumi. In the morning, Haruka took her from teahouse to teahouse to greet the teahouse owners and the ancient "older sisters" who would make up the audience and beg their indulgence.

"The timing is so hard," piped Harumi in her little-girl voice. "If you arrive too early they scold you. If you speak too softly, they scold you. Haruka taught me about that."

"If I become a geisha and have my own apartment, Harumi will come every two or three days to visit," Haruka told me in firm, responsible, big sister tones. "It's not like being friends. It's a special relationship."

Graduation:
The Collar-Changing Ceremony

Downstairs in the living room, the nerve center of the house, the witching hour was fast approaching. The lapdog, now confined to a large cage, yapped hysterically, the television blared, and a roomful of ex-geisha sat laughing and chatting. One, in her thirties and married, bounced a large baby on her knee, crooning in English in my honor, "Hap-pee, hap-pee." Haruta, the large, gregarious house mother, was on the phone, juggling a timetable covered in multicolored scribbles and a book of phone numbers.

"We need a shamisen player for tomorrow night," she barked. "No, no, she'll be busy . . . No, not that one either, she's not good at keeping up a conversation. We need someone who can play the shamisen and knows how to chat too."

Harumi disappeared into the kitchen to have a quick meal of boiled beef on rice. Geisha and maiko ate twice a day, at twelve, after classes, and at four, before getting ready for the evening's parties. They might drink with the guests. In fact they were expected to; a geisha who did not drink was almost a contradiction in terms. But they never ate with them. Thus it was important to eat before starting work so as not to suffer too many pangs at the sight of the mouth-watering dishes being served up. If a maiko was really hungry she might snack at midnight when she got back from her last engagement.

There were no parties that night for Harumi's "older sister," Haruka. Relaxing in a T-shirt and shorts with her long hair tied back in a ponytail, she was noticeably more mature and confident than the child-like Harumi. She lacked the younger girl's porcelain prettiness but she had an engaging candor of manner. Squashed around a corner of the table that filled the living room, we tried to ignore the noise and bustle as we chatted.

Haruka had her own decision to make. She had already been a maiko for five years and now this stage of her life in the geisha world was nearly at an end. She had reached the most important turning point of her career. If she stayed on, the next step was *erikae,* "changing the collar," when the maiko's thick red embroidered undercollar—*eri*— was replaced with the *geiko*'s—Kyoto geisha's—white one and her long maiko locks were cut in preparation for putting on the wig of the geiko. If she wanted to leave, now was the moment to do so. Otherwise she would be committed for at least two years. It was akin to deciding whether to go on to postgraduate study at university.

Lots of young women became maiko for five years. It was like going to finishing school, acquiring gloss and grooming and also meeting a pool of wealthy and influential men, one of whom might turn out to be a prospective husband. Geisha were much less flamboyant, part of the dark fabric of the place. Instead of the brilliant peacock colors of the maiko, geisha wore simple, elegant kimonos. Instead of the maiko's waxed coiffure, they wore their hair in a bouffant bun except on special occasions, when they would don a wig. They were also in much less demand. Customers would ask for a particular geisha whom they knew; but they would just ask for a maiko, any maiko. If she was not particularly charming or entertaining or a particularly good dancer, a geisha might find herself out of work; and no parties meant no income.

Being a geisha was a vocation. You only went through the changing of the collar if you really wanted to, perhaps because you loved traditional dance and music and wanted to take it up as a full-time profession or because you enjoyed the life and didn't want to leave. But if you did choose to carry on, you would end up spending your most eligible years studying dance and music and entertaining old men at parties. If, after all that, you decided that you wanted to marry, you might well find yourself on the shelf.

"I'm wondering whether to give up," confided Haruka. "I like the geisha look; but if you become a geisha, the classes get much more difficult. When you're a maiko, everyone treats you like a child. If you make mistakes, the customers think you're cute. But after *erikae* you're an adult, you can't make mistakes anymore. In any case, I really want to get married. You only have one life. I don't want to go on being a geisha forever.

"I'd like to marry someone who's not fussy about household stuff, someone manly. An ordinary guy would be fine, I don't need a company chairman's son. The only trouble is, you get spoiled as a maiko. You get used to having presents and being taken to good restaurants. I couldn't marry a poor man. I might not make a good wife."

Haruka was the daughter of a truck driver from just outside Kyoto. Becoming a maiko had opened doors for her into worlds she could never have imagined.

"My father didn't want me to become a maiko," she said. "He was worried about me. He didn't know what I would have to do. But my mother said it was okay. I still go home quite often, but this is my family now; we eat rice from the same pot. I love it. I love classes and I love 'work' [the evening parties]. Last night we danced at the International Hotel opposite Nijo Castle. The night before that we were at a restaurant on the river in Takao for an outdoor party. There were jetties out above the water. Three of us were there. We went from table to table, chatting to all the customers. That's how it is most nights in summer, outdoor parties. I love the traveling too, I love seeing new places. I've been everywhere. I've been to Tokyo, I've been to Nagasaki."

Maiko are in huge demand. Kyoto is the only place in the country that still has them and they are often invited to brighten up a party for particularly important guests at a classy traditional restaurant in another city. They travel first class on the bullet train and stay in five-star hotels. They are also often hired to look decorative and be charming at conferences or exhibitions of, for example, kimono fabrics. Added to which, everyone who visits Kyoto and has connections or a bottomless purse wants to meet maiko. They are the symbol of the city. As one self-styled connoisseur put it, "maiko are the flavor of Kyoto."

"I meet famous people all the time," beamed Haruka. "I've met kabuki actors, TV actors, sportsmen . . .

"You know Masahiro Nakai?" she added, mentioning the boyish heartthrob whose photograph dominated the wall in the room she shared with Harumi. "I met him! He was starring in a TV drama and came to film in Kyoto. They ended up at a teahouse run by a friend of our house mother. The master of the teahouse knew I was Nakai-kun's fan.* He didn't say anything, he just called and asked me to entertain. So I got to meet Nakai-kun. He was really fun, even better-looking than I thought."

Six o'clock was approaching, the magic moment when the first parties always began. Harumi reappeared, poised and ready for the evening's work. The mask was in place. She was no longer a wide-eyed innocent child but a porcelain doll, wrapped like a Christmas gift in layer upon layer of kimonos and obis. Her eyes and eyebrows were drawn in black, the corners of her eyes defined in red, and her lips a perfect bow, startlingly red on the alabaster white of her face. Her kimono of light, loosely woven silk was a vivid shade of royal blue with a design of irises. Her thick brocade obi was of pale orange and gold with a red-and-silver under-obi beneath it. Her hair, in the *ofuku* style of the mature maiko, was decked out with a dangling silver comb and a frieze of stylized silk hydrangeas in pale pink and blue, appropriate for the month of June.

She stood rather uncertainly in the entrance like an actress in the wings, composing herself to step out into the spotlight. Outside a taxi had pulled up, almost filling the narrow street with its dark wooden houses. Tucking her wicker-bottomed silk handbag under her arm, she stepped into her high *okobo* clogs and, bells tinkling, slipped gracefully into the taxi, piping *"Oki-ni, oki-ni"* as she left. For a moment the geisha

---

*[-kun is an affectionate suffix used for boys, rather like abbreviating Robert to Bobby; literally something like "young Nakai."]

soap opera on television was interrupted by the face of Leonardo di Caprio, advertising Orico, a credit card company.

The Wigmaker

One day, during a break in the weather, I took a bus across town to the other side of the city, near the Nishijin weavers' district and the Kamishichiken geisha district, to visit one of the three wigmakers who among them serviced all the Kyoto geisha. Mr. Imanishi had turned a wing of his rambling house behind Myoshinji Zen temple into a busy workshop where he sat on his heels alongside his two sons, his apprentices in the trade. Here and there about the room were what looked at first glance like human heads stuck on poles. They turned out to be wigs, some with long bedraggled locks, others neatly coiffed, set on egg-shaped wooden molds.

"Wigs used to be all Japanese hair, you know," said Mr. Imanishi breezily with a grin. He was a roguish man in his sixties with a face like a walnut, a cheeky upturned nose, and a mop of curly gray hair. The hair of the wig on the stand in front of him hung in unappetizing rat's tails which he was sectioning and combing energetically, slapping on globs of white *bintsuke* wax.

"But these days Japanese girls are rich," he went on. "They don't need to sell their hair. So we use imported Chinese hair, plus yak's hair for volume. But Japanese hair is the best. That's what we say, us wigmakers."

He looped, folded, and pinned the tresses in a process very similar to dressing a maiko's hair until he had created the glossy coiffure of the geisha, with a swatch of hair at the back, held in place with a stiff silver ribbon. Then he handed me the finished wig. The glossy hair was sticky with wax but the wig itself was astonishingly light and hard. Inside was a framework of duralumin, a sort of aluminum, lined with netting, like the inside of a crash helmet. Western wigs, conversely, have a rubber base.

"Once they decide to change the collar, that's when we measure them up for their first wig," explained Mr. Imanishi, wiping his hands on his uncannily clean white linen apron. "I meet the maiko and decide what shape will flatter her face. A round face, I make it look thinner; a thin face, I make it plumper. Those geisha all look pretty, right? That's the wigmaker's art, to make a wig that flatters the face. That's what keeps them coming back."

Unlike a Western wig, a Japanese wig had a widow's peak at the front like Mount Fuji. It took, he said, two weeks to make a wig and required several fittings. For the first five days after the changing of the collar, one of his sons went to the geisha house every day to teach the fledgling geisha how to put it on. Once the first parties were over and she had time for more fittings, she ordered a second wig so that she always had one to wear while the other was being reset.

No geisha would dream of being seen in a wig that had a single hair out of place let alone one that was a bit flat or misshapen. In order to ensure that they always had that fresh-from-the-hairdresser look, geisha stored their wigs carefully in wig boxes and had them combed out and reset once a month, a job which took half a day (one and a half hours plus fetching and returning the wig) and cost 23,000 yen ($230) a time. Added to that, a wig had a lifespan of about three years, after which a geisha would need a new one. Each new wig cost 500,000 yen, in the region of $5,000. All in all, it was a sizable expense for the geisha and provided a thriving business for Mr. Imanishi and his fellow wigmakers.

Wigs came into vogue well after the end of the war, around the watershed year of 1958. Before then they had been used mainly in the kabuki theater. Geisha used to go to the hairdresser as maiko do still. For maiko, who were in the process of being trained, it was essential to live the flower and willow life twenty-four hours a day. But geisha were modern women, adults who had chosen to continue the life while it suited them. In their time off, they preferred to have the option of wearing Western clothes and having their hair in a less conspicuous style. Wearing a wig enabled them to switch between the geisha world and everyday life with ease. They could treat being a geisha as a job and the geisha's outfit as a uniform, to be put on when they started work and taken off afterward. It was a liberation. Thus as the profession itself changed, wigs soared in popularity.

But how on earth, I asked, could one tamp down the enormous

amount of hair which most geisha had, and fit a wig on top? Perhaps, said Mr. Imanishi, I should try it myself. Without more ado he swept my hair back and twisted a stretchy net over it, then wound a bandage-like tape around the edges. In seconds my head was as smooth as the egg-shaped molds on which the wigs rested. Then he lifted a wig out of its box. After he had tied a few ribbons and made a few adjustments it fitted perfectly. It felt tight, secure, and heavy, like wearing a crown. He added an ivory comb and some tortoiseshell hairpins and gave me a mirror in which to admire his handiwork.

The effect of a black, glossy, and absurdly stylized geisha wig perched above my European features was, it has to be said, far from flattering, like wearing an enormous piled-up Louis Quatorze wig without the gown, flounces, powder, or perfectly placed round black beauty spot. I hastily dabbed on the reddest lipstick I could find. A good thick layer of white makeup, I could see, would make all the difference. As is normal in Japan to mark the occasion, I lined up with Mr. Imanishi and his family, his baby grandson on my knee, for a group photograph.

I had a final question. He had been boasting of how many geisha he knew and how well he knew them.

"What would you say if your daughter wanted to become a geisha?" I asked.

He looked taken aback.

"Hmm," he said finally, with an uncertain chuckle. "That's a difficult question." It was, it seemed, as outrageous a suggestion as if I had asked a stern Victorian patriarch if he would allow his daughter to become an actress. I could almost hear the music hall refrain: "Don't put your daughter on the stage, Mrs. Worthington!" In turn-of-the-millennium Japan, geisha still had the rakish, not-quite-respectable image that actors and actresses used to have a century ago in Britain. To drop their names and boast of how many one knew was one thing. To have one's own child join the ranks of these glamorous but nonetheless somehow disreputable creatures was quite another.

A hole in the paper wall,
Who has been so guilty?
Through it I hear the breaking of a shamisen string,
Meaning bad luck.
Yet the prediction-seller says
That mine is excellent.

Geisha song[2]

Every now and then a friend of a friend named Mr. Mori would phone me and invite me out on a bar crawl. He was a flamboyant character who had taken me under his wing because I was foreign and therefore a guest of his country and, like him, a writer. He loved the company of geisha; but he also knew how to spend time with them without bankrupting himself.

The secret was the "home bar" (*homu baa* in Japanese). A full-blown geisha party was so exorbitantly expensive that unless one had unlimited means, it was only feasible to throw one when there were very important business guests to be entertained and the whole thing could be paid for on company expenses. In modern Japan, to take over a tatami room in a teahouse in order to down a few flagons of saké with a geisha was insanely expensive. Thus, in order not to price themselves out of the market, most teahouses had developed "home bars," a small bar with sofas, tables, and a karaoké machine where men could go without booking (provided that they were not first-timers) and have a very expensive but still affordable drink. When Mr. Mori took me out on bar crawls, that was where we went.

One evening around midnight we ended up at a small bar on a quiet backstreet behind Yasaka Shrine, right in the lee of the Eastern Hills. From the outside it might have been a private house.

"This is a very special geisha," Mori-san assured me as he slid the door open, slipped out of his shoes, and stepped into the hallway. The mama-san came out to greet us and ushered us into the bar.

A dignified, rather stiff woman, she might have been sixty or seventy. She had a plump round face with even, delicate features which must once have been beautiful. Her hair was swept into the unnaturally black bouffant hairstyle which all the geisha wore and her kimono, crossed high at the neck in matronly style, was a sober dark blue. I felt a little uncomfortable. Her smile was icy. She was perfectly pleasant, yet she seemed to be just going through the motions; she needed our business but in fact would much rather that we had not come. It was as if she was reining in her true feelings with almost noticeable effort.

Mori-san, a buoyant character utterly impervious to subtleties of atmosphere or feeling, was chatting cheerfully about business in the geisha world. Then his face lit up as two young women appeared. These were not maiko but bar girls, leggy students in tiny skirts whose job was to entertain the customers. While he teased and joked with them, the mama-san was left to entertain me.

"Gion must have changed quite a lot since you were first here," I ventured, carefully avoiding impertinent personal questions. I was amazed at the vehemence of her reply.

"It's completely different," she exploded. "Everything has changed. Those days were dark. It was a dark life."

"Could I ask . . ." I murmured politely, "would you mind telling me . . . I've heard music and dance classes were much harsher in those days."

Suddenly the floodgates opened. I didn't need to be polite, I hardly needed to speak. With Mori-san distracted by his two companions and no one but a foreigner, utterly outside the geisha community, to hear her, the mama-san poured out her story. Harsh? The classes had been terrible. The older sisters had been tough on her and the house mothers too; and her "older sister" had died suddenly at twenty-five, so there was no one to stand up for her.

"I thought I'd commit suicide many times," she burst out. "My house mother was famous for her cruelty. Everyone knew it. She was always in a rage. I was like the maid. I did all the cleaning in the house by myself. She'd give me a list of jobs, then go out. If I hadn't done them all when she got back, she beat me."

Her father, she said, disappeared when she was four. Her mother was alone and poor. She hadn't intended to send her child to the geisha district. But her aunt knew of a good position in a geisha house and when she was ten she was packed off to Gion.

"I didn't know anything about it," she said fiercely. "I didn't know anything when I was brought here. I lived in Gion, I went to school, and I never saw my mother again."

In those days there were no big decisions about whether to stay on or leave. A child who had been purchased from her parents was effectively an indentured slave. She labored under an enormous debt—the money used to pay for her purchase plus the exorbitant costs of the hair-styling and gorgeous kimonos and obis which were an essential part of the job. Until it was repaid, which might be never, she was the property of the geisha house. When the time came for her to go through with her debut and become a maiko, she did so. She had no choice in the matter. And later when the time came to change her collar and start wearing the *ofuku* hairstyle, she had no choice in that either. Added to which, changing the collar was not simply a colorful ritual as it is for modern maiko. It meant growing up and becoming an adult in a very literal sense.

"It was against the law to force you to have sex with a patron if you didn't want to, even in those days," blurted out the mama-san. I hadn't even dared mention *mizuage*. "But no one paid any attention. Of course I had it, we all did. It was horrible, he was a horrible man. He was a specialist, a professional deflowerer."

Amazed at her outburst, I was burning to ask her what a professional deflowerer was. But she obviously thought she had said enough. Then Mori-san and the two students joined in, chatting blithely, and a few minutes later he decided it was time to leave. As we strolled through the dark streets to our next port of call, a late-night noodle shop, I commented with due politeness on how nice she had been.

" 'Nice'?" chuckled the irrepressible Mori-san. "I wouldn't call her 'nice.' She's hard—*kibishi*—tough as an old boot." There were reasons for that, I thought. I was beginning to understand why so many of the older women of the geisha community were harsh and sharp-tongued.

The mama-san was the first but far from the only "older sister" to talk to me about *mizuage*. For women who were maiko before prostitution was made illegal in 1958—in other words, anyone aged over about fifty-five, which included many of the older members of the community—compulsory deflowering at an early age was simply a part of life. It made no difference whether they were the spoiled children of generations of geisha and had grown up in a wealthy geisha house with maids and servants, or whether they were the children of starving peasants, brought in weeping from the countryside. Children in those days did not have choices. The option of leaving before one's debut or before the change of collar was simply not available.

Which is not to say that they were unhappy. Japanese practice *gaman*—"endurance," "getting on with things," "putting up with things." When it is cold, you are cold, you don't waste energy heating your house. When it is hot, you are hot. Widespread central heating and air-conditioning are recent developments in Japan and older people still do not bother much with them. And if you were told that you had to have *mizuage,* you just put up with it.

When I asked the older women of the geisha community if they had had *mizuage,* they looked at me with astonishment as if they could not imagine how anyone could ask such a stupid question.

"Of course," they would tut impatiently. "Otherwise I wouldn't be a geisha."

Before the 1958 watershed, *mizuage* was not simply something that everyone took for granted but the most crucial step in the maiko's career. Like a young man's circumcision, painful but unavoidable, it was an initiation ritual. It marked the transition from maiko to geisha, from girl to woman, and was a prerequisite for changing one's collar, synonymous with growing up. Until you had had it, you were not a woman. A virgin geisha would have been as much a contradiction in terms as a virgin wife.

From the customer's point of view, of course, the chance to deflower a maiko was an irresistible opportunity. As everywhere, virgins were highly desirable. And a maiko was the apogee of virgins, the crème de la crème, selected for her beauty, highly accomplished, and trained to be compliant with whatever a man desired. Men were prepared to pay a small fortune for the privilege of deflowering one. It cost several million yen in today's money, one elderly geisha told me, enough to buy a house.

As for the geisha house, they had invested a lot of money, what with the initial purchase and the costs of raising the girl—classes, training, kimonos, housing, and the rest. The first step toward recouping it was *mizuage,* one of the most lucrative transactions in the girl's entire career.

Mizuage began with the courtesans. For the geisha as for them, the cost of the debut was prohibitively expensive. It was simply not possible unless a wealthy sponsor could be found to pay for it. As a bonus, whoever was prepared to lay out the money would have the privilege of being the fledgling courtesan's first patron. The payment was not for deflowering her but to cover the cost of the debut; though for the young woman the distinction must have seemed academic.

Sometimes by the time a courtesan or geisha came to have her debut, she was not really a virgin. Saikaku, the great seventeenth-century chronicler of the pleasure quarters, wrote rollicking stories about girls who were sold for "deflowering" time and again. The deception could be perpetrated if the girl moved to a new district where no one knew her and she could celebrate her "debut" for the second, third, or fourth time. The customer would not find out the truth until it was too late and would never dream of losing face by broadcasting his humiliation. To this day a sponsor or sponsors have to be found to pay for a maiko's debut; though, post–1958, the position no longer carries the same bonus.

In her charmingly self-deprecating autobiography, *A Drunken Story of Gion,* one of the grand old ladies of the geisha district, Haruyu, who recently passed away in her late eighties, described the terrible embarrassment of being unable to find a *danna*. She was, she wrote candidly, not hugely attractive. In fact, as the photographs in the book reveal, she was downright plain. But she was the daughter of a teahouse owner and, attractive or not, automatically became a maiko. She came from a family of four sisters and two brothers, though her brothers were sent away practically as soon as they were born to be brought up by their father.

Otherwise they would have become shamisen players or dressers; those were the only jobs for men in the geisha district.

At eleven she became a maiko. But when she reached fourteen, the magic age when all her contemporaries were losing their virginity and changing from the *ware-shinobu* to the *ofuku* hairstyle, month after month passed and her hair remained resolutely the same. She was so plain that there were no applicants to deflower her. Walking the streets of the geisha districts wearing the little-girl hairstyle that told everyone she was still a virgin, she felt more and more embarrassed and ashamed.

Eventually her "older sister" went to one of the professional de-flowerers to beg him to perform the *mizuage*. Haruyu reported the conversation: " 'I don't want people thinking there's something wrong with her, like a disability or some sort of physical problem. So would you mind . . .' asked Older Sister. 'Do you think you could . . . ? Just so people will know she's normal.' "

Finally the owner of a big department store agreed to do it. By now Haruyu was fifteen, old for *mizuage*. Afterward she had the even greater embarrassment of having to walk around with her hair in the *ofuku*—"just deflowered"—style. The house mothers kept stopping her on the street to congratulate her. She was so embarrassed that she ran home.

At the time, she wrote, there were two "professional deflowerers" who took care of Gion. She gave them pseudonyms: "Mr. Kawada" and "Mr. Kimura." Once a maiko was getting past her sell-by date, if she still hadn't been deflowered, the mother of her geisha house would go to one of them and suggest he do the honors.

Once, she wrote, all the maiko of the district were performing at the annual Cherry Dances. There were two pathways like catwalks—*hanamichi,* "flower roads"—stretching through the middle of the audience from the back of the theater to the stage. For one piece there was a line of maiko dancing on each. "This catwalk is Kawada-san's," yelled a wag in the audience. "That one's Kimura-san's!"[3]

One woman, frail but still lovely, had been the child of a famous geisha and remembered the twenties, when there were 2,500 geisha and 106 maiko in Gion alone. When I met her she was ninety, a little hard of hearing and slow on her feet but imperious still and beautiful, with silky skin as fine as parchment and delicate features. She was perfectly turned out in a kimono of watered silk with a pale-gray swirled ink pattern. She spoke not just Kyoto dialect but archaic Kyoto dialect. It was rather like meeting someone who speaks in Dickensian English.

She had grown up in one of the most prosperous teahouses in the district, with maids to serve her. "Thanks to the money of our patrons," she said in her thin but piercing voice, "we ate very well, better than people outside the geisha districts."

The daughters of geisha and of teahouse owners were in a highly privileged position, very different from girls who had been recruited from outside the geisha areas. They had no debts, they were not in bondage, they had the family house to live in. So she had no need of a patron to support her. In fact, she had no need to become a geisha at all if she didn't want to. She could have simply taken over as the mama-san of the teahouse, the family business. But in those days it would have been unthinkable for a beautiful young girl not to have become a geisha, particularly if she came from a geisha background.

But even though she came from a privileged background, she had *mizuage,* which suggests that it was seen not as a terrible ordeal from which a mother would wish to protect her daughter, but a necessary rite of passage.

"*Mizuage* is when you become a woman for the first time," she said. "In those days everyone had *mizuage* around fourteen. I was late, I was fifteen. I was embarrassed. I changed my hairstyle, so everyone knew I had had it. It was like getting married. Everyone congratulated me and I gave celebratory presents to everyone. I gave gifts of food to my teachers and seniors."

As for the perpetrator, "in those days it was just a man who makes a woman for the first time. He only did it once. Some customers were *mizuage* specialists. Mostly they were honorable senior citizens, rich and old. I don't know about nowadays. Young maiko do as they please! *Mizuage* is really awful; but afterward you celebrated. The *danna* paid a lot of money but the family spent it all on celebrating. It certainly wasn't embarrassing. It was normal; it would have been embarrassing to have been late in having it. It would have looked as if you couldn't find a *danna*."

To a modern woman, the concept of being deflowered on a one-night stand by a rich old man who paid a lot of money for the privilege and liked to spend his time going around deflowering virgins is unspeakably abhorrent. But, barbaric though it may seem, it needs to be seen in context. One way or another, most Japanese women who grew up before 1958 wound up having to have sex with someone they barely knew and didn't care about. If they were of the social class that had arranged marriages, often they had met their prospective husband only once or twice before the wedding and most probably had been so shy they had not dared raise their gaze higher than his shoes.

Japanese women in their seventies have told me that the first time they saw their husband's face was at their wedding. For them their wedding night could not have been much different from *mizuage*. They too had no choice but to have sex with someone who was virtually a stranger. The difference was that at least they could expect him to look after them economically in the future. They certainly did not expect fidelity or love. As for the old men who carried out *mizuage,* ghastly though they were, they were quite likely practiced and expert. If the fumbling upper-class youths whom respectable women had to marry had any idea what they were doing once the lights were out, it was because their fathers had packed them off to the geisha district to be taught.

Good Days for Men

Daytimes in the geisha district were often quiet but evenings were busy. One night I was out with Sara, who was Japanese-American, looking for Ishibei Koji, Stone Wall Alley, the small enclosed quarter where, Mori-san had told me, rich men had built houses for their concubines. He had shown me the entrance, a tiny stone doorway, like the entrance to the Secret Garden, hidden in a long wall. We were strolling around the backstreets behind Yasaka Shrine when I spotted the discreet sign.

Stepping through the doorway was like walking into a fortress. There was a long paved alley lined with high stone walls ending in a massive gateway which led to the inner sanctum. There, well away from the main road and almost impossible to find unless you knew where to look, was a cluster of imposing houses like miniature castles barricaded behind sturdy buttresses of hewn stones topped with wooden palings or brushwood fences. There were no front gardens, only a few spindly pine trees peeking over the tops of the palings which closed in around the path. It was a strange, isolated, claustrophobic little place, a tiny hidden city. There the concubines must have lived rather a peaceful, sociable life awaiting—with pleasure or distaste, depending on their feelings—the visits of the men who were paying for all this.

As we strolled on I realized that we were just around the corner from the home bar of the formidable mama-san in the severe navy-blue kimono. Mori-san had given me her phone number so, on the off chance, I called. I was sure that, despite his introduction, I would still count as a first-timer and be roughly rebuffed. I was pleasantly surprised when she said, all affability, "By all means; do come round!"

In the small bar with the rows of whiskey bottles along the mirrored wall, business was a little brisker. Some businessmen, rather the worse for wear, were sitting around a low table, jackets discarded, ties akimbo, enjoying an evening of karaoké. One by one they rose unsteadily to their feet to belt out a sentimental ditty, following the neon words on a video screen.

The mama-san was as buttoned up as ever, smiling glacially, arranging dishes of snacks. I had been hoping to continue our intriguing conversation but was not sure how to set about it. I had been reading Haruyu's autobiography, I told her, trying to break the ice.

"Haruyu-san," she smiled. "Everyone knew her. She was 'main' "—using the English word—"she was a very important person in Gion society."

"There was something we couldn't understand," said Sara. "Did you ever hear of *mirare*?"

The mama-san's face changed. Yes, she knew all about it.

In her book Haruyu wrote about *mirare*—literally "being seen"—without ever making it clear exactly what it was. In Ichiriki-tei, Gion's famous terra-cotta-walled teahouse, there was a small enclosed room called Kako-i where maiko would go "to be seen." It was dark and shadowy. Usually four or five maiko were sent for at one time. The customer would look them over and decide on one.

"*Mirare* was not nice for the maiko," wrote Haruyu. "If you were chosen it wasn't nice; and if you weren't chosen it wasn't nice. If you didn't like the person who had chosen you, in theory you could say no. For a girl born in a geisha house, it was not so difficult to do that. But if you were a maiko who came from far away and were working hard to make money, you couldn't afford to say no."

"That was the difference between *tayu* courtesans in the old days and geisha," said the mama-san. "*Tayu* chose who they slept with. They'd say to a customer, 'You! I'm sleeping with you tonight!' But geisha couldn't choose. They were chosen."

"Being seen" was the process by which a customer picked a sleeping partner, either for the night or as a long-term arrangement. First he informed the mistress of his regular teahouse that that was what he wanted to do. She sent for a selection of geisha and maiko who clattered over to the teahouse accompanied, as always, by the "boy" (the dresser/assistant).

"You always knew it was *mirare*," said the mama-san, "when you got one customer asking for a group of maiko and geisha. When we were getting ready, we'd tuck a comb backward in our hair at the back, where the customer couldn't see it." She demonstrated slipping a small curved comb back to front into her hair. "It was like a charm to ward off being chosen."

It was a little like an audition. After the customer had looked them over, he would inform the mistress of the teahouse or her maid of his choice. She passed the message on to the "boy." He took the message back to the mother of the geisha house where the maiko in question lived. Then, when she had given formal consent, he returned to the teahouse and the teahouse mother told the other maiko they could leave. Until then none of them knew which it would be. The chosen maiko was left alone.

In theory she had the right to refuse the customer. In practice, said the mama-san, there were times when you could refuse and times when you couldn't. Meanwhile the customer and the mistress of the teahouse would negotiate the price. There was a sliding scale, depending on what the customer wanted, ranging from a single night to some sort of long-term arrangement.

If a customer decided he wanted to become a *danna,* the patron of a maiko or geisha, that was often how he chose her. In those days, as far as a geisha or maiko was concerned, she needed a *danna* in order to survive. Whether he looked like a monster or was young and handsome, it would have been absurd of her to refuse. In any case, she could always take a lover in secret or trade him in for another patron if she got a better offer.

If, as the phrase went, she was "pulled [out of the geisha world] by a *danna*"—*danna-san hika sareru*—in other words, if she decided to take up his offer and become his concubine, she removed her name from the geisha registry. As a farewell, she handed out dishes of white rice called *hiki-iwai*—"celebrating being pulled"—to her teachers, seniors, friends, and colleagues in the geisha community. The whiteness of the rice symbolized that she would be with that *danna* until her hair was white. If, however, she had had her debts paid off by a *danna* whom she did not love and wanted to keep her options open, there would be red aduki beans scattered among the white rice, hinting that this was not forever and that she would most likely be returning to the geisha world one day. The customer, of course, never saw the rice. Most women slipped in a few red beans just in case.

Another permutation popular with the customers was sleeping over—*zakone,* "sleeping huddled together like small fish." At the end of an evening's partying, the customers might ask the teahouse mistress to call the geisha house and ask if the maiko could sleep over. The payment was the hourly rate for each maiko's company times twelve—in other words, very expensive.

The dresser arrived with the maikos' nightwear, put all their combs and hair ornaments into a box, then took the combs and kimonos back to the geisha house. He would reappear the following morning with fresh kimonos for them. Meanwhile the maids at the teahouse were spreading futon bedding around one big room. The maiko and customers slept together, spread out around the room, with a pinch-faced old maid awake all night to make sure that nothing untoward took place. Sex, after all, was to be properly arranged and paid for, not stolen. The men could chat to the maiko and the maiko could chat to each other; but the rule was no touching. Still, men loved sleeping surrounded by beautiful young women. For the maiko it was a chance to steal a customer's heart. With luck he might be sufficiently entranced to go through the proper channels and buy her for a night or even become her *danna*.

One elderly teahouse "mother" I met remembered "sleeping over." "We used to have it in the big room upstairs," she told me rather indiscreetly, smiling wistfully at the memory of those jolly days long gone by. "In the summertime. There'd be three or four guests, five or six geisha and maiko, and a maid or two. The fun was to try and grab the girls' breasts."

For the customers it was expensive fun, for the maiko an edgy combination of fun and desperation. The customers, after all, were at play. They had left the real world of home and work behind to enter this world which operated by different rules and where there were no real responsibilities. That was why it was so expensive. But the maiko were not at play. They had a living to make and, until 1958, a frightening debt to pay off. For them it was deadly serious. As for the steely mama-san in her dark-blue kimono, she had long since put all this behind her. It was a bad memory from the distant past. She had survived. In fact, she had done better than that, she had managed to acquire a teahouse of her own. She had become not just independent but a successful businesswoman. Maybe she had inherited the teahouse from the cruel house mother who had tormented her; or maybe she had had a *danna* to help her out.

" 'Being seen,' 'sleeping over'—all that came to an end in 1958," she said with an edge of pleasure in her voice. "Those were good days for men. Now it's good days for women. These days girls become maiko because they want to and leave when they want to."

With that she presented us with our bill. For a glass each of whiskey and water, a small dish of snacks (dried squid, unappetizing crackers) which we didn't touch and about an hour of the mama-san's time, not to mention the cost of sliding open the door and walking in, the bill for myself and Sara came to 14,000 yen, about $140. Sara, who knew about these things, said that we had got off lightly.

geisha in the victorian age

And west you'll sail and south again, beyond the sea-fog's rim,
And tell the Yoshiwara girls to burn a stick for him.

Rudyard Kipling, *Rhyme of the Three Sealers*, 1893

The Black Ships

One fateful day in 1853, four warships bristling with cannon and trailing clouds of smoke appeared on the horizon, steaming toward the coast of Japan. They dropped anchor in the shadow of Mount Fuji, threateningly close to Edo. Fishermen at work in the placid waters fled panic stricken for shore.

The Japanese called them the Black Ships. Their commander, Commodore Matthew C. Perry (1794–1858), carried a golden casket containing a letter from President Millard Fillmore of the United States of America demanding that Japan open its doors to trade and friendship forthwith. He sent a message that he would speak only to the highest-ranking man in the nation. After waiting a week he finally stepped ashore. Bedecked with medals and gold braid, flanked by two burly black sailors and accompanied by an escort of marines and a brass band, he presented his letter. He would return the following year for an answer, he declared, and with a much larger fleet.

The night of Perry's arrival, a comet flashed across the sky like a harbinger of doom. Until that moment, it might have seemed to the Japanese as if nothing would ever change. For a quarter of a millennium Japan had been able to develop a rich and idiosyncratic culture almost entirely free from prying eyes and unwanted influences. One of the cornerstones of the shoguns' policy was isolation, keeping the country sealed against the many dangers—both literal and ideological—which the outside world might present. Apart from a tiny enclave of Dutch and Chinese traders who were forbidden to leave the foreigners' compound in the distant city of Nagasaki, Japan had been closed to foreign contact. The flower and willow world of the Yoshiwara and the geisha had bloomed in this hothouse atmosphere.

But the last years had been marked by a growing sense of malaise. The country was wracked by economic crises, and famines sparked riots among the peasantry.

In the Yoshiwara courtesans and prostitutes continued to ply their trade but the balance had shifted decisively. The real heart of the demimonde was now the spirited women of Fukagawa, not Yoshiwara, and in Kyoto, Shimabara had long since yielded in popularity to Gion. In 1811 one observer had written that "the Yoshiwara has fallen on hard times nowadays . . . It seems to me that the courtesans are fewer and the number of famous ladies halved." There were, he had said, only two women of *yobidashi* rank (the top rank which had replaced *tayu*); in fact there had been almost no high-ranking courtesans at all.[1]

Another batch of reforms in 1841 had only hastened the Yoshiwara's decline. Once again several thousand prostitutes and geisha had been rounded up from the unlicensed districts. The prostitutes had then been dumped in the Yoshiwara, thus filling it to overflowing with untrained low-grade women. But the geisha had been allowed to return to work so long as they promised to restrict their activities to music and dancing. It was the first time that geisha had been officially recognized as different from prostitutes. By 1851 the Yoshiwara, once the exclusive domain of the super-rich, had been reduced to trawling for trade with discounts and special offers. The writer who chronicled this with disgust added grimly that veritably it marked "the end of the world."[2] The arrival of the foreigner was the last straw.

Early in 1854, half a year after his first visit, Perry was back, this time accompanied by a squadron of eight well-armed vessels. Hopelessly out of touch with Western technology and modern warfare, Japan did not even have a navy. The government had no option but to sign a treaty opening two ports to American ships. That same year an earthquake leveled Edo and the shogun who had signed the treaty died shortly after his brush left the paper. The omens were bad.

Okichi, the Foreigner's Concubine

> As they depart,
> Passing the sampans and spreading their eight sails,
> They think of beloved Shimoda
> And let their tears fall.
> Whilst along the river side
> The dirty water flows from the hovels,
> Behind the doors the sound of the prostitutes' voices rises:
> "Oh! how grateful we are to the honorable foreigner
> Who gives two dollars for the one-dollar whore."
>
> Shimoda boatmen's song[3]

The key had been turned and the Western boot was firmly wedged in the door. Across the Pacific, a man named Townsend Harris (1804–1878) saw an opportunity to make his name and, with any luck, his fortune too. As the Americans saw it, the 1854 treaty signed by the shogun provided for a consul general to take up residence on Japanese soil. Harris petitioned the American president to give him the post. In August 1856 he arrived at the newly opened port of Shimoda. He raised the Stars and Stripes above Gyokusenji, a beautiful old disused temple, and settled in there with his interpreter and secretary, Henry Heusken. His brief was to conclude a proper commercial treaty.

The weeks and months that followed were filled with wrangling, interspersed with long periods of inactivity while the Japanese negotiators awaited instruction from Edo. Often ill and with only Heusken for company, Harris needed some way to alleviate the gloom. The red-blooded young Heusken knew the answer. What they needed was women.

Heusken lodged the request for "nurses" with the burghers of Shimoda. Perfectly natural, they all agreed once he had left. But where was the woman of whom they could ask such a sacrifice? Who would ever voluntarily consent to be fondled by a hairy barbarian who reeked of meat and butter? (The Japanese ate no meat or dairy products and referred to foreigners as *bataa-kusai,* "stinking of butter.") Who would want to take on the stigma of being a *rashamen,* "foreigner's concubine," a word whose alternative meaning was "sheep"? The visits of Perry's American sailors and a Russian fleet had resulted in a rash of pale-skinned babies, all of whom had been clandestinely disposed of in a graveyard in an isolated little valley.

Heusken had asked for a geisha named Okichi whom Harris had noticed as she was walking home from the bath, looking fresh and comely. Seventeen or eighteen, an adult by the standards of those days, Okichi was a beautiful and popular young woman, famous for her sweet voice and in particular her unforgettably lovely rendition of "Raven at Dawn," a plaintive ditty about a Yoshiwara courtesan. She has become a legendary heroine in Japan, revered, practically deified—there is a temple dedicated to her in Shimoda—as the first lamb to be sacrificed on the altar of foreign relations.

Naturally she was reluctant to take on the assignment but the town elders were insistent. On June 13, the consul's large black-lacquered palanquin, specially made to fit his long legs, arrived to carry her to his residence at Anegasaki. She jolted off on the shoulders of the bearers, escorted by equerries and samurai who cleared a way through the crowds. As she sat inside, hidden behind the bamboo window blind, she could hear the townsfolk jeering, "Here comes a sheep for the consul!"

The crossroads at Madogahama was the point of no return.

Shimoda children still sing a ditty evoking the fear and indecision which Okichi must have felt:

> *Shall we go to Anegasaki?*
> *Shall we return to Shimoda?*
> *Here is Madogahama. We must decide!*

Harris had had carpenters in to turn the disused temple into a Western home, throwing away the rice straw tatami matting which had become infested by American beetles from the Black Ships and replacing it with Western carpets and furniture. To Okichi it must have been unimaginably alien, full of strange and repellent odors—woolen carpets instead of the familiar new-mown-hay smell of tatami, the whiff of polish on the heavy wooden furniture and, worst of all, the reek of searing animal flesh from the kitchen. Then there was the consul himself with his big, hairy, smelly body; though in the end there was not much difference between what he did on the large uncomfortable Western bed and what other men had done to her in the past.

After three days Harris discovered that Okichi had a suspicious skin eruption and told her not to visit again until it was cured. She carried on receiving a sizable allowance. But even after the sore had disappeared, whenever the subject of a visit was broached, Harris always decided he was unwell. Two and a half months later he terminated the contract.

For Okichi the experience must have been utterly traumatic. She had had to sleep with an old and repugnant barbarian, she had had to abrogate her right as a geisha to choose her customers, and then she had been publicly humiliated and found wanting. On top of all this, as her widowed mother pointed out in a letter to the town council, she was ruined. Having been polluted by the touch of the barbarian, no Japanese man would ever touch her again. Not surprisingly, she turned to drink. She became a beggar and years later drowned herself in the river.

Harris may have forgotten her but the Japanese never did. If you visit Shimoda today, there is a temple dedicated to Okichi Kannon, Kannon being the mother goddess, complete with a sex museum. Here you can see the cliff from where, according to the much embellished legend, Okichi jumped into the sea, having done her bit for international relations.

The First Madame Butterfly

The Westerners who poured in to populate the foreign settlements in the country's growing number of treaty ports ranged from diplomats, missionaries, and scholars to adventurers, misfits, roisterers, and sailors. They had all heard rumors of the legendary geisha and of the walled city of delights, the Yoshiwara, and were eager to learn more.

In 1885 a languid, rather unpleasant French naval officer who wrote under the pen name of Pierre Loti (1850–1923) sailed into Nagasaki harbor with the express intention of marrying a Japanese wife and writing about it. He had already titillated the world with tales of his exotic love affairs in Turkey and Tahiti. Now, for his Japanese period, he wanted "a little yellow-skinned woman with black hair and cat's eyes. She must be pretty. Not much bigger than a doll."

He spent a mere five weeks in Nagasaki, quite long enough to marry, gather the material for his opus, become bored, and leave again. The object of his brief affections was Kiku (Chrysanthemum), a tea-house girl whom he called Madame Chrysanthème and married for a price of 20 piastres a month. They seem to have had a relationship of mutual contempt. Loti described his wife's irritating habits, the incessant tap of her tiny pipe bowl against her porcelain smoking box, her bored yawns and mirthless laugh. Asleep, at least, he wrote, she did not bore him. As he was making his farewells, he was horrified to find her cheer-ily counting the coins he had tossed to her and hitting them with a mallet to test that they were real silver.[4]

Unromantic though Loti's account was, he had touched a chord. The Western world was thirsty for tales of sweet, gentle Japanese child-women who gave themselves adoringly to Western men, even if the reality was a good deal more mercenary and sordid. John Luther Long's tragic *Madame Butterfly* of 1903, pining away for the caddish Lieutenant Pinkerton, was exactly the heroine that Victorian readers had been wait-ing for. The story was immortalized in Giacomo Puccini's opera in 1904 and the Western myth—or should we say cliché—of the "geisha" was born. As for the real geisha, living their lives out in Japan, they were made of considerably sterner stuff.

Plotters in Gion

> *Drunk, my head pillowed in a beauty's lap;*
> *Awake and sober, grasping power to govern the nation.*
>
> pre-Restoration popular ditty[5]

The coming of the barbarians threw everything into chaos. First there was Perry, then Harris, installed on Japanese soil with his interminable and infernal demands, and behind them the menacing Black Ships lurking just across the horizon. What on earth was to be done? As far as the newly installed twelve-year-old shogun, his regent, councilors, and court in Edo were concerned, there was nothing for it but to concede on every point. Rusty samurai swords and antique muskets were useless against the might of the foreigner's firepower.

It was a matter of national survival. But national pride was also at stake and for the first time in centuries, a sizable proportion of daimyo warlords chose to disagree with the shogun. Some called for war, others argued that the country's seclusion must at all costs be maintained. The matter was so critical that the emperor himself—normally utterly outside politics—took a stand, in favor of continuing the policy of isolation. The real reason Harris was left twiddling his thumbs in Shimoda for so long was that the emperor refused to sign his treaty.

In the end, under intolerable pressure, the shogun's regent signed the document and those presented by the other Western powers without the emperor's consent. It was an action which sparked an explosion of anger among samurai of all ranks and men of other classes too.

Disaffected samurai, particularly from the distant provinces of Satsuma and Chofu, followers of the dissident daimyo and others who opposed the shogunate, began to gather in Kyoto. For centuries the political center of the country had been the shogun's capital, Edo. But now there were two hubs, not one. Kyoto was abuzz with passionate political debate.

These young blades, mainly in their twenties, united under the twin slogans of "Restore the emperor, expel the barbarian." Their avowed aim was to oust the shogun and return the emperor to his divinely appointed place at the heart of the nation. For them the natural place to meet, argue, plan, and eventually foment revolution was Gion with its rabbit warren of tiny lanes lit with glowing white lanterns and lined with teahouses and geisha houses. There they could pretend to be wastrels, drinking their lives away. Many also fell in love with geisha who returned their love and were to prove every bit as brave and stubborn as they.

The young braves on the shogun's side, meanwhile, spent their evenings carousing in another of the geisha quarters—not Gion but its archrival, Pontocho, on the other side of the river. It would have been far too risky for both sides to have had their plots and secrets overheard by the same geisha, even though the geishas' code of secrecy theoretically prevented them from ever divulging what they had heard.

One of the leaders of the rebel imperialists, a romantic, driven young samurai called Takayoshi Kido (1833–1877), held rabble-rousing meetings in Gion, where he fell in love with a beautiful and spirited geisha named Ikumatsu. In August 1864, when fighting broke out on the streets of Kyoto, the shogun's men came hammering on Ikumatsu's door. She stood in the entrance, arguing with them long enough to give Kido time to sneak out and escape across the tiled roof. By the time they shoved past her, swords glittering, he was gone.

For five days, disguised as a beggar, he hid among the down and outs who lived on the riverbank under Nijo Bridge. Ikumatsu crept out by night to take him rice balls. After that he disguised himself to try and shake off his pursuers. One day he was a shampooer, the next an attendant at a public bathhouse or a porter at a coaching inn on the highway out of town. Finally, with Ikumatsu's help, he escaped from the city and lived under a false name as a shopkeeper in a country town.

The final push came in 1868. The old emperor had died and been succeeded by his fifteen-year-old son, Mutsuhito, known to history as Emperor Meiji. In Japan the years are named after the reigning emperor; it was Year 1 of the Meiji Era, the beginning of a new age. Kido, Takamori Saigo, and the other rebel leaders, backed by a large military force, seized the imperial palace and declared an end to the rule of the shoguns. Hereafter the emperor would be their titular head and the figurehead of the nation.

On the outskirts of Kyoto, there was heavy fighting. In the evenings the youthful rebels—who now constituted the imperial army—would be back in Gion, relaxing in the teahouses, arguing, singing, and dancing with the geisha. One night a geisha plucked out a rousing tune on her shamisen. A Choshu samurai, Yajiro Shinagawa, composed the lyrics:

Miya-sama, Miya-sama, o-uma no maeni
hira hira suru no nanja ya ya!

Your Highness, Your Highness,
What can that be, fluttering before your horse! . . .
It's the imperial brocade banner
that attacks the enemies of the court.

We'll shoot down the scoundrels
who would raise their hands
against the Mikado,
emperor of the firmament.

When the shogunate's samurai hear the noise
which way will they run?
They'll throw away their castle and their spirit
and flee eastward.

The next day Shinagawa handed out copies of "Toko Ton Yare Bushi," as he called his song, meaning something like "To the Death!" or "Go for Broke!," and the samurai marched into battle singing lustily. It was Japan's first war song. Seventeen years later, in 1885, it was hijacked in its entirety by W. S. Gilbert and Sir Arthur Sullivan to use as the overture and the song of the Mikado's troops in their operetta *The Mikado,* in which it is sung in the original Japanese.[6]

From Kyoto the imperial troops marched east, heading for Edo.

Shortly afterward the young emperor was installed in the shogun's palace which would hereafter be the imperial palace. Edo became the new capital and was renamed Tokyo, the "Eastern Capital."

The young men who had led the rebellion were the leaders of the new government. They settled in Edo and many brought their geisha lovers to join them. Kido, now one of the most powerful men in the Meiji administration, did not forget his brave and devoted geisha lover, Ikumatsu. First he arranged for her to be adopted into a samurai family, a traditional procedure to make a geisha into a respectable woman, essential in a society where marriage was a matter of creating an alliance between families rather than of individual preference. She was given a new name, Matsuko, and shortly afterward he made her his wife. (To this day when a man wishes to marry his geisha lover, he has first to find an older man from a respectable family who will agree to "adopt" her and act as her "father" at the wedding.)

The eminent Victorian Algernon Mitford (1837–1916), grandfather of the celebrated Mitford sisters, met her in 1869 and described her as "a bonny little lady, though eyes less familiar with the custom than mine would have objected to the disfigurement of shaved eyebrows and blackened teeth." He commented on her "ease and grace" as a hostess and added that as a former geisha she had "none of the shyness which I have usually met with in Japanese ladies."[7]

Thus a Gion geisha rose to the pinnacle of Japanese high society to be the woman behind one of the most powerful men of the realm. Many other rebel leaders married their loyal geisha lovers and all of them, from the bull-like Takamori Saigo to Hirobumi Ito, the country's first prime minister, kept geisha mistresses.

The geisha had proved their mettle and, with their unique ability to span the social hierarchy, were poised to become the leading women of their day. The courtesans in their gorgeous cages and the wives of rich men, trapped in their homes, offered no competition. The years that were to come would be the heyday of the geisha, when geisha were at the forefront of society as trend setters, fashion leaders, and the companions and confidantes of powerful men.

For the Edo-ites who turned out in their tens of thousands to watch the emperor's grand entry into the city in his palanquin, the Phoenix Chair, on November 26, 1868, it must have seemed as if the world had turned topsy turvy. Was the future to consist of rule by country bumpkin samurai married to geisha lovers? It was as if these queens of the counterculture, who had hitherto played at being great ladies so that merchants could play at being gentlemen, had suddenly turned respectable.

Still, business was business. In recent years the Yoshiwara, with its population of imprisoned courtesans, had fallen far behind the times. Fashionable young men about town much preferred the chic geisha of the illegal quarters; it was geisha the new oligarchs married, not courtesans. By now all but one of the Yoshiwara houses were small and low class, offering little more than sex. Still, seeing a new market in the influx of provincial males flocking into the new capital, the Yoshiwara brothel-keepers quickly upgraded 120 courtesans to the top *yobidashi* rank, thus enabling them to charge far higher fees than for a humble prostitute.

The enthusiastic young samurai who ran the new government recognized the needs of the city's growing populace by giving licenses to six areas which had been semilicensed. Whereas the illegal quarters had sprung up around shrines and temples, the natural gathering places under the shogunate, these new licensed quarters were in the bustling population hubs of the new order, at the points where roads from the provinces entered the city, soon to become railway termini: Shinagawa, Shinjuku, Itabashi, Nezu, and two at Senju.

They also, rather touchingly, attempted to provide for the many foreign gentlemen who were expected to come and work in the city. For despite the slogan "Revere the emperor, expel the barbarian," it had become apparent not only that the foreigner was here to stay but that he had a myriad of interesting things to teach the fledgling state.

Shortly after the emperor arrived in Edo, he put his signature to a memo from the leading daimyo recommending that Japan abandon the attitude of "the frog looking at the world from the bottom of a well" and resolve instead to learn from the foreigners, "adopting their best points and making good our own deficiencies." The Japanese forthwith embarked on a love affair with all things foreign. Young Japanese steamed off on P & O liners to the West to study and the Japanese hired foreign experts—British engineers to share the secrets of the industrial revolution, French to teach them law and military affairs, Germans to teach them about their parliamentary system, and Americans to teach commerce, agriculture, and technology.

One of the first of the Meiji government's projects was a pleasure quarter for foreigners. Named the New Shimabara, after the famous quarter in Kyoto, it opened not far from the imperial palace, near present-day Ginza, in 1869. It operated according to the Yoshiwara system, with teahouses serving as houses of assignation for clients to make appointments for the grander brothels. A total of 1,700 courtesans and 200 geisha, including 21 male geisha, moved in from the Yoshiwara to populate its 130 brothels and 84 teahouses.

Unfortunately all these brothels and teahouses remained largely empty. Foreigners, it became apparent, preferred more illicit pleasures. Many came to sightsee but few stayed on to enjoy themselves. The project was particularly overambitious given the small size of the foreign settlement at the time and the fact that a large proportion of the foreigners were missionaries.

By now the Japanese were beginning to get the measure of the foreigner's prudery. They had already discovered, to their astonishment, that foreigners not only thought there was something wrong with male-on-male sex but punished it with death. It was utterly different from the Japanese notion that when it came to sex, anything went.

Shortly after the ignominious closure of the New Shimabara, an extraordinary event occurred which focused Japanese attention on the gulf between foreign attitudes and their own. In June 1872 a Peruvian ship, the *Maria Luz,* dropped anchor in Yokohama Harbor for repairs. A Chinese coolie jumped overboard to try and escape, revealing that the ship was carrying a cargo of 230 Chinese slaves. Thirteen were children, including one, a little girl, who was under ten. There was international uproar and the captain was arrested and put on trial. The slaves were finally declared free and sent back to Hong Kong.

In the course of the furor the Peruvians pointed out that the Japanese too trafficked in slaves—the women of the Yoshiwara. This was not strictly accurate. The sale of human beings had been declared illegal in 1612 and services in the Yoshiwara were known as "term employment." Nevertheless, the women were not free even to leave the quarter, let alone give up their "employment" there.

Having been a closed society for so long, the Japanese now squirmed under the eyes of the world. The Meiji government was eager to persuade the Western powers that Japan was every bit as civilized and modern as they. Four months after the *Maria Luz* incident, the government passed the Prostitute and Geisha Emancipation Act, prohibiting the sale and trade of human beings. "Said prostitutes and geisha," went the wording, "have lost their human rights and are treated no differently from cows and horses. Human beings cannot logically demand payment of obligations from cows and horses. Therefore the said prostitutes and geisha should not pay debts or the balance of installments." The act became known humorously as the Cattle Release Act. (The Japanese, incidentally, were early by international standards in this respect. In Britain, for example, the Public Prostitution Law was repealed only in 1886.)

Many prostitutes went home and brothels were forced to close though, as the individual members of the government knew perfectly well, there were plenty of "cattle" who did not wish to be emancipated and had no idea how to make a living if they were. Many brothels quickly reopened for business under the designation "rental parlors." Before emancipation, according to the census of the time, there were 5,759 prostitutes and 280 geisha in the seven licensed districts. Afterward the figures show that the number of prostitutes had quartered to a mere 1,367. Geisha conversely had increased to 417.

The act in fact gave a fillip to the geisha, who were already far more popular and chic; there were always fewer geisha than prostitutes because of the stringent artistic requirements for the geisha. The government also recognized a distinction between geisha and prostitutes. Hereafter prostitutes who wished voluntarily to carry on their trade were required to have a license. Geisha who also practiced as prostitutes had to have two licenses, one for the sale of *gei*, "entertainment," the other for *iro*, "sex."

The Yoshiwara continued to do business right up until prostitution was made illegal in 1958. But it had long since ceased to be the cultural center it once was. It had become a splendid relic of a bygone age, the sort of place where Victorians went to gape and the hoi polloi went for sex. A decade after the Cattle Release Act, in 1883, cognoscenti were dismissing the geisha of the Yoshiwara as low class compared to their sisters in the unlicensed districts. By then all the most fashionable geisha were to be found in the romantically named Yanagibashi (Willow Bridge) and Shimbashi (New Bridge), while the second-rank of geisha were those of Sukiyacho and Yoshicho. The Yoshiwara geisha came a poor third.

Yanagibashi took on the mantle of Fukagawa as the home of the most elegant and witty geisha who entertained the merchants of old Edo. This was an area of boathouses along a tributary giving on to the River Sumida whence the *chokibune*—light swift boats with a single long oar—set off to carry customers to the Yoshiwara. Enterprising boathouse-keepers turned their properties into stylish teahouses and restaurants so that customers need not even bother with the journey.

The chronicler of Yanagibashi wrote under the pen name Ryuhoku, meaning "North of the Willows." The last of the great *tsu* sophisticates, he wrote scathingly of the uncouth ways of the country bumpkin samurai, of ghastly post-Restoration parties where people were so boorish that they talked politics or even spoke in English and ignored the geisha and their singing and dancing. He complained of modern geisha, little better than prostitutes, who were more interested in money than art and bought copies of the official gazette to find out how much their clients were earning.

But Yanagibashi was too thoroughly imbued with the decadence of old Edo under the shogunate. The men who had spent their youth rabble-rousing in the teahouses, the industrialists, politicians, bureaucrats, and businessmen who ran the brave new Tokyo, now found Shimbashi, New Bridge, more to their taste. With all things Western coming into vogue, Shimbashi had the advantage of bordering on the Ginza, where the first street of brick buildings with a long colonnaded arcade was built in 1872. And, as it happened, it was also where many of the Gion geishas who had followed their lovers the 250 miles to Tokyo had set up teahouses.

There, men like Hirobumi Ito, the country's first prime minister, and Taro Katsura, one of his successors, would spend the evening after a day of wrangling over the fledgling constitution in the Diet, the country's new parliament. And there, in their crass, forthright, country samurai way, they would discuss matters of state between nibbling on delicacies, exchanging banter with the geisha, and showing off their own skills at singing and dancing.

The larger-than-life women whose names were on every tongue, and whose stories gripped the popular imagination of the time, were mainly Shimbashi geisha—women like Okoi, "Honorable Carp," who was the mistress of, among others, a famous kabuki actor, a sumo grand champion, and prime minister Katsura. Connoisseurs of the old school, nevertheless, continued to favor the Yanagibashi geisha, who were much admired for their elegance and stylish femininity.

The most celebrated geisha of the era was Sadayakko Kawakami, who rose to become the concubine of the country's first prime minister and later the first woman to tread the boards as an actress. Her story casts light on the women who became geisha, the life they led, and the way in which becoming a geisha opened doors that would otherwise have remained firmly shut. It was the only way in which a woman could hope to take control of her own destiny.

The Story of Sadayakko

Sadayakko or Sada (as she was known at the height of her career) was born in the Nihombashi district of Tokyo just four years into the new era, in 1872. Her father had been a successful businessman but when she was six his business collapsed. Desperate, the family took her along to a geisha house in the Yoshicho geisha district and arranged for her to be adopted by the proprietress, a woman named Kamekichi, who became her geisha "mother." Undoubtedly money changed hands and the family finances benefited from the transaction. Still, it was an adoption, not a "sale of persons," considered a perfectly normal way in those days to ensure the future of one's child.

Mother Kame too did well out of the deal. Not only was the child "of good family," which would make her more salable as a geisha, she was also strikingly lovely, with translucent white skin, lustrous black tresses, and extraordinary eyes. The left was flat like an Asian eye, the right had a crease like a Western one. And she was very quick; she could "learn one thing and pick up ten," as the saying went. At the age of ten she demanded to learn to read and write, an outrageous request for a young girl training to be a geisha. The first high schools for women had opened only in 1870 and they were certainly not for the likes of Sada.

Had it been any other child, Mother Kame would have said, "What are you trying to do? Reading and writing is for men!" But she had high ambitions for Sada. She could win, she thought, not just a good *danna* but the very best in the country. To groom her, she arranged classes in riding, swimming, billiards, and martial arts as well as reading and writing.

The word *danna* means "master" in the sense of "patron" or "husband," though the geisha's patron will almost always already be married to someone else. Until the enormous changes brought about in Japan by the Second World War and its aftermath, it was a matter of prestige, a mark of a man's wealth and success in the world, to be known as the patron of a beautiful and famous geisha. Even the dashing rebel samurai leader Kido, devoted as he was to his wife the ex-geisha Matsuko, was the patron of a Gion geisha named Okayo, who had been one of Matsuko's friends. And, as he wrote in his diary, he also spent much time carousing in geisha quarters.

For the geisha house "mother" and "older sisters" who had the future of a young geisha in their hands, their most important task was to find her a suitable patron. In the course of her career, a geisha would probably have several. The first would have the unique privilege of introducing her to the ways of love through *mizuage*.

At sixteen, Sada, who, as a virgin geisha, had been given the name of Ko-yakko (Little Yakko), was an exquisite girl with feathery eyebrows, delicate features, and those extraordinary mesmerizing eyes. As the proprietress of a top geisha house, Mother Kame had many connections in high society. One day she met up with Eiichi Shibusawa, a great industrialist, real-estate magnate, and banker who lived in a splendidly baroque faux-Moorish mansion. To him, Mother Kame confided her ambition for Sada. He suggested the prime minister himself, Hirobumi Ito, and said he would put in a word on Sada's behalf.

Like Kido, Ito (1841–1909) had been a swashbuckling gallant from Choshu. Under the stern rule of the dying shogunate he risked execution by smuggling himself aboard a British ship in 1863 when leaving the country was still a capital offense. (According to another version of the story, it was actually the shogunate that sent him and his colleagues on a secret mission to find out how things were in the West.) With four friends he sailed via Shanghai to London, where he lodged in Hampstead and studied at University College for a few months. Reading one day in the *Times* that an international coalition led by the British was planning to attack his home province, he rushed back to Japan to mediate. By 1880 he was the leading figure in the government and in 1885 became the first person to take the title of prime minister. He was instrumental in developing the country's constitution and served four different terms as prime minister.

A short, stout man who loved to strut around sporting a chest covered in medals, he had a broad forehead, turned-up nose, and straggling goatee beard. He was a notorious libertine. Pompous in public, in private he loved nothing better than the company of a group of charming geisha, whom he would regale with an endless flow of improvised songs, finally driving all but the one who struck his fancy out of the room with a favorite ditty such as "Oh, what a boor and nuisance are you!"[8]

A great dancer, he once hosted a magnificent masked ball at his Western-style mansion, to which all the foreign diplomats in the city were invited. He went as a Venetian nobleman but the evening degenerated into an orgy of ribaldry and bawdiness, after which his cabinet became known, rather unflatteringly, as "the dancing cabinet." Of his incessant love affairs, the most scandalous involved a Japanese nobleman's wife.[9]

On his raffish nights out in the geisha districts, Ito had already noticed the ravishing, precocious child who shyly filled his saké cup. He was not the sort of man to turn down a proposal to deflower a girl like this. His wife, however, being, he said, something of a dragon, he suggested that the encounter should take place at his villa on an island outside Tokyo. He also handed over a very substantial amount of money to Mother Kame.

As for Sada, she was already in love with a swarthy thickset farm boy turned student but knew well that as a woman, her private feelings were utterly irrelevant. One summer afternoon in 1888 she boarded a boat for Ito's palatial villa, where she had a bath and carefully applied her makeup. The tubby, bewhiskered Ito, who at forty-seven must have seemed like a grandfather to her, arrived in time for dinner. Knowing her charmingly eccentric interest in reading and writing, he had brought with him, so the story goes, a Chinese book full of extremely explicit instructions on lovemaking. He read to her before putting the instructions into action.

Having now officially become a woman, Sada was entitled to wear the kimono of an adult geisha and took the name Yakko to mark her change in status. Given his wife's no-nonsense attitudes and the need to avoid scandal, explained Ito, he could not openly keep her. But he bought her the latest fashions, new-fangled Western items like a bathing suit, riding costume, boots, and spurs of 14-karat gold. Whenever he could, he arranged clandestine visits to continue his lessons in sexual techniques. When a policeman questioned her for swimming in the Sumida in her glamorous bathing costume, she tossed her black tresses and said, "I am Yakko, Count Ito's concubine."

As Ito's mistress, Sada was a celebrity, one of the most famous faces in the country. When she went to meet her student lover, she had to go in disguise, hiding her face in her shawl. She in her turn initiated him in the arts of love. But he, like her, could not afford to be ruled by sentiment. Offered the chance to marry into one of the country's most powerful and wealthy families, he took it and was sent to the United States to study.

Sada knew there was no point pining. Beautiful and famous, she took a succession of lovers, including two kabuki actors, heartthrobs of their day, and a mountainous sumo wrestler. Then one fateful day in 1892 she was summoned to entertain Ito and his guests, among them the real-estate tycoon Shibusawa who had introduced them. He had brought along a young man who was the talk of the town, an actor and satirist named Otojiro Kawakami.

Eight years older than Sada, Otojiro came from a rough rural background and had spent time in prison because of his scurrilous tongue and subversive speeches. Making a living by his wits on the streets, he had become a *rakugo* comedian, the Japanese equivalent of a stand-up comic. He quickly became famous for his savage but very funny stories in which he targeted pretentious city dwellers who made a fad of all things Western, right down to Western government, but somehow always got it wrong.

Shibusawa expected Otojiro to do his piece in front of the prime minister but the young man refused. "If you want to see my performance, you'll have to come to my theater and pay for a ticket," he said cheekily. It was the kind of effrontery that Ito, who had been a rebel himself, rather liked.

Entranced by this brusque young man, Sada saw him to the door, introduced herself, and a few days later went to see him perform. The result was a love affair which was to last for the rest of their lives.

It was the end of Sada's career as a geisha. It was one thing for a geisha to have a professional relationship with a *danna,* quite another for her to have an all-engrossing personal relationship. It gave her a different flavor. Men could no longer enjoy the pleasures of an innocent flirtation with her. Thus if a geisha wished to marry, she had to leave the profession immediately.

As for the *danna,* the only course was to respond with a good grace. Normally he would offer to be the official go-between, a key part of the formalities of marriage in Japan. Given Ito's position he could not do so; instead he did the next best thing and arranged for a friend of his—a man of rank—to perform the role.

Otojiro became a famous (some would say infamous) actor, director, and impresario and built his own theater while Sada busied herself in time-honored Japanese fashion being his wife. Some years later he started planning a world tour in which, as was usual in Japan, *onnagata*—male actors—would take the female roles. Ever since Izumo no Okuni and her followers had been banned from the theater in the seventeenth century, women had been forbidden to perform as actresses in public. Not that this meant there were no actresses. Geisha and courtesans were, as it were, "parlor actresses," performing on a small stage to a select audience, and just as famous and celebrated as if they had performed on the public stage.

But, said the promoter, in order to attract an audience in the United States Otojiro would have to have a female star—and who better than his own deservedly celebrated wife, the beautiful Sadayakko!

So Otojiro, Sada, and their troupe of twenty actors set sail for San Francisco. It was 1899, the cusp of the new century and Sada was twenty-seven.

The West which they were on their way to seduce had been enjoying a love affair with "olde world" Japan ever since Commodore Perry opened the doors of this extraordinary feudal society. Japonisme was all the rage. In Britain Victorian artists, notably James McNeill Whistler, were painting in the Japonesque style and collecting Japanese art; Arthur Lasenby Liberty spent much time in Japan studying fabrics and buying goods for his store on London's Regent Street; and Victorians avidly bought kimonos, fans, and blue-and-white porcelain to decorate their homes. "In fact, the whole of Japan is a pure invention," commented Oscar Wilde in his supercilious way. "The Japanese people are simply a mode of style, an exquisite fancy of art."

In England, *The Mikado* had been a smash hit, with a thousand performances over an eleven-year run. Across the Atlantic on one particular night in 1886 there were 170 separate performances going on simultaneously all over the North American continent. A pin-up that same year of the much-adored star Marie Lloyd showed her dressed as the Westerner's notion of The Geisha in a red long-sleeved kimono open like a coat, waving a fan, with hairpins in her hair and an enormous bow on her back. The chorus to her song was inscribed beneath the picture:

> *Every little Jappy chappie's gone upon the Geisha—*
> *Trickiest little Geisha ever seen in Asia!*
> *I've made things hum a bit you know, since I became a Geisha,*
> *Japanesey, free and easy Tea house girl!*[10]

In those politically incorrect times, such lyrics seemed utterly inoffensive.

But no one apart from those who had been posted to Japan, and certainly no one in San Francisco, had ever seen a real geisha. When they arrived Sada was astonished to find that her fame had preceded her.

There were posters, not of the famous actor but of his humble wife, all over the city.

The troupe performed a melodramatic piece called "The Warrior and the Geisha," fusing together a couple of different kabuki dramas and ending with a death scene derived from "Musume Dojoji" (The Maiden of Dojo Temple) in which a maiden, maddened with jealousy and rage, dies of a broken heart. Sada's dancing thrilled audiences across the country. "Mme. Yacco's death scene at the end of the play revealed tragic force," enthused the *New York Times* of December 6, 1899, after the troupe performed in Boston.[11] (Western writers of the day, unused to Japanese names, referred to her as Sada Yacco—romanized thus rather than the more modern "Yakko"—and assumed mistakenly that Yacco was her surname.)

Then they sailed for London where they played at the Coronet, the leading theater of the day. The artist William Nicholson painted a portrait of "Sada Yacco" as an old-style courtesan with foot-high lacquered patens and a splendid coiffure spiked with hairpins. She looks somber and dignified, utterly unlike the pin-up of Marie Lloyd.

In France their visit coincided with the Paris Exposition of 1900, where Japanese arts and crafts excited huge interest. A journalist called Louis Fournier conducted a lengthy interview with Sada and later described her long black kimono and "delicate and childish melancholy face." As a romantic Frenchman, the question he was most interested in was "What is love in Japan?" This was her reply:

" 'Different—so different,' she exclaims. 'In this country men and women love each other freely; it is the custom. Japanese girls do not declare their love so frankly. Often they will die rather than confess it . . . Ah! to me, my friend, love in Japan is very noble, sublime, and sacred!' "[12]

Even the young Pablo Picasso did a painting of her in india ink and gouache, entitled *Sada Yacco*, in which he portrays her dancing in a rather wild and abandoned way, her arms flung over her head, wearing a kimono and obi with a sinister black cloak coiling, serpent-like, around her.

In Washington President William McKinley had commandeered a box to see the troupe; in Paris, they performed at the presidential palace, where President Emile Loubet had personally presented Sada with a bouquet; and in London the Prince of Wales requested a command performance on a specially built Japanese stage inside Buckingham Palace. Japanese government officials, however, were outraged that their country was being represented by these geisha and actors. As far as snobbish traditional-minded Japanese were concerned, such people were riverbed folk, no different from prostitutes and beggars. To have fun with them and use them for pleasure was one thing. But for such people to be adored and treated as symbols of the mysterious Orient by Westerners, whose opinion the Japanese were very sensitive about, was a scandal. In the long run it just went to show that Westerners would never be able to grasp what Japan was all about. It was a matter for national shame.[13]

Abroad Sada played a geisha or a courtesan in productions specially tailored to suit Western taste. But at home, along with Otojiro, she was instrumental in introducing Shakespeare to the Japanese public. She played Ophelia, Portia, and Desdemona, among other roles, and also founded a school for actresses.

On one memorable occasion the troupe gave a performance of *Othello* before a packed house. At the time Otojiro was engaged in an intense affair with a Shimbashi geisha, Kyoka, whom he had seated in the front row. When the time came for Otojiro, as Othello, to smother Sada, who was playing Desdemona, she refused to die. "I don't want to die, I'm innocent," she screamed.

"Please die," whispered Otojiro desperately. "I swear I'll never see her again."

He kept his word. The couple remained together until Otojiro died in 1911. Later Sada re-met her student lover, the thickset farm boy, now a successful businessman, and lived with him until his death in 1938. She lived to see the Second World War and the devastation that followed and died in 1946 at the age of 74. Thus thanks to her beauty and talent and the doors opened to her as a geisha, Sadayakko was able to rise from impoverished beginnings to become Japan's first actress and real star. She is celebrated as such to this day.[14]

chapter 7

inside the pleasure quarters

Geisha Life

The night is black
And I am excited about you.
My love climbs in me, and you ask
That I should climb to the higher room.
Things are hidden in a black night.
Even the dream is black
On the black-lacquered pillow,
Even our talk is hidden.
    Geisha song[1]

The Ichiriki Teahouse

Ichiriki-tei—"One Strength Teahouse"—is the most splendid tea-house in Kyoto, renowned across Japan. It stands proudly on the corner of Shijo Street, the main shopping area, and Hanami-koji, "Flower-Viewing Alley," the heart of Gion. The teahouses which press side by side along Flower-Viewing Alley are dark and forbidding, with slatted wooden fencing in front, bamboo screens concealing the windows, and little sign of life except for the red lanterns which hang in the doorways and the discreet wooden plaques which give the names of the geisha and maiko who live there. Behind them stretch warrens of shadowy lanes lined with faceless houses and closed gates. Ichiriki, conversely, is large and showy, a grand two-story edifice whose distinctive terra-cotta-colored walls are a symbol of the city. Nonetheless, it is every bit as firmly closed to all but the most privileged of insiders.

Whenever I passed by I admired the imposing red walls with their beams and buttressing of blackened wood and peeked wistfully through the heavy brown curtain which hung across the gateway, emblazoned with the characters *Ichi riki,* "One strength." Everyone assured me that the outside walls and the curtain were the most I would ever see; as a rank outsider in this closed community, I could never even dream of crossing the threshold.

Then one day I was in the hair-oil shop on Shijo Street, talking to the elegant, very modern young woman behind the counter whose family had dealt in heavily scented camellia oil for generations. She had grown up on the edge of the geisha world; she was in it but not of it. She was not determined, as the geisha were, to maintain its exclusivity even if that meant it would die out entirely. Almost in passing she asked if I would like to meet the mistress of Ichiriki, whose son happened to go to school with hers. There and then she took me around the corner, brushed through the brown linen curtains, crossed the cobbled court-yard, slid open the doors, and introduced me.

The mistress was a plump, pretty, confident woman in a pink jumper who wore her hair in a bun like a geisha. There was nothing much, she said with Japanese self-deprecation, just tatami rooms, but if I really wanted to see them, I could. Amazed at my luck, I followed her in stockinged feet as she padded along the dark corridors, glossy with pol-ish, and led me into a large, airy banqueting hall, empty but for acres of straw-colored tatami matting and a few low tables. Ancient wooden screens, brushed with a design of purple irises, concealed the sliding doors. Above another set of doors was an ink sketch of a bald-headed samurai, wearing a blindfold, chasing a bevy of laughing geisha.

"Oishi Kuranosuke?" I asked.

She nodded with a glance of approval; I was not just an ignorant foreigner. Oishi Kuranosuke is a romantic hero akin to Bonnie Prince Charlie in the West and quite close to him in dates. A real historical character, he is the protagonist of the much-loved *Tale of the Forty-Seven Ronin* [leaderless samurai]. According to the story, he whiled away two years in Ichiriki teahouse, play-acting a life of debauchery, in order to put his enemies off the scent before exacting a terrible vengeance for the death of his lord. Purists complain that in his time, around 1702, Gion barely existed and had certainly not reached its apogee of splendor; the Ichiriki he knew must have been in the south of the city. But no one in Gion pays the slightest attention to such quibbles.

Thanks to the Oishi connection, Ichiriki was by far the most successful of the Gion teahouses; there were always people wanting to dissipate an evening at the scene of the most celebrated partying in Japanese history. Ichiriki, the mistress added firmly, had definitely existed in 1702. I didn't argue the point.

Beyond the glass doors which formed the outside wall was a small garden laid out like a picture with moss-covered rocks around a stone lantern and a gnarled tree. The mistress showed me the air-conditioning ducts cunningly concealed behind a veneer of ancient bamboo piping and wooden latticework. The teahouses of Gion had been among the first places in Japan to install it. It was a profitable business.

She too was in the geisha world but not of it. She had moved to Ichiriki when she married Seiichi Sugiura, the thirteenth generation of the Sugiura family which had dominated Gion throughout its history. The ninth, Jiroemon, had been instrumental in reviving Kyoto's geisha culture when the emperor and his court moved to Edo in 1868, establishing the annual public dances which now formed the pinnacle of the geisha calendar. For three hundred years, the master of Ichiriki had been in charge of the geisha union in Gion. He was like the lord of the manor. The ultimate responsibility for the prosperity and well-being of the whole of Gion rested on his shoulders.

Seiichi had never had any choice in the matter. No matter what he did or where he went, he was always branded with the mark of Ichiriki. He was "the Ichiriki boy." Rumor had it that he had been something of a playboy in his youth, who drove fast cars and holidayed in Hawaii. But eventually when his grandfather died he joined the family firm and set to work to learn the business. He was now a pillar of the Gion community.[2]

But the future, said the pretty pink-sweatered mistress, was a worry. In the eighteen years in which she had been at Ichiriki, the number of geisha and teahouses had fallen disastrously. Once upon a time customers used to bring their sons and introduce them. But now most customers were over sixty and their numbers too were plummeting. Instead of going off on a bar crawl for a "second round" and a "third round" of drinking as they used to, people tended to go home after a geisha party. Some of the smaller teahouses were closing down. Ichiriki still thrived. Anyone would grab the chance to spend an evening with the most glamorous geisha in Gion at the historic teahouse. But it could not survive in isolation.

"If we were a restaurant, it wouldn't matter if we were the only one left," she said. We were in one of the upper rooms, looking down on the dark wooden houses along Flower-Viewing Alley. One by one, lanterns began to glow in the dusk. A line of taxis was building up, half blocking the narrow street, ready to ferry the geisha and maiko to their nightly assignations. "But we need geisha and maiko coming and going. That's the flavor of Gion.

"It used to be a special world here where patrons—*danna-san*—took care of the geisha. Geisha ran teahouses but that was just pocket money. Now they have to make a living by that alone. It's impossible. So they end up closing down."

Then she was called out. I sat alone in the banqueting hall, imagining the rowdy parties that had punctuated the last three centuries and the days when glamorous dissidents, from wealthy but powerless merchants in their silks and finery to hot-headed young samurai forced to leave their swords at the door, had gathered here to while away night after night with their geisha lovers.

After a few minutes the door slid open and a woman slipped in. She folded herself onto her knees in a corner of the big room and sat silently looking at the tatami, nervously twisting her bony hands. She was a wisp of a woman, painfully thin with a graying bun.

As the guest, it was not my place to begin the conversation. But when the silence became heavy, I tried a little small talk. She must have known Ichiriki for many years, I said. She started reminiscing about how it had been after the war when they tried to get the business going again but everyone had sold their kimonos.

"I'd just arrived," she said. She had a thin, reedy voice. "I hated it here. I cried and cried. The maids tormented me. It was so hard to learn all the different ways of doing things."

She must be, I realized, the "old mistress," the mother-in-law of the pink-jumpered young mistress. I never ceased to be amazed by the passion with which older women poured out their feelings. At first I thought it was because I was such an outsider. As a non-Japanese, I was barely human and rendered harmless by my childish foreign accent. Perhaps this was why they felt able to speak of things which could not be shared with their peers. But then I read an interview in an obscure Japanese magazine in which the "old mistress" had said many of the same things. Perhaps it was the privilege of age. She had handed on the mantle of responsibility. No longer "the mistress of Ichiriki," she was free to be herself.[3]

A couple of visits later, she was delegated to tell me her memories of the history of the place. I waited in the banqueting hall for her to arrive. She slipped in, birdlike and nervous.

"Customers used to summon their favorite geisha and maiko and sleep with them in those small rooms upstairs," she began, almost before she had folded to her knees. "Black marketeers would ask for geisha. Most of the patrons were the owners of the weaving factories in Nishijin. They spent the night here with their geisha, or they went to an inn. Some of the wives had horns [the demon horns of jealousy] or pretended not to know. In those days keeping a geisha was a mark of status. It was natural. But after the war all that stopped. That way of thinking was abolished."

A Tokyo girl, she had been evacuated to Kyoto with her family during the war. Her father knew a man who had a saké shop and he knew the old master of Ichiriki. The two met up at a tea ceremony and decided that their children should marry. She was eighteen, the "young master" of Ichiriki thirty-three. After the formal introductions, before anything had been decided, she sneaked off to the teahouse to have a look around. It was huge and intimidating. The last thing she wanted was to marry into this famous family with such a long history and weighty place in Kyoto society.

"I didn't want to enter a world I didn't know," she said in her thin reedy voice. "But my parents said I had to. The Sugiura family promised that I would not have to go to teahouse parties. But as soon as I moved in, I had to. I was the young mistress, I had to."

Fresh from Tokyo, she had no idea how things were done in stiff, rather formal Kyoto society, let alone in the arcane world of the geisha. It was a bit like moving from New York to the salons of Washington high society or arriving from Manchester to marry the son of a lord with a luxury home in Mayfair. Even the high-falutin' dialect of Kyoto was barely comprehensible to her Tokyo ears; worse still, her dowager mother-in-law spoke old Kyoto dialect, like fearsomely posh Victorian English.

"The maids bullied me. I wasn't used to dealing with customers. When I made mistakes, they scolded me. The most difficult thing was knowing what to talk about at parties. I couldn't just sit there and say nothing. My mother-in-law gave me instructions but she spoke old Kyoto dialect and I couldn't understand, even when I asked her two or three times to repeat it. I used to hide in the toilet and cry. I cried and cried.

"Right after the war we had lots of foreigners coming. The geisha refused to sleep with foreigners."

She led the way up the steep wooden staircase to the upper floor and showed me the big rooms where customers used to "sleep over" with groups of pretty maiko and a couple of maids to make sure things did not get out of hand. There were also several smaller, cozier rooms for *danna* who wanted to spend the night with a geisha. If a customer had booked a *mizuage,* that was where he did it.

"Some of the maiko and geisha hated having to sleep with the *danna.* They used to complain to me. But they had to do it."

One balmy night I went for a stroll along the River Kamo. Behind the teahouses of the Pontocho geisha district, below the platforms where drinkers caroused with geisha in the heat of summer, right at the edge of the water there was a broad stony esplanade lined with cobbles, popular with sunbathers, cyclists, and courting couples. That evening it was crowded with the city's youth in shorts and trainers, letting off fireworks, laughing, and jostling.

Walking along, I came to a group which seemed to be from another world, though to a seasoned Kyoto-ite, they were such a common sight as to merit barely a second glance. The men were in business suits but looked as if they had been enjoying a well-lubricated evening out, ties askew, faces flushed and glistening with sweat. They yelled with as much abandon as the youths in shorts. With them were four or five maiko, their painted faces glowing white in the reflected neon light, the decorations in their hair sparkling and swinging, their brilliantly colored kimonos absurdly cumbersome, like fancy dress. Some of the men were chasing the maiko, brandishing sparklers. The maiko ran about adroitly on their high clogs, shrieking and giggling.

It was just innocent fun, young men and women enjoying a summer evening together. But there was one thing that made that group a little different from all the others. The maiko were being paid for every second of their time.

There was a story I heard about a businessman who had been on his way back to Tokyo. Happening to meet three maiko at Kyoto station, he invited them to join him in the Green Car, the first-class carriage in the Bullet Train. Geisha and maiko always travel first class on any mode of transport and stay only in five-star hotels. It is part of the flower and willow lifestyle. Even an aging geisha who is no longer in huge demand at parties and has limited means would not dream of traveling economy class. She has to keep up appearances even if it bankrupts her.

Charmed to find himself in such delightful company, the businessman bought the maiko snacks and drinks and enjoyed their girlish chatter. The three-hour journey passed like a dream. When they arrived at

Tokyo Station, he bade them farewell, wished them all the best, and went off to his meetings.

Several days later—when, no doubt, he had almost forgotten the encounter—a letter arrived in the post. Puzzled, he opened it. It was from a Kyoto teahouse and contained an enormous bill for the time spent with three maiko: three hours each, plus additional charges. It was, said the geisha who told me this story, nothing to do with greed. It was not that the teahouse mistress wanted money. In the geisha world, things have to be done properly. Time spent with a maiko or a geisha has to be paid for, even if it is distasteful to have to ask. It was a matter of doing things with style.

Another story in the same vein concerns an elderly professor who was strolling across Shijo Bridge one day when he happened to meet some maiko he knew. They were off duty, pattering along in cotton yukata, their glowing young faces unpainted.

"Big Brother," they greeted him. Geisha and maiko always address their *danna* as "Father" and other customers as "Big Brother," no matter how old they are. "Where are you going?"

"I'm going to have lunch," he beamed. "I don't have any classes today."

"We haven't had lunch either," chorused the maiko.

Thrilled at the prospect of several hours in the company of these charming young women, he took them to the best French restaurant in Kyoto, wined and dined them. But alas, for all his generosity, he suffered the same fate as the unsuspecting businessman.

A man who "knew how to spend money and have fun with geisha"—that was the kind of man a geisha liked. Quite apart from the no-strangers rule, this meant that the geisha world would be eternally exclusive, the realm of the very, very rich. For no one else could possibly keep up with the spending required.

In modern times, elderly geisha grumbled, standards had slipped badly. These days you got vulgar types throwing around not their own but company money and who were so déclassé as to ask for a receipt. "The receipt society," they called it, wrinkling their elegant noses in disdain.

Back in the eighties, when the Japanese economy was on a roll, big spending was all the rage. In those days there was a coffee shop, legendary in Tokyo, where you could get a cup of coffee for $200. You could buy exactly the same cup of coffee in the same shop for $5 but that was no fun. The thrill was in spending $200 on a cup of coffee. In the geisha world, that mentality continues. As in the days of the courtesans, it is a world where money speaks.

From the moment a maiko or a geisha slips her dainty feet into her clogs and slides open the geisha house door, she is at work. The meter clicks on. It continues to run as she moves from party to party until she is back in the geisha house at the end of the evening. Whether you take a geisha out for dinner, for a trip to the theater, or a day of golfing, no matter how relaxed and informal the occasion, she is still at work, earning an hourly wage.

Geisha were quite unembarrassed to talk about money, though of course one never called it "money." The word for the maiko's or geisha's fee was "flower money"—*hana-dai* or *o-hana,* "honorable flower." In the old romantic days, when Japanese clocks pursued a rather eccentric course and the pleasure districts ran on a different time from other parts of the country, a geisha's or a maiko's time was measured by the number of incense sticks which burned down while she was working. The incense sticks in different areas were different lengths. In Gion, twelve sticks equaled an hour; in Pontocho an hour was four sticks. The nomenclature continues, even though the practice has ended. In theory all geisha in any particular area earn the same. There is no sliding scale for seniority. In other words, as geisha were at pains to point out, being a geisha is not a career. It is a calling.

As for the actual rate, it varies area by area but is in the region of 10,000 yen ($100) an hour. For an evening's work, a geisha might average 30,000–40,000 yen ($300–$400). On top of that there are tips, invariably lavish. No one would dream of insulting a maiko or geisha by giving her less than at least 10,000 yen ($100). Often by the end of a single evening she will have slipped 40,000–50,000 yen ($400–$500) into the collar of her kimono.

As one maiko told me with a candid smile, she made a far better living than her schoolmates who had taken jobs as OL—"office ladies" or secretaries. At the geisha house, everything was paid for. Her kimonos, her fans, her bags, her taxi fares, and the costs of her trips to the hairdresser were all supplied by the house. The house mother kept all the maiko's earnings as repayment of what was effectively her debt, though she did give her pocket money in the region of 30,000–40,000 yen ($300–$400) a month. And the tips were hers to keep (although in some houses the maiko were required to hand over their tips too). For both the maiko and the house mother, it was a very profitable business.

But if the maiko were to decide to stay on and become a geisha, she would move out of the geisha house and set up on her own after a year or two. Unlike a maiko, she would no longer be in such enormous demand. Men loved the company of the doll-like maiko in their brilliantly colored kimonos, giggling artlessly; that was why they came to Kyoto. The geisha, however, had a serious profession. A geisha's success depended on her skill in conversation, music, and dancing; it was not enough just to have a pretty face. As a geisha, she would keep all her own earnings; but she would have to try to make a living from that alone. Life, in fact, would be much easier if there were a *danna* around.

The amount a customer paid, of course, bore little relation to the amount a geisha received. When a customer wanted to organize a geisha party, he began by calling the proprietress of the teahouse where he was a regular customer. Customers were expected to observe teahouse loyalty. Most businesses, particularly those in Kyoto and Osaka, always used the same teahouse, as did many families. It was like being a member of an exclusive private club. Fathers would take their sons to their teahouse when the boys were in their teens and introduce them to the teahouse mistress and their regular geisha. "Teahouse crawling" was frowned upon—though, if you were the customer of the venerable Ichiriki teahouse, you had such kudos that you were welcome in any teahouse in Gion.

Most probably the teahouse mistress had known the customer for decades and could plan the perfect party for him on the basis of his tastes and requirements. That was why he had entrusted the job to her. Teahouses were not restaurants. If he had asked for food, she ordered it in from one of the outside caterers.

Then she set about planning the best mix of geisha and maiko.

There would have to be geisha who could dance, geisha who could sing, and geisha who could play the shamisen. The shamisen in particular took years to learn. The best shamisen players were old and were in huge demand. Then there would need to be shy pretty maiko to sit around looking decorative and filling saké cups. The union office at the large concrete Kaburenjo was the center of operations for the whole district. There they pored over detailed charts showing where each geisha and maiko would be at any particular time in the evening. There was frequently feverish juggling of names as last-minute calls for geisha came in.

The system varied district by district. Sometimes the teahouse mistress called the Kaburenjo to sort out geisha for the evening, at others she would call the geisha house direct to book a particular geisha.

The first party of the evening was from six to nine P.M. Invitations in Japan usually tell you what time the party will end as well as what time it begins and formal parties invariably end precisely when they say they will; geisha are being paid by the hour and running over would be extremely costly. Popular geisha might not stay for the whole evening but might flit from party to party. After the party was over, everyone relaxed. A guest might take a maiko or a geisha out for dinner or to a karaoké bar and later on they might come to some private arrangement for the night. But no matter how relaxed the evening became, the meter ticked relentlessly on.

On such occasions, nothing so crass as a bill would ever appear; neither would money ever change hands—unless it was a tip proffered to a maiko or geisha. At the end of the evening, the customer thanked the geisha for their hospitality, they thanked him for his patronage, and he left. From time to time a bill from the teahouse covering the last few months would arrive discreetly at the accounts department of his company. He would probably not even see it. If he did, he would not dream of checking it, let alone—perish the thought!—asking for a receipt.

In any case, there would be no itemized charges, no hint as to how the final figure had been arrived at, though one could be sure that that final figure would be earth-shatteringly huge. Quite apart from the costs of the geisha, there was the fee to the teahouse owner for organizing the party. Each tidbit or sip of liquor that passed a guest's lips cost a fortune and the expense, if a meal was ordered, can barely be imagined. A geisha party I attended along with two other guests, which included four geisha and a light meal for the three of us, cost the host more than $3,200. I heard of parties costing $8,000 to $16,000, as much as a new car. But then again, the kudos for the party-giver was to show that for him this was a mere nothing. As in the old days, when a dashing young fellow would happily ruin himself for pleasure, it showed that he was a man not only of means but of style.

When the payment arrived, the teahouse mistress took a percentage that included the cost of paying the caterers who had provided the food. She also sent an agreed sum to the union to cover the costs of the maiko and geisha. The registry office would take a percentage of that and send the requisite fee on to the geisha house.

The Danna

The geisha world was always awash with gossip and rumors. There was the house a few doors up from mine, built of shiny new wood, half-hidden behind a bamboo fence with a permanently closed gate pressed up almost against the front door, adding a symbolic extra barrier against intruders. The houses to each side were bustling with life. Maiko would slip in and out in their cotton yukata, the house mothers would emerge and bow to passersby as they went to tidy the small shrine across the road or went off to the coffee shop for breakfast. I would hear the plangent notes of the shamisen as the same riffs were practiced uncertainly over and over again. But the house in the middle was always silent and the door firmly shut.

"That was her *danna* had that house built for her," people told me.

"Is it a geisha house?" I asked.

"Nah, she doesn't have to work at all. Doesn't do a thing."

Then there was the story of the beautiful geisha who had had an affair with the popular singing star which had been blazoned all over the weekly magazines (the Japanese equivalent of the tabloids). And there was the oil magnate who had given his mistress—complete with her house—to a government minister as a "gift," in exchange for which the minister had turned a blind eye to some illicit activity he was engaged in.

All these stories were impossible to confirm and, like most such tales in Japan, probably true.

The geisha I knew were canny, down-to-earth, working-class girls. But once they put on their makeup and the last cord of their obi was in place, they became fantasy creatures in a dreamworld which existed solely for the pleasure of men. There they were expected to be the epitome of femininity, dizzy doll-women who understood nothing of the harsh realities of life. As one ex-geisha told me, if a man asked about the cost of anything, she would say—smiling a sweetly helpless smile and speaking in a breathy Marilyn Monroe voice—"Oh, I really don't know anything about that!" Though, of course, she added, she knew perfectly well.

Until recent years, most geisha had not had to bother their pretty little heads with such distasteful matters as money because almost all of them had *danna* who supported them. As the young mistress of Ichiriki had said, tips from customers, entertaining at parties, running a teahouse, all that had been mere pin money. The real financial backing had been provided by the *danna*. All the older geisha had had *danna* as a matter of course. Love did not come into it. It was a practical arrangement.

My seventy-nine-year-old neighbor, a gracious and still beautiful woman with lacquered white hair and a twinkling smile, had been a geisha before the war. "If you didn't have a good *danna,* you couldn't live," she told me. The mistress of the teahouse where she worked had arranged a *danna* for her when she was twenty-three.

"You could tell immediately," she said, "if someone would make a good *danna.* They'd approach the teahouse mistress. You could refuse if you wanted." In those days a *danna* was almost like a husband except, of course, that he already had a wife. The geisha would be his concubine, his number two wife, or, if he was a wealthy man, his number three or even number four wife. My neighbor's *danna,* who was in the ceramics business, supported her for thirty years and she bore him two children. She also at one point had a lover. Once, she recalled, they talked about marriage.

"But I told him, 'I can't get married.' It's part of being a geisha. If you become a geisha, you don't think about marriage. I never think now, 'I wish I'd got married.' "

A Tokyo geisha I met, who was seventy-three, lived alone, rather sadly, in a small house where she subsisted by giving shamisen lessons. "You have to have a *danna*," she told me. "You need money." Her *danna* had been the president of an iron company. "Some people kept their relationship secret," she said. "But ours was open. His wife met me; she understood.

"He gave me a monthly allowance of 200,000 yen [$550–$700 at the exchange rate of the time, equivalent to $4,800–$6,400 in modern currency], plus money for kimonos and classes, and bought me presents. It was about the same as you'd make in your first job after leaving university. I lived in the geisha house. I often used to visit his house. He took me to the cinema and to restaurants and to see kabuki and we traveled together to Hokkaido and Kyushu.

"I saved up and bought a house for myself. He said he'd have it repaired for me, but the economy was bad. If the economy had been good he would have bought it for me just like that.

"I remember one day he said to me, 'It'll be fifteen years we've been together soon.' Soon after that his health got worse and he stopped visiting. Then he died. He was in his sixties, I was in my thirties. At least I got to go to his funeral. I was lucky. A lot of women I know couldn't go to their lovers' funerals. The wives wouldn't allow it. That was always a painful thing."

The patronage or *danna* system was—and, to some extent, still is—the essence of the flower and willow lifestyle. The first requirement was a man who had a sizable amount of money to spare (extra, that is, after he had paid all his living expenses, his mortgage, provided for the needs of his family and dependent relatives, paid for school fees, holidays abroad, pension plans, and regular investment commitments). Such a man was likely to be at the pinnacle of his career and rather elderly. Most likely he owned his own business and could do as he pleased with his money, rather than being a salaried president, at the beck and call of the shareholders. One businessman reckoned that it would cost 20 to 30 million yen ($200,000–$300,000) a year to keep a geisha.

Following the proper route, he would approach the proprietress of the teahouse where he was a long-standing and trustworthy customer and mention his interest in a particular geisha. The proprietress would discuss the matter with the geisha and her house mother. If all were in agreement, the "mothers" would settle the practical details with the patron and agree on the level of financial assistance he was prepared to give.

Usually the *danna* paid a monthly allowance to cover the geisha's rent and living expenses and also bought her kimonos and obis. He paid all the tuition fees for her lessons in dancing, shamisen, and singing. When she appeared at a public dance performance, he covered the considerable costs. He would be given the seat of honor and a batch of tickets to distribute to his influential friends and colleagues. If he summoned her to entertain for him at a banquet, he took priority over other guests, though he still had to pay the usual hourly rate for her services. She was also available for sex if required, though, as he was rather elderly, it was not a foregone conclusion that he would exercise his rights.

As to whether geisha or maiko ever slept with customers for money, as prurient Westerners like to imagine: "Geisha don't do that," one maiko told me firmly when I dared to ask her. "A *danna* and a customer are quite different. The *danna* is like your husband. You have a proper arrangement with him."

Maiko, she pointed out, lived in a geisha house watched over by a strict *okasan;* they did not have the opportunity for freelancing of that sort. In any case, they were too busy with their classes and work even to have boyfriends. The maiko confessed that for a short time she had had a boyfriend, not a customer but a young man of her own age. But she had not had the time to see him and eventually the relationship collapsed. Such affairs were strictly against the rules. In the old days, sex had to be arranged through the proper channels and paid for in the proper way; freelance sex was out of the question. The customer had to approach the teahouse mistress who would consult the geisha house mistress before informing the young woman in question. These days, of course, licensed prostitution was illegal.

"Some geisha have *danna*, some don't," the maiko added. "It's much easier if you do. It's too expensive otherwise."

Men with the wealth and leisure to become *danna* were often highly cultured, with a keen interest in the traditional arts practiced by the geisha. They would spend a considerable amount of time and money, educating her with tender care so that she became the male ideal of accomplished and talented womanhood. At its most exalted, it was not so much "Lolita" as "Pygmalion," with the *danna* as a kind of Professor Henry Higgins, choosing his Eliza Doolittle and putting her through finishing school to create the perfect woman, with no ulterior motive other than the pleasure of seeing her grow and develop. Or he might be a sort of connoisseur, a collector of beautiful items with her as his prize possession, demonstrating his wealth, taste, and status.

There is a very simple reason why the geisha world is under threat. The Henry Higgins generation, who saw becoming the *danna* of a geisha as a mark of success and an ideal to strive toward, is dying out. For a start, no one has the money anymore. In modern Japan there are very few family-owned businesses left. Most top executives are employees of large impersonal corporations and cannot help themselves to several million yen of the company's money in order to spend it on a geisha. Added to which, the baby-boomers are rapidly growing into society's grand old men. But these are modern Japanese men in their fifties. They have grown up in a world where people go to the ballet and the opera or listen to jazz or techno, rather than the melancholy plink plonk of the shamisen. They spend more time in French restaurants or hostess bars than teahouses. Many have never even seen a geisha. Far from seeing them as objects of desire, they think of them as gorgeous fossils or cultural dinosaurs, if they think of them at all.

Nevertheless, teahouse mothers told me that a good proportion of geisha were still supported by *danna,* maybe one in five. But no one I knew would ever admit to it. It was too sensitive a matter. Geisha knew very well what their image was outside the confines of their small enchanted world. One very popular geisha told me, in tones that brooked no argument, that in the old days maiko had had enormous debts to pay off and that was why they needed a *danna*. Now there were no debts—the 1958 bill had seen to that—so there was no need for patrons any longer.

That was not strictly true. Constructing a world where men can live out their dreams is not a cheap matter. To play her part to the full, a geisha has to be a walking work of art, gorgeously attired, her wig, makeup, and kimono all of the most exquisite quality. Yet to buy the most basic kimono can cost anything from 200,000 yen ($2,000) up to several million ($20,000 upward); the average kimono costs 350,000–500,000 yen ($3,500–$5,000). And it has to be worn with an obi of equal value. Added to which, one kimono is far from enough. Teahouse customers are regulars who come again and again and it would certainly not do to be seen in the same kimono too many times.

All the geisha adored kimonos and collected them with passion. My white-haired neighbor confessed to having two hundred. As a famous Japanese saying goes, a native of Osaka will bankrupt himself for a great meal, but for a Kyoto-ite the fatal weakness is fine silk. None of this is a problem for a maiko who lives at a geisha house where the house mother lays out her kimono each evening. But for a newly hatched geisha setting up on her own, the initial costs might run as high as 20 million yen ($200,000). Geisha need three kimonos a month—one to wear, one to go to the cleaner's, and one spare, in case a customer spills his drink over your priceless silk. And each month they need different kimonos. All in all, it comes to about 3 million yen ($30,000) a year for kimonos alone.

Then there are classes, which might come to 100,000 yen a month, plus the exorbitant costs incurred for the various ceremonies marking the rites of passage in a geisha's life—the debut and the changing of the collar, when a maiko graduates to become a fully-fledged geisha. These cost hundreds of thousands of yen for the proper kimono, fans, bags, and other equipment, for tips to the dressers and other helpers, and gifts to members of the community. There are also enormous costs whenever a geisha takes part in one of the grand public dance performances such as the Cherry Dances. Far from being paid like a professional dancer, she has to pay for the honor of appearing and for her costumes and equipment, plus enormous sums in tips for all the helpers and assistants and monetary gifts to her teachers.

In recent years customers have started offering to sponsor part of the cost. One might pay for the kimono and obi, another for the wig for the new geisha, another for the cost of printing the scarves with the geisha's name which she hands out to everyone. One very popular maiko who decided to give up before the turning of the collar had had promises from sponsors to pay for everything for the ceremony and been showered with expensive bags and gifts. Nevertheless well into the 1990s there are still men who maintain the tradition of the big spender. Those who can afford it pride themselves on being the sole sponsor for a maiko's debut or turning of the collar. As to whether the maiko chooses to reward her benefactor in the traditional way, that is strictly between her and him.

Geisha Chic:
The Art of the Kimono

One day when I got back to my inn, I found a note, prettily written on handmade paper with a drawing of a *maneki nekko* (a lucky "money-beckoning cat") on the envelope. It was from Koito. There was a journalist from a women's magazine coming to interview her, she wrote. Could I, the local foreigner, please be there to add a touch of international color to the photograph?

In her idiosyncratic way Koito was the epitome of the modern geisha. She was a star not of the silver screen or the television but of the Internet. She regularly featured in articles in newspapers and magazines and had a lively fan club. Three years ago she had started a website to put across the geisha lifestyle and philosophy, describe its arts, customs, and history, correct misconceptions, and persuade new customers to come.

Rather than Koito, it was Komaki, her maiko, who was the star of the website. She was the first maiko of the cyber age. She had seen Koito on television, looked up her website, and been captivated by the images and descriptions of life in the flower and willow world. She persuaded her father to send Koito an e-mail asking if she could become her apprentice, was accepted, and moved into Koito's house. But like many maiko, she discovered that there was a lot more to the life than just looking pretty. Her story—her hopes, her disappointments, her growing frustration—formed the gripping day-to-day substance of the website. Even the house cat featured on it. But now, a year later, having gone through with her debut, she had disappeared.

"It's not easy raising a maiko," complained Koito, addressing the plump young journalist who was busy scribbling notes. She too was a fan of Koito's and regularly checked her website. "She got pimples. Everyone was always watching her and passing comments. It made her self-conscious. No one ever told her she was doing well. So she got depressed. I think she might have run away for good."

We had been sitting rather stiffly on cushions around the low table in one of the tatami rooms upstairs. Koito led us into a dressing room and began lifting flat cardboard boxes out of the shallow drawers of a tall wooden dresser. She took the lid off one to reveal a package of textured handmade paper. Carefully she undid the ribbons. Inside, within another layer of tissue paper, was a swathe of lustrous silk, quail's-egg gray. She lifted the folds of fabric to reveal a pattern of white grasses. We fingered the soft silk.

"It's a geisha's kimono for autumn," she said. "Autumn grasses."

Next she brought out a pale mauve kimono, the color of wisteria, then a dark mauve one with a pattern of maple leaves in dark greens and rusty oranges sprinkled with golden and orange chrysanthemums, and put them both aside. The first, she said, was a summer kimono, the second for autumn. Then she showed us a summer kimono of netlike silk in a delicate leaf green the color of a cicada's wing, with a river specked with leaves rippling along the hem. Finally she brought out a kimono of a rich midnight blue. Wisteria blossoms tumbled in mauve-and-gold fronds around the skirt and across the sleeves. The cat was rolling on its back, playing with the loose ribbons.

"I'll wear this one," she said. We helped her refold the others, carefully wrapping them in layers of tissue paper, replacing them in their envelopes and retying the ribbons.

"How do you choose?" we queried. A maiko living in a geisha house had no need to worry about which kimono was appropriate; her house mother would lay out a different kimono each month for her. But Koito was herself a house mother. For her, life was a succession of day-to-day decisions.

It depended, she explained, on the customers, the teahouse, and the occasion for the party. For a congratulatory party or a celebration of some sort, she might wear something dressy, for a small quiet gathering, something more subdued. It went without saying that she would wear a geisha's kimono, much more subtly colored than a maiko's, with sleeves that hung to her hips, not to the ankle, and with the obi tied in a knot without the heavy, swaying ends of the maiko's.

For a geisha, the art of choosing and wearing a kimono is as important a part of her training as learning traditional dancing or studying the shamisen. The kimono is an art form in its own right, as subtle and complex as tea ceremony, flower arrangement, or brush painting. Woven of the finest, most luxurious silk, kimonos are dyed with designs which are exquisite and often enormously complex; landscapes of palaces, bridges, streams, trees, and birds scroll across a kimono skirt in lavish detail and jewel-like colors.

Traditional arts in Japan are to do not with expressing oneself but learning the form, the *kata,* the proper way of doing things. The aim is perfection, a perfect promulgation of tradition, the right kimono worn in the right way for the place, the season, and the occasion. A geisha is an artist who transforms herself into a perfect work of art according to rules laid down by tradition.

Everything in traditional Japanese life reflects the season, from the flowers arranged in a vase to the brush painting on a wall to the words one uses when writing a poem. If you visit a teahouse, a geisha house, or a private home in spring, there will be a sprig of spring flowers in a wicker vase and an ink painting, perhaps of a sprouting bamboo, on the wall; in winter there might be a sprig of plum blossoms artfully arranged in a section of bamboo. And every haiku includes a word which refers to the seasons—irises, rain, or a frog to evoke June, a cicada in high summer, snow in winter. In the same way, a geisha naturally chooses a kimono proper to the season. For the cool months, from the typhoons of September through the winter snows to the end of April when the cherry blossoms fall, she wears a double-layered *awase* kimono of thick silk lined with crepe. In May and June she wears lighter single-layer kimonos and when the steamy days of July and August come, she switches to *ro,* a silk so fine it is almost transparent.

More muted colors are suitable for winter, fresher ones for the hot months. There are also traditional color combinations for each month: pale green layered on deep purple for January, rose backed with slate blue for October. The designs on the kimono, whether dyed (as in the dressier garments) or woven in, always reflect the season. A geisha naturally selects a kimono with the appropriate flowers, plants, insects, or birds: sprigs of pine in January, plum blossom in February, cherry blossom in the spring, small trout in summer, maple leaves in autumn, and snowflakes in the winter. It is all part of the process of living one's life as art.[4]

Koito had changed into a white cotton under-kimono patterned with red chrysanthemums. Scooping her hair into a net, she knelt in front of the tall narrow mirror of her dressing table and opened the tiny drawers overflowing with brushes and tubs of unguents. She took a breath and settled down to begin her makeup. Absorbed, we watched the transformation, all the more dramatic because this was not a beautiful young maiko but an aging, rather plain woman.

Having covered her face in a layer of eggshell white, she turned her back to the mirror and, using a hand mirror to help her, skillfully painted her back in white, leaving the provocative V of unpainted flesh at the nape of the neck. She penciled in two feathery eyebrows, adding a surreal touch of lipstick to define them, edged her eyes in red and added a line of black, then painted her mouth the color of a ripe cherry.

Then she lifted an enormous box like a hatbox from a cupboard and brought out a gleaming coiffed wig on a stand. She combed it, tidied it, and fitted it over her head, adjusting it until it was perfectly centered and balanced, combed it again, added a few hairpins and turned to look at us. The wig had performed its magic. The "Mount Fuji" widow's peak and the strange unnatural wings of the wig had transformed the shape of her face, accentuating the delicate pointed chin. The frumpy thirty-year-old had disappeared and a startlingly alluring creature emerged, like a butterfly from a chrysalis, not beautiful, but indubitably sexy and fascinating. Coquettishly, she picked up the mewing cat and held it up to her face, gazing into its sharp black eyes. It put its paws on her shoulders and tried to lick the immaculate alabaster of her face.

Standing up, she put on a red-and-white under-kimono, followed by another of pale pink scattered with small red chrysanthemums, and the thick white brocade collar marking the adult geisha, tying them all in place with ribbons.

"I used to have a dresser," she said. "But now I do it myself. If you get someone in, you have to fit in with their timing."

Then she took the lustrous midnight-blue kimono with its mauve-and-pale gold design of wisteria and slipped it over her shoulders, pulling it down to reveal not an ample expanse of bare back like a maiko's but a titillating flash of white-painted shoulders. The fabric swirled about her feet like water.

In old Japan, sex appeal was all to do with mystery. Far from revealing swathes of naked bosom, midriff, or leg like a Hollywood star on Oscar night, the epitome of desirability was the *tayu,* the courtesan, swathed in layer upon layer of sumptuous fabric like a Christmas present, with just her tiny bare feet to remind you of the frail flesh of the woman inside. To the Japanese eye, there was an enormous difference in the way geisha and wives—the two poles of Japanese womanhood—wore their kimonos. The geisha was ineffably sexy; but it was a subtle sexiness, a matter of hint and suggestion.

In time I began to be able to see the difference between the kimono a geisha wore when she was dressed to kill with white face and wig and an ordinary one such as a wife would wear. The geisha's was more ornate, bolder, and more decorative with a strong pattern on the skirt and hem where it would be most visible. It was the same shape and size as a standard one; the kimono is a one-size-fits-all garment which you adjust by folding and tying. But there were a myriad subtle ways in which a geisha tied hers to make it very different from a wife's, and infinitely sexier.

For a start it was worn looser than a wife would ever dream of, leaving a suggestive flash of pale under-kimono, spangled with red, clearly visible at the sleeve and hem. It sat lower on the shoulders with the collar pulled well down to reveal the painted back and the erotic tongue of bare flesh at the nape of the neck. It was also worn much longer so that it draped to form a train on the ground, eddying gracefully about the feet. A wife, conversely, would wear a kimono with a discreet pattern on the chest or thigh. She would fold and tie it so that it stopped just at the ankle to make a prim asexual cylinder with barely a bulge for bottom or breasts. When walking the geisha held the skirt of her kimono gracefully with the left hand; if a wife needed to lift her kimono skirt, she would hold it with the right hand.

Koito had wrapped herself in a long green obi, winding it round and round her waist and tucking in pads of stiffening and a cushion at the back to give extra bulk, until she was cocooned as thoroughly as an Egyptian mummy. The last touch was a narrow white silk cord. She turned with a coquettish downcast glance. "It's a long time since I've dressed like this," she confided. Normally she wore the understated kimono and subtle makeup of the day-to-day working geisha. The white makeup, wig, and sumptuous kimono were party wear, for special occasions only.

It was not only her appearance that had changed. Her bearing and the timbre of her voice had changed too, though she was still as chirpy as a Cockney sparrow. As she opened the front door, the cat darted out and disappeared under a nearby parked car. She slipped on a pair of wooden clogs, lower and lighter than a maiko's hooflike ones, and minced after it, lifting her trailing kimono skirts with her left hand and trilling, "Kitty, Kitty"—*"Nekko-chan, Nekko-chan"*—in a girlish falsetto. Together we set off down the street to pose for photographs, Koito tripping along, bowing and calling out greetings to everyone we met.

chapter 8

from the flapper years
to the age of neon

No matter what happens
I am in love with Gion.
Even in my sleep
Beneath my pillow
the waters ripple.

　　Isamu Yoshii (1886–1960)[1]

Cherry Dances in
Turn-of-the-Century Kyoto

Throughout the centuries of the shoguns' rule, there had always been two hearts in Japan. Although Edo was the center of power where the shogun had his castle, Kyoto-ites could console themselves with the thought that theirs was the emperor's city, home to the imperial court. They were the upholders of taste, class, and the aristocratic old ways.

For a few years as valiant young samurai crowded the teahouses of Gion, plotting and roistering, Kyoto had seethed with passion and politics. Then suddenly a deathly hush fell. Dust began to gather on the white-walled imperial palace with its red pillars and silent expanses of raked sand. The emperor, the courtiers, the princes, the lords, even the flunkies had gone. The swashbuckling samurai and their geisha mistresses, merchants, writers, and artists packed their possessions, hired palanquin bearers and headed for the glittering streets of the new capital, Edo, now renamed Tokyo.

What was to become of Kyoto? What role did the ancient capital have to play in this brave new world? For a while a pall of gloom hung over the beautiful valley with its purple hills and crystalline rivers. Then the city fathers put their heads together.

They came up with the idea of an international exposition to show off the city's traditional arts and crafts, already much admired abroad, and build up business. The Kyoto Exposition, the first in Japan, took place in 1871 but had only limited success. Something extra was needed to brighten up the city and bring it back to life.

The answer was to bring the geisha out of the closet. They were, after all, one of the city's chief glories and, having played such a heroic part in the recent struggle, might finally be considered almost respectable. Some had married the country's new rulers; they need no longer suffer the stigma of being branded "riverbed prostitutes" by polite society.

So the vice-governor consulted the two most powerful people in Gion: the ninth Sugiura, the owner and direct descendant of the founder of Ichiriki-tei, the venerable teahouse where the ronin Oishi as well as the heroes of the recent revolution had reveled; and Haruko Katayama, the legendary dancer and teacher who, under her professional name, Yachiyo Inoue III, was responsible for establishing the Inoue style as the exclusive dance form practiced in Gion. (The Inoue School might be considered the Bolshoi of the geisha world in Japan; the present principal is Yachiyo Inoue IV, now ninety-six.)

Once a year, they decided, the public should have a chance to see the geisha perform their famous dances. The first public performance of Miyako Odori, "Dances of the Capital" (known as the Cherry Dances in the English-language brochures published for Victorian tourists), took place in March 1872 as part of the second and much larger Kyoto Exposition. They lasted seven weeks and have been repeated in some form annually (increasing to semiannually in 1952) ever since. Two other geisha districts also performed public dances. Gion's archrival, Pontocho (still rather subdued, having been the quarter favored by the losing side), called theirs the Kamo River Dances, while Kamishichiken, in the north of the city, performed the Kitano Dances.

Until then the geishas' charms had been reserved for those who could afford to pay for them. Many, along with courtesans, were famous and adored among the populace. Everyone knew their names and might even own a woodblock print pin-up of a favorite; but few ever had the chance to see them close up. Now, once a year, the dancing, which had previously been only for the eyes of a select and wealthy few in intimate tatami-matted rooms, was on display for the general public. It was, of course, rather different. It was large-scale, not small-scale, involving many geisha. In the 1872 performance, there were seven groups each of 32 dancers, 11 singers, 4 hand drum players, 2 flautists, 3 players of smaller drums and gongs, and one player of the large drum, who performed for a week each, 371 performers in all.[2]

It was the beginning of a new role for the geisha. They were still regarded with ambivalence. They were still on the outskirts of society, being either the children of geisha, part of a demimonde beyond the pale of the respectable world, or having been sold by impoverished country parents into a sort of servitude. But they were also stars; they had a recognized place in society and an aura of glamour. And every year crowds flocked to buy tickets for their brilliant and colorful dance spectaculars.

Thus both Kyoto and the geisha continued to flourish. When, that same year, the Cattle Release Act was passed, geisha stood in line at Kyoto City Hall to buy their two licenses, one for entertainment, the other for sex. The enthusiastic reformers of the young government, out to emulate Western ways, instigated various experiments. For a few years there were compulsory workshops for geisha so that they could learn a skill and, in theory, at least, be equipped to pursue a decent living. There they sat in glum rows spinning and weaving or learning reading, accountancy, dancing, or music. The only escape was when they were summoned to a teahouse to entertain. Eventually attendance was made optional and classes immediately stopped apart from dancing and singing. So began the vocational schools which each geisha district in Kyoto still runs.

The American Millionaire and the Icy-Hearted Geisha

One spring day in 1902 a world-weary American named George Dennison Morgan, whiling away a few weeks in Kyoto, went to see a performance of the Cherry Dances. A nephew of the millionaire financier J. Pierpont Morgan, he was wealthy enough that he would never have to work. Disillusioned with New York society after a soured romance, he moved to Japan and settled in Yokohama where he started collecting antiques.

No doubt he thought of taking a Japanese concubine. For a Western man it was the simplest of financial arrangements and one Japanese girl was much like another, or so the average Western chauvinist might have thought. But then at the Cherry Dances he saw a geisha so beautiful, so feminine, and so graceful that he had eyes for no one else. Another, only slightly less romantic version of the story is that he met her at a Gion geisha party. In any case, he fell utterly and incurably in love.

It was a story which was to set tongues wagging and newspaper presses whirring furiously on both sides of the Pacific. To this day, if you ask a Kyoto geisha to name the most famous geisha of all time, she will say, "Oyuki Morgan."

O-yuki (Honorable Snow) was at the height of her career, an exquisite young woman of twenty-one. In photographs she looks like a porcelain doll, with a long strikingly aristocratic face, fine nose, delicate mouth, tapering almond eyes, and a disdainful lift to her eyebrows. She is the eternal feminine, woman personified, remote, aloof, and mysterious. As far as Morgan could see, she was completely perfect.

In fact she was not at all aristocratic but the daughter of a Kyoto swordsmith. There being less and less call for swords in the bright new Japan, the family business had gone disastrously into decline when she was in her teens. For a good-looking young Kyoto girl, it was the most natural thing in the world to go and work in Gion to help her family out. Missing out the trainee maiko stage (she was too old for that), she went to live at a geisha house run by one of her relatives.

George was thirty-one, not handsome but impeccably groomed and rather stolid in appearance, with a faintly lugubrious spaniel air. He wore his hair with a neatly combed center parting, in the fashion of the time, and had a bristly mustache which covered the sides of his pursed, rather stubborn mouth. His deepset eyes were a little sad, his nose slightly bulbous.

To Western eyes he looked unremarkable enough. But in the Kyoto backwoods, where Westerners were a rarity, the round-eyed long-nosed foreigner seemed like a visitor from another planet. When Oyuki was summoned to the teahouse to entertain him, she was shocked and repelled by his pallid skin, coarse compared to silky Asian skin, and colorless hair. Maybe he wooed her through an interpreter, maybe he had picked up a few words of barbarically accented Japanese. In any case, at the end of the evening he asked the maid of the teahouse to arrange for him to spend the night with her. Oyuki was aghast.

"Sleep with a foreigner? I'd rather die," she exclaimed in the privacy of one of the teahouse's back rooms.

But George had no intention of giving up. Even though she rejected him, he gave her an outrageously extravagant tip—20 yen, at a time when a one yen tip was unheard of and a ticket for the Cherry Dances cost 10 sen (one tenth of a yen). So Oyuki, having a family to support, accepted him as a regular customer.

She had other financial pressures too. As it happened, she was in love with a student named Shunsuke Kawakami. One of the customs among geisha until well into the modern era was to invite university students to have fun at the teahouses after hours without charging them *hana-dai,* "flower money," the geishas' fee; they only paid for their drinks and sometimes not even for those. After midnight when the formal geisha parties were over and the customers had been packed off home to their wives, the dashing students of Kyoto's Imperial University would pile into the teahouses to chat, drink, and carouse.

The geisha loved the company of these handsome young gallants.

They also knew that one day they would undoubtedly be among the country's elite. The first universities had only recently been founded and the gilded young men (it was only men) who succeeded in entering were guaranteed positions among the country's movers and shakers, whether in the financial, bureaucratic, or political spheres. When they were rich and powerful, they would automatically continue to patronize the teahouses where they had been so kindly treated as students. Japanese society worked (and still works) on the basis of loyalty. Once a man had set up a relationship with a teahouse, he would maintain it throughout his life; indeed, he would probably pass it on to his son.

Thus Oyuki had met her student. She also, very secretly indeed, broke all the rules by sleeping with him when she got the chance. Shunsuke had promised to take her out of the geisha world and marry her when he finished his studies. But in the meantime he was struggling to find the money to pay his fees. George, knowing nothing of all this, persisted in his suit. By now, he wanted more than just a night of sex. He wanted to possess this exquisite creature; he wanted to marry her. Night after night he went to the teahouse and asked for Oyuki to entertain him then plied her with gifts and tips. Oyuki smiled her cool mysterious smile, icily played her shamisen and the antique bowed *kokyu*, danced with grave but unmistakable eroticism and accepted his money, most of which ended up in Shunsuke's pocket. Beyond that, she kept poor George at arm's length.

By now the story of the fabulously rich foreigner and the icy-hearted geisha had become big news. The *Osaka Daily News* published a series of sixteen articles under the title "The Lovelorn Foreigner," reporting breathlessly on events as they unfolded and padding the story with colorful details, some true, some distinctly dubious.[3] There was, for example, the matter of the 40,000 yen (about $20,000 at the exchange rate of the time, equivalent to $350,000 in modern currency) which, rumor had it, Oyuki had demanded of George in order to fend him off, telling him that she needed it to pay off her *danna* (the *danna* was, of course, fictitious). But far from giving up at being asked for such an exorbitant sum, he set off for New York to raise the money. True or false, Oyuki became known as "40,000 Yen Oyuki" and a stage play entitled *A Single Night's Dream for 40,000 Yen* was a great success.

George became more and more desperate. He also, say Japanese sources, whiled away the time by visiting other teahouses and even became the *danna* of a Shimabara courtesan named Hinamado whom he set up in a house with her mother. He was, after all, only a man. But although he found sensual satisfaction with others, his heart was Oyuki's.

Then Shunsuke graduated and took himself off to Osaka where he immediately got a fast-track job in a bank. Suddenly his love for Oyuki evaporated. The last thing an ambitious young man wanted was a scandalous relationship with a geisha, let alone a geisha as notorious as Oyuki had become thanks to George's much-publicized attentions. As for marrying her—that did not even bear thinking about. When she went to see him in Osaka, he offered to pay back the money he owed her.

For Oyuki it was a terrible shock. Suffering the pangs of rejection, she was also overwhelmed with remorse at the way she had exploited the lovelorn foreigner on behalf of this perfidious lover. It seemed like karmic retribution for her cruelty to him. Even while she had been using him, she herself was being used. George had been so constant in his devotion no matter how cruelly she treated him; surely the proper thing to do was to give him what he wanted and marry him.

So she did. The 40,000 yen story pops up at this point too. George, it was said, handed over this outrageous sum—enough to start a bank—to Oyuki's family for the privilege of marrying their daughter. George himself denied any such rumors, as did Oyuki's family. But even American papers reported that he had paid $25,000 (equivalent to $440,000 in modern currency) "according to Japanese tradition."[4]

In 1904, the year that the Russo-Japanese war began, the couple had a very quiet wedding in Yokohama. Shortly afterward they boarded a steamer for New York. During the voyage, he taught her a few words of English and explained how she would be expected to comport herself as a member of one of America's most powerful and snobbish dynasties.

George's immediate family was on the quay to meet them, together with the American press, buzzing with curiosity about this outlandish match. The family, his stepmother was reported to have said, was far from happy with George's choice. The woman was, after all, Japanese and not even a Christian. In those days Westerners were unabashedly chauvinist when it came to other races. No matter how clever their fans and pretty their kimonos, the Japanese were still nonwhites and therefore inferior; it was only after the Japanese armed forces had shot a few Russians in the ongoing Russo-Japanese War that, as one Japanese diplomat commented with heavy irony, the West began to concede that they might be remotely civilized.[5]

The prodigal son and his Madame Butterfly bride who could barely speak a word of English found themselves ostracized not only by the Morgans but by all of New York polite society. There were no invitations to Mrs. Astor's balls or to soirees with the Vanderbilts or dinner with the Goulds. After a few uncomfortable months, the couple set sail for Paris. By 1906 they were back in Japan, with the intention of settling there. But in the aftermath of the Russo-Japanese War, antiforeign sentiment was running high. The "slut" who had given herself to a "barbarian" was far from welcome. Finally they took a house on the Champs-Elysées in Paris, a city both relaxed and bohemian enough to welcome a wealthy American and his geisha wife into chic society.

There they lived happily for a decade. Madame Morgan, famous for her porcelain-like Oriental beauty, learned French, studied the piano, and was regularly seen at the salons of the top couturiers. She was never dressed in anything less than the height of Paris fashion. With an ample purse at their disposal they visited Oyuki's family in Japan several times, though when George had to go to New York to settle financial matters, he went alone. Still, his family, who summered in Europe and there spent time with George and his wife, gradually came round to the marriage.

Then came the First World War. In Japan it was a distant war in far-off countries whose main effect was to provide bottomless markets for Japanese munitions, ship-building companies, and other industries. Foreign businesses having tied up all their resources in the war effort, it was an unprecedented opportunity for Japanese companies to gain the edge—a bonanza, in fact.

George and Oyuki, however, were caught up in the middle of it. When war broke out, George was in New York where he had gone to deal with family affairs. Trying to get back to Paris, he discovered that the direct route was impassable because of German submarine warfare. So he boarded a ship for Gibraltar. After a long and circuitous journey he was traveling overland toward Paris when he died of a sudden massive heart attack. It was 1915 and he was 44.

Utterly shocked by his death—he had never even been ill before—and all alone in a foreign country in the midst of a major war, Oyuki waited as bravely as she could for the body to be sent back for cremation. When the will was read it transpired that George had left enough to support her, in considerable style, on the interest alone for the rest of her life.

The legend of Oyuki Morgan has it that she then returned to New York bearing his ashes where, as his widow, she was more kindly received than when she had been his wife. She settled down there, goes the story, and became a prominent figure in fashionable society, entertaining her guests with her eloquent piano recitals.

A Japanese journalist, however, looked into Oyuki's life, studied her letters and diaries, and came up with a completely different end to the story. In fact, it seems, she stayed on in Paris where she lived with a French legionnaire who had been sending her love letters from China for some time before George's death. Oyuki had complained that she was "a widow" even then. So perhaps, ponders the journalist, George, having captured his prey, lost interest and went in search of new lands to conquer. Perhaps he had reasons other than business for going to New York. In any case, Oyuki was only thirty-four when he died, very beautiful still and enormously wealthy, a most eligible prospect.[6]

In 1938, the ex-legionnaire (by then an elderly academic) having died, Oyuki decided it was time to go home. She was still such a celebrity in Japan that long before she got there, when her ship docked at Shanghai, Japanese journalists were crowding the quay to get a glimpse of her. Back in Kyoto, she settled near the teahouse where George had first gone to woo her, in the oldest section of Gion north of the Shirakawa stream. By then she was practically a foreigner herself. She could barely speak Japanese and wore her outlandish Parisian hats even inside the house. When the Second World War broke out a few years later, people in Gion joked that they would not be bombed "because Oyuki Morgan lives here." She died in 1963 at the age of eighty-two. Even before that, in 1961, her extraordinary life had been celebrated in a Japanese musical entitled *Morgan Oyuki*.

Katoro, the teahouse run by her cousin's family, is still there on the corner of a quiet cobbled street shaded with willows beside the Shira-kawa stream. In the evening a white lantern glows outside and the wooden doors slide open and close again as customers come and go. The plangent notes of the shamisen, plucky but somehow sad, can be heard faintly from inside.

New Geisha for a New Age

In 1922 the handsome young Prince of Wales, later to rule briefly as Edward VIII, toured Japan on a state visit. At the time Britain was Japan's staunchest ally and he was greeted with boundless enthusiasm. Wherever he went enormous crowds turned out to cheer him. In Tokyo he reviewed the army, took in an opera at the imperial opera house, and viewed the cherry blossoms in the grounds of the imperial palace.

One of the most memorable celebrations took place on the small rural island of Shikoku. Here, in the city of Takamatsu, Count Matsudaira, a scion of one of the country's most ancient aristocratic families, had spent more than $45,000 (equivalent to $415,000 in modern currency, a veritable fortune) to provide suitable entertainment for such an important guest. After a feast prepared and served by a staff of three hundred, the climax of the evening came when twelve of the city's most renowned and beautiful geisha glided demurely into the room. Clad in specially woven silk kimonos with a design of Union Jacks intermingled with the Rising Sun, they performed a series of elegant dances.

Much had changed since a couple of decades earlier when the conservative Japanese establishment had been horrified at the success of Sadayakko and her husband Otojiro—a "riverbed prostitute" and a low-grade actor—on the stages of Europe and America. Having started out as countercultural heroines on the fringes of society, geisha had now reached the acme of respectability, being wheeled out as proud representatives of their country to entertain visiting royalty.

Where once the licensed pleasure quarters had dominated the demimonde, it was now the geisha districts that people referred to when they spoke of the "flower and willow world." There were still highly accomplished geisha in the Yoshiwara; geisha from all over town went to

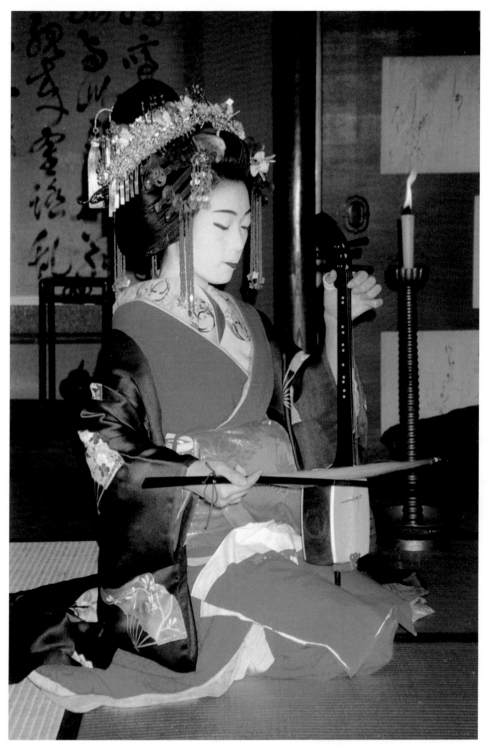

A *tayu* courtesan in the Shimabara pleasure quarter uses a loosely strung bow to play the *kokyu*, the classic instrument of the *tayu*. Her headdress and kimono are far more ornate than those of a geisha or maiko. (LESLEY DOWNER)

The main street of Miyagawa-cho geisha district, too narrow for cars. (LESLEY DOWNER)

The Great Gate of Shimabara. The willow tree outside marks the flower and willow world. (LESLEY DOWNER)

Stone Wall Alley with its high walls, where rich men used to house their concubines. (LESLEY DOWNER)

Harumi, the maiko, in her room in Haruta geisha house. The mirror is lined with photographs of famous geisha. (LESLEY DOWNER)

Harumi in full maiko regalia, ready for a night out. (LESLEY DOWNER)

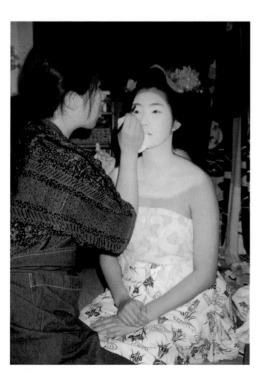

Masami preparing Kanosome for her *misedashi* debut. (LESLEY DOWNER)

Kanosome in black ceremonial kimono, ready for her debut. Only her bottom lip is painted. (LESLEY DOWNER)

Mr. Imanishi resets a wig. (Lesley Downer)

Koito, the geisha with the website, prepares to put on her wig. (Lesley Downer)

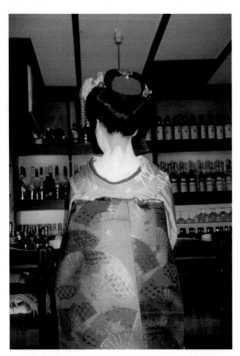

A young maiko in the "home bar" of a geisha house reveals the titillating fork of unpainted flesh at the nape of her neck, which Japanese men find the most sexy. (Lesley Downer)

Harem, a soapland in the old Yoshiwara quarter, modeled on an old geisha house, offers "baths" for ¥20,000 ($200). (Lesley Downer)

The author (in wig) with Mr. Imanishi, the wig maker, and his family. (LESLEY DOWNER)

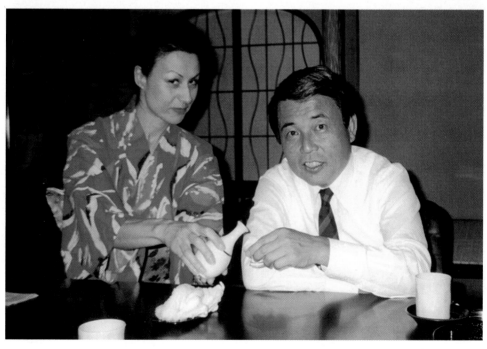

The author in geisha mode, tending to a customer. (LESLEY DOWNER)

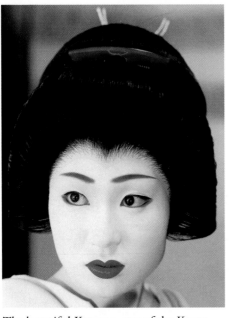

The beautiful Katsuno, star of the Kyoto geisha. (Chris Steele-Perkins/Magnum)

The maikos' room in a geisha house. Maiko can be as young as thirteen or fourteen. (Chris Steele-Perkins/Magnum)

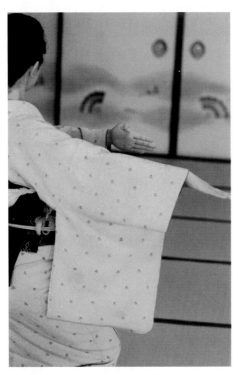

The Nihon buyo dance form is as controlled and precise as ballet, though not as athletic. (Chris Steele-Perkins/Magnum)

A maiko, on high clogs, her obi reaching her ankles and her hair in the maiko coiffure, carries a red oiled-paper umbrella. A geisha, on lower clogs, wearing a wig and with her obi tied into a knot, follows behind.

(Chris Steele-Perkins/Magnum)

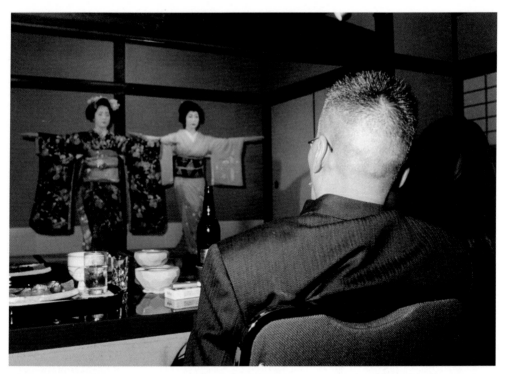

Teahouse party. A maiko with swinging sleeves and a geisha dance before the customers. (Chris Steele-Perkins/Magnum)

Geisha musicians perform for the annual Cherry Dances. (Gideon Mendel/Network)

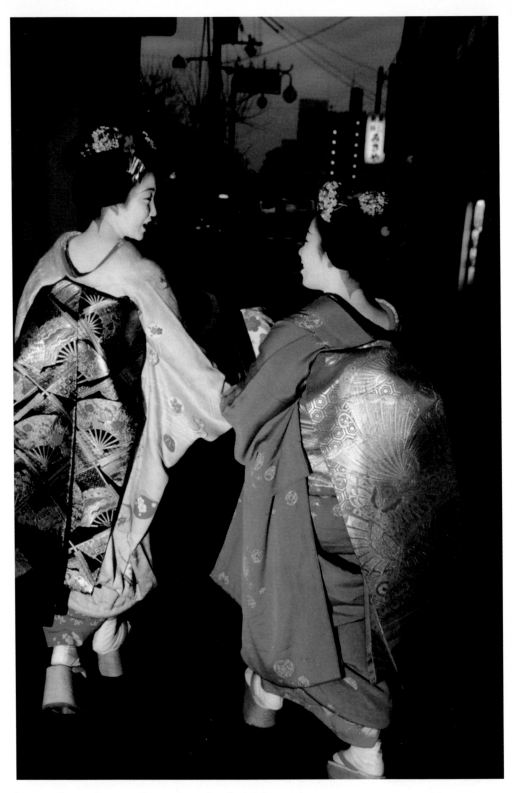

Two maiko on their way home after a hard night's partying. (CHRIS STEELE-PERKINS/MAGNUM)

them for lessons in dancing and music. Nevertheless, in the popular mind the licensed quarters had become little more than red-light districts. For high culture in the traditional Japanese mode, for exquisite shamisen playing, graceful and subtly erotic dancing, and witty conversation, men visited the teahouses and high-class restaurants of the geisha districts. For the geisha it was something of a golden age. At the turn of the century there were 25,000 geisha in Japan, by 1929 close to 80,000. It was a thriving profession.[7]

The 1920s, however, were to be the pinnacle. Already people were asking where exactly geisha fitted into the wild new era of speed, sport, and sex, with its fast cars, American movies, gramophones, ice cream, Marxism, *moga* ("modern gals" with short hair and flapper skirts), and *mobo* ("modern boys" with slicked-back Harold Lloyd haircuts).

Geisha had always been fashion leaders. In the nineteenth century, they set the trends in kimono and obi styles which townswomen enthusiastically followed. Geisha had been the first to try Western hairstyles, carry umbrellas, and learn Western dancing. In 1915 the geisha district of Pontocho in Kyoto established a ballroom dancing school and the geisha houses there had on their books "dance geisha" who could offer the tango and the waltz among their *gei*.[8] Nevertheless the chief pleasure geisha still offered connoisseurs was their mastery of the high arts. Their company could transport the harassed salaryman in his uncomfortable Western suit and prickly haircut back to the romantic days of old Edo. With them, he could imagine himself a swaggering samurai, a wealthy merchant, or a dashing rake.

Moreover, for men who wished to enjoy the company of women, or possibly more than just their company, there was now a plethora of choices. The roaring twenties spawned cafés (really bars) across the country and, most famously, up and down the Ginza. There young women, in time-honored fashion, poured men's drinks for them and chatted flirtatiously. Unlike geisha, they did not need years of training to learn their skills. Nor did a man have to be a *tsu* connoisseur to appreciate them. Particularly in the years following the great earthquake of 1923, which leveled Tokyo and destroyed what few buildings remained of the old city, cafés were all the rage.

The favorite tippling place of Kafu Nagai (1879–1959), a famously decadent novelist who reveled in recording the low life of the time, was the Café Tiger. "The interiors and exteriors of Ginza cafés take me back to the days when I was in Paris," he recorded nostalgically in a published essay.

In his personal diary he was less diplomatic. "The cafés that are so popular throughout the city are to all appearances like Parisian cafés," he wrote. "The reality is much different. We try to imitate everything Western and we always make a botch of it. The girls go to work every day and yet they do not receive salaries, and they must depend on gifts from customers for their livelihood. It is quite evident, therefore, that they actually live by prostitution. Fearing rumors and the threats of newspaper reporters, they must appear unwilling to surrender to the blandishments of drunken customers."9

He had personal experience of "rumors and newspaper reporters," having had problems with a waitress named Ohisa with whom he must have shared a bed. By then he was a famous author. After newspaper and magazine reports linked their names, Ohisa decided that she was entitled to share his wealth and badgered him relentlessly.

As the ranks of café girls grew, the number of geisha began to fall, until by 1934, there were over 100,000 café girls to 72,000 geisha. It was time for a radical rethink of geisha and their place in society.10

What exactly were they? Leaving aside the more dubious country geisha, the grand ladies of Tokyo and Kyoto could in no way be confused with prostitutes, high class or otherwise. They could hardly be counter-cultural queens, for, with the neat class system of Tokugawa society shaken out of place, there was no longer a counterculture—or, if there was, it was not the sort that would be ruled by geisha.

Perhaps they should follow the same path as their fellow entertainers, the kabuki actors, who were in the process of undergoing a distinctly ironic transformation from disreputable members of the underclass, frequently prostitutes, to doyens of the public stage. Until the departure of the shoguns, kabuki had been a living, changing theatrical form. But, with the coming of the modern age, it became a historical relic. When new plays were written, they were always set in a timeless, nostalgically remembered Edo Never-Never Land.

The music and dance of the geisha too had been a living art form, the popular music and dance of its day. Should they now move with the times or, like kabuki, become repositories of the much-loved past? Were they too doomed to live forever in Edo?

In the mid-1930s, there was much debate on the subject. Geisha, being women, did not contribute. But intellectuals, poets, restaurateurs who employed geisha, politicians, actors, and the director of the Shimbashi Association of Geisha Houses all had their say. Their comments were published as a series of essays in a book called "The Geisha Reader."

In it the poet Sakutaro Hagiwara expressed in a neat paragraph what was to become the accepted definition of the role of the geisha: "Our wives at home are engrossed in cookery and children, and our conversations with them are quietly serious, mostly concerning household affairs. Outside of this, men need a totally different sort of companion: a woman with whom we can talk about affairs of the world, about the arts, about ideas. We need someone who is entertaining, knowledgeable, educated. This is what a geisha should be." He went on to say that they should wear Western clothes, give up the shamisen, and learn the piano. The ideal for the modern geisha, it seemed, was to be the Japanese equivalent of the ancient Greek *hetaera,* an accomplished companion for gentlemen.[11]

But there were more serious things to worry about than the role of the geisha. Japan had plunged deep into an era which people later spoke of as "the Dark Valley." The army had grown more and more powerful. Defying the ineffective and corrupt civilian government, troops invaded China and occupied Manchuria. There they set up a puppet state and, as a matter of course, shipped out geisha and prostitutes to entertain the soldiers.

As army and politicians clashed, there were several attempted coups d'etat and a rash of assassinations. In the growing mood of patriotic fervor, the "thought" police were out in force, clamping down on anything that smacked of subversion. The infatuation with all things Western evaporated. Speaking English and playing the piano were frowned on, while the geisha, a potent symbol of the old days when Japan was great, found business booming once more. Politicos and the

1
9
5

military gathered in the grand geisha restaurants of Shimbashi and Akasaka to discuss policy and celebrate victories.

While intellectuals like Kafu kept their heads down, and sales declined in the grand department stores of the classier sections of town, in the back streets on the wrong side of the river—which had been the heart of the old city of Edo—life went on much as before. There the great event of 1936 was the apprehension of a woman called Sada Abe, known to history as O-sada, who was found wandering the streets with her lover's severed penis wrapped in a *furoshiki,* a large kerchief. A low-grade geisha, she had fallen in love with her employer, a restaurant owner, and spent a week with him in a house of assignation. According to one version of events, the grand climax to a week of fevered love-making came when she strangled him. Another has it that he was a philandering pimp and that she strangled him to ensure that he would remain eternally faithful to her.

In any case, hers was judged to be a crime of passion and she was sentenced to a mere five years' imprisonment. The public, tired of gloomy news, latched joyfully onto her story and she became something of a romantic heroine. Freed in 1941, she opened a bar in the old city and some years later, in traditional fashion, ended up in a nunnery. Her story was made into one of Japan's most famous films—*Ai no Corrida (In the Realm of the Senses)* by the celebrated director Nagisa Oshima.

The Writer Who Yearned for Old Edo

The bamboo was withered and the stalks were eaten at the base by insects. Chokichi thought they would probably disintegrate if he poked them. An emaciated willow tree drooped its branches, barely touched with green, over the shingled roof of a gate. The geisha Yonehachi must have passed through just such a gate when, of a winter's afternoon, she secretly visited the sick Tanjiro [hero of *The Plum Blossom Calendar,* an early nineteenth-century romance]. And it must have been in a room of such a house that Hanjiro, telling ghost stories one rainy night, dared to take his sweetheart's hand for the first time. Chokichi experienced a strange fascination and sorrow. He wanted to be possessed by that sweet, gentle, suddenly cold and indifferent fate.

Kafu Nagai, from "The River Sumida," 1909[12]

In 1909 a young writer named Kafu Nagai (1879–1959) published an achingly lyrical short story entitled "The River Sumida." It established him as a master of exquisite prose and defined him as the chronicler par excellence of the demimonde—the last remnant of the misty world of old Edo which was being blasted away by the cold winds of Westernization. Looking for some romanticized past, he found it above all in the shadowy world of the geisha, prostitutes, strippers, bar girls, and chorus girls.

The son of a successful Meiji businessman and bureaucrat, Kafu could afford to slum it. Instead of following in his father's footsteps, he spent most of his youth in the Yoshiwara and the Yanagibashi geisha quarter, devouring old romances and—most shocking of all—writing fiction, an activity which he did his best to conceal from his family. In Edo times, writers and artists had been considered as disreputable as the geisha, actors, and prostitutes they portrayed, an attitude which persisted among conservative families such as Kafu's.

Despairing of his son's feckless lifestyle, his father packed him off to the United States to learn banking, but instead he hung out on the seedier edges of society. The only place where he felt even slightly at home was New York's Chinatown, in those days a slum teeming with brothels and opium dens. He wrote of the bestiality he saw there, "I thought I had never before heard so poignantly the music of human degradation and collapse." As for the ragged prostitutes, "I do not hesitate to call them my own dear sisters. I do not ask for light or help. I only await the day when I too shall be able to offer myself to a grain of opium."[13] Only amid scenes of abysmal depravity and deprivation could his romantic yearnings be satisfied.

After a few years in Paris and a short stay in London, he was back in Tokyo, pouring out in a torrent of writing his horror at the brutal new

Japan. The only place where he glimpsed anything akin to the beauty and passion he had found abroad was among the denizens of the demi-monde who still lived the life of old Edo. His diatribes against the loss of the old ways and his swooningly elegiac tales full of decadence and overblown passion soon won him a huge following.

Urged on by his father, he made a respectable marriage to a merchant's daughter. But for love he went to geisha. As soon as his father died, he divorced his wife in a matter of weeks (and, as he recorded grumpily, at considerable expense) and married a geisha called Yaeji. They lived in a small ramshackle house with paper screens and doors where they practiced the shamisen together and she helped him prepare paper on which to brush his stories; he wrote contemptuously of "the modern scribbler who does his polemics with a fountain pen on Western-style paper."

But less than a year later, when he got home one day, she was gone, unable any longer to tolerate his serial infidelity. He never married again. Instead he lived his life in or near the geisha areas and found his pleasures among geisha, bar girls, dancers, and "waitresses" (who were really unlicensed prostitutes) at the new-fangled cafés. In his fifties he bought a pretty young bespectacled geisha out of indenture and set her up in a little house which became a gathering place for journalists and literary people. Later he bought her a house of assignation with, rumor had it, peepholes through which the aging Kafu could watch the customers and geisha at play.[14]

In many ways he was a strange, misanthropic, rather unattractive character. Apart from his girlfriends he professed to hate everyone except for one writer friend who turned down a top position on a newspaper in order to have more time to drink himself to death, an ambition which he duly achieved. Nevertheless Kafu was a magical writer. He captured better than anyone the disappearing romance of Edo.

Rivalry is the work which most vividly portrays the suffocating claustrophobia and desperate passions of the world of the geisha.[15] Set in the classy Shimbashi geisha quarter, it is the story of Komayo, a gentle, guileless young woman very different from the stylish, sophisticated Shimbashi geishas of legend. Utterly at the mercy of her feelings, she seems to live life balanced precariously on the edge of disaster. Already a widow at twenty-six, she bumps into a man called Yoshioka who, when he was a student many years before, had been her lover. He has become a successful, rather cynical businessman and is already the *danna* of a senior and celebrated geisha, as well as of an ex-waitress whom he has set up in her own house of assignation. Meeting the lovely, childlike Komayo, he remembers the innocent days of his youth. Smitten with unaccustomed and unexpected passion, he determines to make her his own.

Yoshioka has every intention of doing the decent thing by Komayo—in other words, buying her. He offers to pay off her indenture, buy her her freedom, set her up in a villa, and become her *danna*. But, to his astonishment and rage, Komayo does not leap at this proposal. Is it worth losing her independence again, she wonders, for a man who, like all the others, will only prove to be unreliable and leave her in the end? For Yoshioka is, of course, not offering her marriage. He already has a wife and children.

Komayo, meanwhile, has committed the one mistake which is fatal for a denizen of the floating world: she has fallen in love. Successful geisha make men fall in love with them; but if they lose control of their own feelings, they are doomed. Seduced by Segawa, a handsome young *onnagata* (a kabuki actor who specializes in women's roles), Komayo finds herself utterly obsessed with him. Recklessly she throws herself into the emotion. At last, she feels (or Kafu imagines that she feels) she knows the essence of what it is to be a geisha, to live on the edge, experiencing the extremes of passion and pain. "Realizing now that bitterness and pleasure alike were part of being a geisha, Komayo felt that she had tasted for the first time the true flavor of geisha life."

She is convinced, against all the odds, that the actor will marry her. Nevertheless, to keep her options open, she agrees to accept as a part-time *danna* a hideously ugly antiques dealer whom she refers to as "the sea monster." He provides her with money and in exchange satisfies two of his proclivities: to sleep with a geisha who also from time to time buys the love of a famous kabuki actor and to entertain himself by having sex with a woman who, he knows very well, finds him physically repellent.

Predictably all this ends in tears. As Komayo behaves in a more and more wifely fashion to the kabuki actor, he becomes bored with her and finally throws her over in favor of a statuesque woman made all the more attractive by being the possessor of a large inheritance. Yoshioka, in his turn, has taken his revenge on the hapless Komayo by buying the freedom of a rival geisha from Komayo's own house and becoming her *danna*.

Thus Komayo has to pay the price for having broken the geisha code by allowing herself to be swept away by her emotions. She is in utter despair. Her life, it seems, is over. She has lost everything. But the way is still open for the story to have a happy ending. The kind old man who runs Komayo's geisha house wants to retire and decides to pass the business on to her. He gives her the deeds to the house, the use of the name, and the business. Once again she has a future. She can run the geisha house and take care of the geisha that live there. She has finally won financial independence, a far greater prize in the geisha world and certainly much more reliable than winning a man.

Rivalry is probably the most complete, lovingly observed evocation of the geisha world ever written. Kafu never questions the values of the geisha, though he does point out that the underlying flaw in their lifestyle is their fatal dependence on others. They cannot say no to a customer no matter what he asks. There is a memorable passage which was excised from early versions of the book and only appeared in private editions, describing an encounter which Yoshioka, an insatiable sexual athlete, has with Komayo:

> When, at eleven o'clock, she finally escaped from his embrace, she was breathing great gasps, she could scarcely speak, and she had no will to get up. Entirely satisfied with this state of affairs, Yoshioka sped off into the darkness . . . She sighed, and chagrin and resentment came back with doubled intensity at the thought of the men who had imposed themselves on her in the course of the evening. She was battered to the very core. She wanted only to die.[16]

Armageddon

In December 1941 Japan launched a surprise attack on Pearl Harbor. The first retaliatory bombing raids by American B-25s came the following April, damaging and demolishing swathes of buildings around the edges of Tokyo. But still the splendid restaurants, where Tokyo's 9,000 geisha entertained, stayed open for business despite the punishing new tax which the government, desperate for funds, had imposed on such luxurious activities.

Anyone who could afford it had every intention of carrying on their hedonistic lifestyle. As for the military, they were still partying at teahouses in the spring of 1943 when—for everyone else—rationing was biting hard. Kafu chose to spend his time among the youthful chorus girls of Asakusa in the city's East End. "In this world apart, there are no ashes of war," he wrote in his diary.

Finally even the geisha had to go. On March 4, 1944, Kafu recorded regretfully, "From tomorrow restaurants and teahouses are to be banned . . . Geisha have not yet been banned, but they appear to be moving into other trades for want of engagements. Without theaters and geisha, the music of Edo, based upon the shamisen, will perish."[17] It was not a matter of morality but of desperate need. The country was on the brink of collapse and every woman and child had to be conscripted to help with the war effort.

On their last night the geisha restaurants stayed open almost until dawn. Then the geisha took off their silk kimonos, folded them carefully, and wrapped them in sheets of crisp handmade paper for storage. They put on smocks and *mompe* (baggy cotton indigo-dyed peasant trousers) and went to work in ammunition factories or to labor through the night sewing uniforms and parachutes. The canniest managed to avoid such a fate by finding someone to marry them, becoming concubines, or persuading their patrons to include them on their lists of company employees. And if, of course, your *danna* was a member of the military, he would ensure that you were properly cared for.

Worst of all was 1945, the last year of the war. People sold everything they had and fled to the countryside. In Tokyo, the air-raid sirens whined nearly every night as swarms of B-29s cruised the skies, raining down firebombs in such quantity that the snowflakes turned soot black. The rundown wooden city stood no chance. In a single night, on March 9, some 78,000 people burned to death and 1.5 million were left homeless. The city was reduced to a sea of ashes, rubble, twisted metal, and charred, broken

stone walls. The pleasure quarters were utterly destroyed and the theaters
(including the beautiful art deco Shimbashi Embujo Theater, built in 1925
for the geisha to perform their annual dances) were reduced to blackened
shells. The Yoshiwara, still functioning in defiance of government orders,
was burned to a cinder together with hundreds of women who had been
locked inside by the brothel-keepers, anxious not to lose their investment.

Kyoto fared better. Thanks to the intervention of American scholars who argued that it was a place of irreplaceable cultural heritage, it
was barely touched by bombing.

As the war intensified, the patriotic geisha of Gion decided to do
their bit. They bought two planes for the extravagant sum of 65,000 yen
each, had the names *Dai-ichi Gion Kogo* (Number 1 Gion plane) and
Dai-ni Gion Kogo (Number 2 Gion plane) painted with a flourish on the
flanks and presented them to the army. The ceremony took place at a
nearby military airstrip, where the troop of beautiful young geisha, clad
patriotically in peasants' working clothes and straw sandals and with
their famous glossy black locks tied up in bonnets, drew much press attention. Being practical women, the geisha also instigated evacuation
training at the teahouses, practiced relaying buckets of water to put out
possible fires, and observed a curfew so that the quarters fell into darkness after nightfall.

The last annual dances, entitled *"Ko-koku no miyabi"* (Elegance of
the Japanese Empire), took place in spring 1943. Shortly afterward the
Gion Kobu Kaburenjo, where dance performances and classes took
place, was commandeered and transformed into a munitions factory
where geisha and maiko who had not fled to the countryside were conscripted to sew parachutes and uniforms for the army. From late in 1944
they were also ordered to produce incendiary balloons (enormous hy-
drogen balloons containing bombs and incendiary devices) which would,
in theory, drift across the Pacific on the jet stream and set America's
cities ablaze. After 17,000 fire bombs fell on Osaka, the city council, fearful that Kyoto would suffer the same fate, ordered swathes of houses,
10,000 in all, to be evacuated and demolished to make fire breaks.
Among them were the beautiful old teahouses of Shimbashi, the northern part of Gion.

The end came on August 15, 1945, after the cities of Hiroshima and Nagasaki had been obliterated by atomic bombs. A few days later, people gathered round their radios, expecting to be exhorted to fight the enemy, with bamboo spears if necessary, to the death. Instead, for the first time ever, they heard the reedy voice of their emperor, crackling over the airwaves. His words were convoluted and the language archaic but the meaning was clear. His people, he said, would have to "endure the unendurable and suffer the insufferable."

After the Deluge

When the American and other Allied occupation forces, under the command of General Douglas MacArthur, arrived in the country a couple of weeks later, many were shaken by the scenes of utter devastation which they saw. They had been expecting violent resistance. Instead they found a nation of shell-shocked, half-starved people, ragged and dirty, who stared at them, blank-eyed, as they drove through the dusty, rubble-strewn streets. Some seemed positively—and astonishingly—pleased to see them.

For the Japanese the first winter was, if anything, even grimmer than the bombing had been. Then they had had wartime spirit to buoy them up. Now they were a nation in defeat. Life had been reduced to the barest essentials—keeping warm and scavenging, thieving, smuggling, or begging for food. In Tokyo 60 percent of the housing had been destroyed. The few buildings that still stood were unheated, and the miserable shelters people put together out of broken bits of wood and rubble offered little protection against the icy winds and snow. Many died of exposure or pneumonia or of the plagues which swept the stricken city—typhus, smallpox, and cholera. Malnutrition and beri beri were rife.

The geisha who had fled to the countryside used their kimonos for barter. One by one they gave them away—a priceless silk kimono with an exquisite gold thread design in exchange for pumpkins, eggplants, and sweet potatoes; a heavy brocade obi worth tens of thousands of yen for some cabbages, spinach, and radishes. Rice was like gold dust, almost never to be found. The farmers got richer and the geisha poorer; but at least they were able to eat.

For the women who remained in the cities, whether geisha, prostitutes, or destitute women who had lost their families, there were other ways of staying alive. The victorious GIs might be well fed with clean uniforms but there was one commodity they lacked. And there were plenty of Japanese men with lengthy experience in the field ready to ensure that this gap in the market was promptly filled.

Mark Gayn, one of the first American journalists to arrive in the country, recorded a "curious tale" reported to him by an American colonel. Barely two weeks after General MacArthur flew into Atsugi air base, on September 9, 1945, the American First Cavalry Division was poised to march into Tokyo. The GIs were nervous about how the Japanese military might react when their capital was invaded and had set up a roadblock on the edge of the city. Well after nightfall, they heard the rumble of an approaching truck.

"Halt!" yelled the sentry when it was within hailing distance. The truck stopped and a Japanese man stepped down. Behind him followed a flock of young women. Warily they walked toward the troops. When they were quite close the man stopped, bowed low to the soldiers, gestured to the women, and announced, "Compliments of the Recreation and Amusement Association!"[18]

It was a bizarrely comic moment which pointed up the enormous cultural gulf between the invaded and the invaders. The Japanese, convinced that the Americans were beasts who would rape their wives, mothers, and daughters, had taken the precaution of sending their women as far away into the countryside as possible before the troops arrived. As an alternative, brothel owners from the Yoshiwara, which had been burned to the ground in the bombing, together with the presidents of the seven major entertainment guilds in Tokyo including the restaurant, cabaret, geisha, and brothel associations, had been commissioned by the Metropolitan Police, under government auspices and with government funding, to set up the RAA. Long before the first American set foot in the country, they started recruiting from among prostitutes, geisha, and bar girls. They were looking for 5,000 women, though only 1,360 initially responded to the poster they had pasted up in the Ginza.

To sternly puritanical conspiracy-theorists like Mark Gayn, the RAA was "the world's biggest white-slave traffic combine" and a prime "item of evidence in the damning record of Japan's efforts to seduce the Army of Occupation away from its purposes."[19] But to the Japanese, it was not unlike the New Shimabara, the licensed quarters set up at the time of the Meiji Restoration for visiting foreigners. Conquering army or not, the Americans were men and had the same needs as any others.

There were plenty of GIs who did not suffer from Gayn's moral scruples. By April 1946, as his doughty researches revealed, there were 668 known brothels in Tokyo alone, with 8,000 prostitutes who did not, one assumes, suffer from lack of customers. But none could compete with the RAA which, thanks to government sponsorship, offered the prettiest women working in 33 "houses of entertainment." The most famous was the Oasis dance hall in the Ginza, which featured an "army prophylactic station" in a Nissen hut. The RAA ran two hospitals for its women and had a network of agents recruiting through Japan.

Gayn also investigated the International Palace, a large ugly factory on the outskirts of Tokyo which had started life producing clocks and watches for the Seiko corporation, then became a munitions plant, and after the war, on the advice of the Tokyo Police, was transformed into "the world's largest brothel." Five concrete-walled dormitory buildings which had housed workers now functioned as brothels. The women Gayn interviewed there told him they had lost their families in air raids, though there were also some who described themselves as geisha. All, he noted grimly, had been forced to buy clothes and cosmetics from the company and were heavily in debt.

Kafu Nagai too went to see this new pleasure quarter (which he knew as the Tokyo Palace) and told a rather different story. It was populated, he reported, by whores from Kameido, one of Tokyo's unlicensed districts, who had packed their bags and moved in en masse. At first the main clientele had been American soldiers; but from October 1946 onward the American traffic stopped and the only customers were Japanese. Painted across the walls were large signs in English reading "Off Limits—VD." He noted, in his dour way, that the women seemed more like factory girls and students than bona fide whores. Perhaps the truth fell somewhere between the two versions.[20]

General MacArthur, whose powers were so all-encompassing that the Japanese called him the "last shogun," was determined to clamp down on this dangerous and unhealthy trade. He declared all brothels off limits to GIs and issued a directive banning contractual prostitution. This was followed a year later, in 1947, by an imperial edict, drafted by the Americans as was everything else at that time, outlawing officially sanctioned prostitution. Like the Prostitute and Geisha Emancipation Act enacted by the Meiji government in deference to Western notions of propriety, it was full of noble intentions but utterly unenforceable. Worse, far from ending prostitution, it made life harder for the women.

No longer publicly recognized and government-sponsored, the Yoshiwara, which had been hastily rebuilt and was operating out of barrack-like shacks, was privatized. The masters and mistresses of the old bordellos became "special purveyors of beverages" and the women became "waitresses." As freelancers, they received a percentage of the brothel earnings and in theory could leave whenever they wished. The law required that they should all be over eighteen, though many were not. The problem was that the proprietors of the new, illegal Yoshiwara required firm assurances that the women would not run off without re-paying their debts. They took to using yakuza—members of the Japanese mafia—to enforce this.

Added to which, officially recognized red-light zones were only the tip of the iceberg. Besides the unlicensed quarters which had always existed side by side with the licensed ones, the ranks of prostitutes had been massively swollen by thousands of desperate women who had lost their families or were waiting hopelessly for husbands who would never return from the front. These women had no means of supporting them-selves except by prostitution. The most visible were the streetwalkers or *panpan* girls ("bang bang girls," referring to the speed of the trans-action). At their height there were as many as five hundred young women thronging the area around the railway arches near the Ginza and within spitting distance of General MacArthur's headquarters, grabbing pass-ing GIs, pulling them into the shadows. For payment they begged for cigarettes, chocolate, chewing gum or, most pitifully, food.

Using a term the GIs could understand, they called themselves "geisha gals." Among Westerners, "geisha girl" became the catch-all term for anyone of dubious morality, from hostesses at bars, cabarets, and dance halls to the lowliest streetwalkers.

The authorities, nevertheless, were perfectly aware that real geisha were a different species. They were excluded from the directive and the imperial edict and on appropriate occasions top American officers enjoyed geisha parties. The government discreetly sponsored the Shinagawa quarter which was popular with Americans. They also offered a subsidy to the Shimbashi quarter, though the proud Shimbashi geisha refused it.

Bars, teahouses, and geisha houses were officially permitted to reopen on October 25, 1945. Little by little, those who had fled to the countryside began to make their way back. Kiharu, once the star geisha of Shimbashi, found herself on a rickety train jammed between scavengers and sacks of illicit rice on their way to Tokyo's black markets. Once in the city, she found work as a translator for a British journalist and every Sunday took food to her son, mother, and grandmother whom she had left in the countryside. From time to time she appeared at geisha parties. She also began teaching English to young geisha so that they could talk to their foreign guests.

With the war, the number of geisha had been reduced practically to zero. Now they gradually began to rise again, though it was a long time before the profession returned to its prewar prosperity. In 1947 there were 1,695 geisha in Tokyo and 2,478 in the whole country.[21] And in March 1948 the Shimbashi geisha were ready to perform their first postwar dance spectacular, *Azuma Odori* (Dance of the East) in their own Shimbashi Embujo Theater, which had been restored to its prewar art deco glory.

During the seven years in which the American and other allied forces occupied Japan, they revolutionized society in a myriad of ways, some expected, some less so. Their brief was to instill democracy and to bring Japan into line with the modern world, and one of the ways in which the country was way out of line was in its treatment of women. The new constitution of 1947, hastily drafted by American officials, recognized men and women as equal in politics, law, and education, which was, in Japanese terms, utterly revolutionary. It introduced universal suffrage, thereby giving women the vote for the first time. Henceforth women—who had been banned in the late nineteenth century from participating in politics at any level—were to be as free as men to run for parliament. Article 24 stated, even more radically, that "marriage shall be based only on the mutual consent of both sexes." The occupying forces also instituted compulsory education for boys and girls up to the age of fifteen and stipulated that all national universities were to be open to women.

A more unexpected development was the introduction of public kissing, on stage and screen. In Japan, of course, kissing was very much confined to the bedroom; it was one of the most esoteric of the geishas' repertoire of outré sexual techniques and considered almost as intimate as the sex act. But if the Americans wanted Japan to imitate their ways, imitate they would. The first on-stage and on-screen kisses took place in 1946, to the considerable embarrassment of the actors called upon to perform them. Traditionalists were shocked but audiences were entertained. Kissing, however, was only the beginning. The following year saw another innovation: the introduction of the striptease. What with all these raunchy American imports and the traditional Japanese laissez faire attitude toward such matters, the way was open for Japan to develop a no-holds-barred sexual culture—which, indeed, it has. Could there be a place for the delicate arts of the geisha in such a world?

Less than a century had passed since Commodore Perry and his men had roughly booted open the door of Japan, exposing its hothouse culture to the cold winds of change. The geisha, who had started out as the stylish queens of a raffish underground, had survived the transition, though, as skirts got shorter and lifestyles wilder in the twenties, they were already beginning to seem like something of an anachronism. Then, in the patriotic years before the war, with traditional Japanese values being reasserted, they found themselves back in favor. Like it or not, it seemed, they were identified in people's minds with Edo and old Japan. No matter how Western the country became, while that core of Japanese-ness remained they would survive. But how long could it remain, as Japan moved inexorably into the modern world?

> After the war two things became stronger—women and nylon
> stockings.
>
> popular postwar Japanese saying

As the clocks struck midnight on March 31, 1958, in the thirty-third year of the reign of Emperor Hirohito (known to history as Emperor Showa), prostitutes and their customers in brothels and bordellos across Japan rose to their feet, linked hands and, swaying rather boozily, broke into the nostalgic strains of "Auld Lang Syne," known in Japanese as *"Hotaru no Hikari"* (The Firefly's Glow). It was one of those moments of exquisite poignancy which the Japanese love to savor. An era had come to an end.

By then, to general rejoicing, the occupying forces had climbed into their airplanes and gone home. In the aftermath of the Korean War, Japan was thriving again, becoming wealthier with each year that passed. New buildings had sprung up on the rubble of the old. It was a country of worker ants busy rebuilding their economy and their lives. In many ways things had not changed much since the prewar days. Many of the same old faces were to be found running the country and its businesses and hobnobbing in geisha restaurants in the evenings, though they wore modern suits and voiced updated sentiments about democracy and the like. Even so, inside their conservative jackets and ties, those men were serving their companies with the same single-minded devotion with which the samurai had served their feudal lords. That old core of Japanese-ness was still there.

But there was one legacy of the occupation which could not be shuffled aside so easily. General MacArthur and his cohorts had given women a voice. It would be generations before Japanese women became as independent as Western women, if they ever even wished to do so. But they had the vote and, after the 1946 elections, there were thirty-nine women lawmakers in the Diet, the Japanese parliament. In the early 1950s militant women's groups, aligned with the Salvation Army, the Japanese Christian Women's movement, and antislavery organizations, lobbied tirelessly to bring to an end, once and for all, what they saw as the pernicious, humiliating, and barbaric practice of licensed prostitution. The imperial edict of 1947 had been singularly ineffectual. What was needed, they argued, was a law to abolish socially recognized prostitution and make it as unacceptable as it was in the West.

Kenji Mizoguchi's moving 1956 film, *Street of Shame,* stirred the national conscience and provided powerful ammunition for the anti-prostitution lobby. In it he depicts life in the Yoshiwara as the law is being debated in the Diet. There the rapacious brothel-keeper of Yume no Sato (Village of Dreams) plays the bluff, fatherly old man as he counts his earnings. "We're social workers," he argues, insisting that he is doing good, providing a home and work for the girls. But the film also shows the desperate lives the women lead: the aging mother, too old to appeal to any but the most drunk or undiscerning of clients, who has sacrificed herself to support her ungrateful son; the bespectacled wife working to support her sick husband who kills himself when he discovers how she has earned their money; and the young women already hardened in a life of vice, heartlessly fleecing men to set themselves up in business.

There were plenty of people struggling to maintain the status quo who argued that prostitution was a social necessity. Brothel-keepers hastily got together the All-Japan Association for the Prevention of Venereal Diseases to show how responsible they were and also smuggled sizable amounts of cash into the pockets of Diet members in an attempt to buy their votes. One was arrested for accepting bribes from them. And thousands of women at risk of losing their jobs united to form the Tokyo Federation of Unions of Women Workers.

But there was never any doubt that the voices raised in outrage against socially recognized prostitution would carry the day. The Anti-Prostitution Law, outlawing public solicitation and management of prostitutes, was passed in 1956—with a year's leeway before it came into force and another before prostitution became a punishable offense. The women who had supposedly been liberated thus joined hands and lifted their voices in a soulful rendering of "Auld Lang Syne" before going home to pack their bags. Some half a million had to go back to their families, look for other work, or—most commonly—find a new job title under which to operate.

After 350 years in business, the Yoshiwara and its ilk were to close their doors forever—at least in theory. Respectable, controllable, government-sanctioned prostitution was at an end. The licensed quarters had, for all their faults, been clean, well organized, and safe for both the women and their customers. Hereafter there would only be unlicensed prostitution which rapidly became the domain of the yakuza. Some of the most famous old houses of the Yoshiwara did indeed close. But most simply carried on under another name, setting up signboards advertising themselves as *"Toruko"* or "Turkish baths." (Later, after protests by the Turkish ambassador, these became known as "soaplands.") Despite the illegality of prostitution, the number of prostitutes actually rose in the years following the passage of the act. After all, as Western observers (invariably male) delighted in pointing out, the day on which the bill went into force was April Fool's Day.

Geisha, of course, being considered an entirely different profession, were exempt. Yet, for them too, the anti-prostitution law of Showa 33 was a watershed. Despite the many pious words which had been spoken and written to the contrary, there had always been gray areas where the geisha and prostitute worlds crossed. In the poorer unlicensed districts such as Miyagawa-cho and Gion Otsu in Kyoto, geisha houses were side by side with houses where prostitutes lived. Geisha and prostitutes were part of the same community.

After the bill was passed, the geisha moved several steps closer toward respectability—though they never made it all the way; the ambivalence remains to this day. Prostitutes who had lived in the same areas faded into the shadows. Some went back to their families in the countryside, some became *nigo-san* (mistresses or "second wives"), while the lucky ones found someone to marry them. Others who were skilled at playing the shamisen stayed on as musicians. Red-light districts developed where illegal prostitution flourished under the vigilant eyes of the yakuza, completely separate from the geisha districts.

Many women who became geisha before the war had been sold by their parents as children. Long after the bill was passed, such practices continued. Despite the law, as late as the mid-seventies, children from impoverished rural villages were still ending up as maids in geisha houses, attending primary school in the daytime, and cleaning and helping the geisha with their makeup and kimonos in the evening. But attitudes had

changed. Such practices were coming to seem more and more unacceptable, and the country's growing prosperity meant that soon no one would
be in such straits that they would need to sell their children.

Likewise, anyone who had become a geisha in the prewar years
had taken for granted that the rite of passage by which one blossomed
into a fully-fledged adult geisha was *mizuage*. After the Showa 33 bill,
this too became strictly illegal. A geisha might continue to have one or
more *danna* to support her, but if she did she kept quiet about it.

The institution of compulsory education up to the age of fifteen
also undermined the profession. Before the war, budding geisha had begun their dancing and shamisen lessons at the age of six years, six
months, and six days. They became maiko at eleven and had *mizuage* to
become adult geisha around fifteen. But now that they had to attend
school, they could not become maiko until the age of fifteen, which
meant that their rigorous training as professional musicians or dancers
had to be curtailed. Standards, it seemed, were doomed. Could geisha
still be geisha when everything that made them unique and distinctive
was changing?

The fourth decade of the rule of Emperor Hirohito, 1965–1975,
was when Japan really found its feet economically and surged into the
modern world. In 1960 Prime Minister Hayato Ikeda had swept into
power, promising to put the economy first and to double the national income within ten years. But long before the decade was out, standards
of living had rocketed. By the 1964 Tokyo Olympics, which marked
Japan's emergence from the struggle of the postwar years, almost every
household could boast the "three treasures": television, washing machine, and refrigerator. Practically overnight Japan became a modern,
wealthy country.

But astonishingly, the geisha continued to flourish. The postwar
decades were a boom period for the geisha. The number never returned
to their 1920s peak but by the mid-1970s there were a healthy 17,000.

For the men who ran Japan, the geisha world was something they
had grown up with. To support a beautiful and famous geisha was still a
measure of a man's success. Industrialists and politicians took it for
granted that after a hard day at work, they would spend the evening at a
familiar teahouse which was practically their second home. There they

could get a feminine perspective on the events of the day by talking them over with their favorite geisha in an atmosphere of intimacy and trust. Their wives, who lived in a much narrower domestic world, bounded by home and children, could not understand such things, they felt, whereas geisha were used to mixing on equal terms with powerful, articulate men. Lesser men might use bars and hostess clubs for the same purpose. But the top men of the nation had earned the attentions of women who they considered the nation's most sophisticated and accomplished. Teahouses, in fact, were very much akin to the gentlemen's clubs of the West, luxurious, ruinously expensive, and closed to all but the elite.

The evening sessions at the teahouse were also where movers and shakers would deepen their bonds with their colleagues, wrangle over business or political matters, and conclude deals which had been barely broached in the formal daylight meetings in the boardroom. When there was a guest to be impressed, rewarded, or entertained, they would call the teahouse, secure in the knowledge that the highly professional geisha would ensure that the party went without a hitch.

Two great scandals shook the 1970s and 1980s—the Lockheed scandal, which culminated in prime minister Kakuei Tanaka's disgrace when he was indicted for accepting more than $2 million in bribes from the American Lockheed corporation; and the Recruit Group shares-for-influence scandal, which involved government officials profiting hugely from the sale of stock acquired before public listing. Many of the key meetings between the plotters took place in the teahouses of Shimbashi and Akasaka where discretion was guaranteed.

But society was changing. Japan was entering the modern world at an unprecedented pace. The men for whom geisha were an essential part of their lives were growing older. A new generation was coming into power which no longer understood or appreciated the gracious old ways. Gradually the numbers of geisha began to fall.

The oil crisis of 1973 was probably the beginning of the decline. Thereafter, although Japan's economic fortunes rose again, the country had changed beyond all recognition. Instead of showing off their connections and limitless expense accounts by hosting teahouse parties, powerbrokers took to entertaining in French restaurants or glitzy hostess clubs in the posh Ginza district or inviting their colleagues for a weekend of golf at a private golf club where the membership alone cost far more than weeks of teahouse parties. In the new world of big money, fads, fashion, schoolgirl prostitution, host clubs, and a bacchanalian world of sexual titillation, the geisha retired deeper and deeper into the shadows, jealously guarding their ancient culture.

In 1945 Shigeru Yoshida, soon to become prime minister and a towering figure of the postwar years, was released from house arrest, where he had been kept in the last days of the war for advocating peace talks with the Allies. He went straight to Shin Kiraku, the famous geisha restaurant in Shimbashi, to see his mistress Korin and stayed there for several days. At the time, such behavior was not even worthy of comment; it was to be expected. Within the Yoshida family, the great man's relationship with Korin was completely open. When he died in 1967, she was an official guest at his funeral. But by then everything was changing. Yoshida was the last politician who could afford to be so splendidly insouciant about his affairs.

The Short, Fat Prime Minister
Who Wanted to Save Money

In June 1989 a woman who described herself as a former geisha sold a kiss-and-tell story to the Japanese media. Her name was Mitsuko Nakanishi and she had, she revealed, had an affair with the short, fat, jowly prime minister, Sosuke Uno, while she was working as a geisha in the Kagurazaka district. He had kept her as a paid mistress for a few months, then ditched her.

In Japan such a story was far from newsworthy. Everyone knew that politicians, along with any other man who could afford it, kept mistresses. Newspapers scrupulously refrained from scrutinizing such matters. "There's no personality below the navel," went the saying; in other words, what goes on beneath the navel is a man's private business and nothing to do with his public persona. But Nakanishi—who by now had a lowly job in a law office and was short of cash—persisted. The editor of the *Mainichi* newspaper finally decided to print the story, arguing that in the late twentieth century the public ought to know about the pecca-dilloes of its leaders.

As well as the *Mainichi* article, Nakanishi also appeared on televi-sion to hold forth in excruciating detail on their relationship. The story was blazoned across the Western press, thrilled to be in on Japan's first-ever sex scandal. At last, wrote Western journalists, traditional attitudes were changing. Japan was falling into line with the rest of the world (or at least the American and British part of it) in condemning men who had extra-marital affairs.

In reality, though a few women Diet members and vocal represen-tatives of women's groups made great play of Uno "treating women as pieces of merchandise," what shocked and amused most Japanese was his meanness. He had paid her, Nakanishi complained, the paltry sum of 300,000 yen ($2,300 at the exchange rate of the time) per month when the going rate had been a million yen. Then she had phoned him on the night that he became prime minister and suggested he pay her to keep her mouth shut. Ten million yen would have shown proper respect. Instead, he gave her three. Infidelity on a grand scale showed that a man was a man; mean-mindedness was the very opposite.

In the geisha world there was fury not against Uno but against Nakanishi, who had brought shame upon the profession by speaking out. Obviously she was not a real geisha, for no geisha with an ounce of self-respect would dream of breaking the fundamental code of silence; indeed, it transpired, she had not done the geisha training and had worked in the Kagurazaka district for only a few months. Uno was guilty not only of meanness but of having had an affair with a geisha so low grade that she would talk about it.

The Japanese take on the business was instructive. It was clear that Uno was incapable of managing his women. And if a man couldn't man-age his women, how could he be expected to manage the country? If a man did not take care of his geisha properly, he was not to be trusted. It was 1989, but among the movers and shakers who ran Japan Inc., atti-tudes were still firmly entrenched in the old Never-Never Land of Edo; that old Japanese-ness was still in place.

From time to time since then, geisha scandals have broken in the press. One very famous geisha is renowned for having had an affair with a louche Japanese heartthrob. But in general the geisha world remains secret and impenetrable.

But these women are still the stuff of romance in Japan. They still shape the Japanese self-image. Novels, films, and television soap operas re-create the romantic age embodied by the geisha, when it was better to die rather than be dishonored and men paused regretfully at the Willow of the Backward Glance, at the boundary of the Yoshiwara, before returning to the real world.

chapter 9

a dying tradition

A dream of springtide
When the streets
Are scattering
Cherry blossoms.
Tidings of autumn
When the streets
Are lined with lighted lanterns
On both sides.

      Koji Ochi (seventeenth-century poet);
      inscribed on the Great Gate of the Yoshiwara[1]

À la Recherche

Not long after I got back to Tokyo from Kyoto, I met up with Shichiko, the male geisha. It was the dog days of summer, so hot and oppressive that it was difficult to move. He was in baggy checked Bermuda shorts, long striped white socks, and an oversize T-shirt. With his mod-ish Henry V haircut and wicked grin, the outfit made him look like a naughty schoolboy—not inappropriate, it seemed to me, for a *taikomochi* jester. We sat in his small apartment—his wife and daughter were out—chatting languidly, fanning ourselves.

Shichiko lived in the rundown East End of the city, a long way from the glittering shops of the Ginza, the imperial palace, and the posh business addresses, and round the corner from the Yoshiwara, which had been established as far as possible from the parts of town where re-spectable people ran their businesses and kept their wives and children. Early in the evening, when the heat was a little more bearable, we de-cided to take a stroll.

There was something irresistibly alluring about the Yoshiwara. After Japan opened its doors to the outside world, everyone who had ar-rived in the great city of Edo, starting with the Victorians, found an ex-cuse as soon as possible to sneak off for a visit. Even though it had been closed down, in theory at least, in the great cleanup of 1958, I was curious just to tread the streets which had seen so much drama, passion, pain, culture, and poetry.

Shichiko had donned a pair of chunky orange schoolkid's sandals. Striding ahead, ice cream cone in hand, he led the way through the back-streets to a wide thoroughfare, lined with unlovely concrete blocks, with cars, trucks, and buses roaring by. Strolling along, we came to a bedrag-gled willow tree, its leaves pale and grimy. To the left, a road zigzagged around a corner and out of sight.

I knew exactly where we were. It was the Looking Back Willow—or rather, a sad descendant of it—where lovelorn merchants and samu-rai had turned to take a last look toward the Great Gate of the Yoshiwara and the glittering streets beyond, before returning to the monochrome world of work, home, and family. The road that zig-zagged out of sight had led to the heart of the Yoshiwara, designed so that passersby could see nothing of what lay within. Right where the narrower road met the thoroughfare, the Great Gate had stood, mark-ing the boundary between one world and the other.

The busy thoroughfare itself had been part of the moat—the Ditch of Black Teeth—which surrounded the walled city of pleasure. On the other side was a quiet backstreet which had once been the Dike of Japan, packed night and day with streams of eager male visitors, jostling along on foot or horseback or, in later years, by rickshaw. Nothing was left. The moat had long since been filled in and the dike absorbed into the warren of streets. Even the name Yoshiwara had been obliterated in the city burghers' efforts to comply with Western puritanism, though the present-day name still recalled the throngs of visitors who had tramped toward the place: Senzoku, "Thousand Feet."

Shichiko and I took each other's pictures in the shade of the legendary willow and turned down into what had once been the Yoshiwara. At first it looked like any nondescript working-class part of Tokyo, with shabby shops and rows of parked bicycles. But once round the bend we saw what had become of the most famous pleasure quarter on earth. The lower end of the business at any rate had not changed, though it had become a fair bit more sordid.

The main road and the side roads—the famous Five Streets—were lined with the fantasy palaces with which Japanese love to fill their red-light districts. The grand wooden edifices within which geisha had danced and courtesans entertained merchant princes and the shacks where the lower ranks of prostitutes had carried out their less exalted trade had disappeared. In their place were street upon street of exuberantly gaudy buildings, bristling with neon and festooned with wires and cables.

Flamboyant red-light districts are part of the scenery in Japan. What was notable was the sheer number and concentration of the brothels. One was modeled on a traditional Yoshiwara house with eaves and bamboo blinds carefully molded in concrete. In front hung a neon picture of a geisha and the name O-oku (Harem) above a sign giving the price: 20,000 yen ($200) per "bath." (Brothels are known as "soaplands" and involve complicated activity with a particularly slithery variety of soap.) Another, called True Love, spelt out in red characters on green neon, was a Spanish-effect mock brick "villa." Others with names such as Love Rose, Acapulco, and Quartier Latin featured snarling stone panthers, Roman columns, or baroque stonework. Mean-looking gangster types with cheap suits and slicked-back hair propped up the walls or lounged outside the doors where the prices and services were listed. There were no women to be seen; presumably they were all inside.

Shichiko strode along, saying little, giving monosyllabic grunts in answer to my questions. Perhaps he was worried about what I, a foreigner, might think of this rather shameful aspect of his country's culture; perhaps he was concerned that I might confuse the world of the "arts people" which he inhabited with this tawdry, exploitative place; or perhaps he just took it all for granted and thought there was nothing to say.

Half a mile further on, clear of the streets lined with brothels, we came to a small graveyard shadowed with trees, with grave markers crammed tightly side by side. Among them were stone images of *jizo-sama*, the deities who take care of the souls of miscarried and aborted children. At the back was a pond—the Benten pond, said Shichiko, where unhappy prostitutes used to jump in to commit suicide. In the middle, on top of a stony hillock, was a statue of Kannon, the goddess of mercy, wimpled like the Virgin Mary, gazing compassionately down on the scene.

In the old days, said Shichiko, before everything came to an end in 1958, the Yoshiwara had been a thriving place where geisha lived side by side with prostitutes. Many of the old geisha, including his own shamisen teacher, had gone there for lessons from dance and music teachers who were considered the toughest and best, if not in the city, at least in the East End. In those days, to have studied at the Yoshiwara gave a working-class geisha kudos. But that was then.

Then around a corner we spied a large ugly plaster tanuki, the stylized badger which carries a flask of sake, wears a straw hat, and a friendly grin and adorns shops and homes. It might be compared to a garden gnome in the West except for its enormously distended testicles which reach to its ankles and are believed to bestow fertility. Here Shichiko was on safer ground.

"My ancestor," he cried, going up to it and flinging his arm round it. Remembering his outrageously priapic act which had shocked me so much when I saw it, I took a picture of the two of them, grinning, side by side.

The party at the riverside house is over, the lamplight dim;
The crowd of painted ladies, tipsy, is departing now.
Their delicate hands have trouble opening snake-eyes umbrellas—
On the banks of the Ryogoku Bridge the rain is mixed with sleet.

Yodo Yamauchi (1827–1872)[2]

Of all the Tokyo geisha districts or flower towns, Yanagibashi, "Willow Bridge," most seemed to preserve the romantic aura of old Edo. I had caught glimpses of its tile-roofed geisha houses and teahouses clustered around the mouth of a narrow canal where it gave onto the River Sumida, its lanterns and softly lit rooms reflected invitingly in the water. In the past mendicant musicians used to row right up to the Yanagibashi gardens, strumming their shamisen and singing romantic ballads.

For years the teahouses of Yanagibashi had been the prime place in the entire city to see the magnificent summer fireworks display that took place along the river. People made reservations to dine there years in advance, but unless you were a top-ranking politico or chairman of a major corporation and, furthermore, known to the teahouse, you had no chance. (Unlike the Kyoto teahouses, which serve only drinks and, if asked for food, order it in from outside caterers, the Tokyo ones—which are called *ryotei,* high-class Japanese restaurants, rather than *ochaya,* teahouses—serve expensive traditional haute cuisine.) To be in a Yanagibashi teahouse on fireworks night marked you out as a member of the ruling elite.

But as the city spread westward, the river, which had once been at the center of life, was pushed off to the eastern edge and Yanagibashi was left high and dry. Politicians looked for their entertainment closer to home, in the Akasaka geisha district on the doorstep of the Diet, the parliament building. Company chairmen and business magnates gravitated to Shimbashi to enjoy the urbane conversation of the geisha there. Few people bothered to go to the eastern reaches of the city any longer. Then came the economic boom of the 1980s. In the frenzy of building that engulfed the country, glass and concrete buildings sprouted around the old wooden teahouses and geisha houses and the banks of the River Sumida were encased in concrete. The Yanagibashi gardens disappeared.

Almost as soon as I arrived in Tokyo I began to hear bad news. Not so long ago there had been a hundred geisha in Yanagibashi. Now, said a businessman who was a devoted patron of the geisha world, he had heard there were twenty left and at most two or three teahouses. But it was worse than that. It was not until I talked to geisha themselves that I discovered the full story. As recently as January 1999 there had been six flower towns in Tokyo: Shimbashi, Akasaka, Kagurazaka, Yoshicho, Asakusa and, most venerable and gracious of all, Yanagibashi. Now there were five. It boded ill for the others.

In the end, only the Inagaki *ryotei* had been left in Yanagibashi, with thirty geisha working there. Gradually it became harder and harder to make ends meet. A teahouse cannot exist in isolation. It needs a community of geisha and a family of customers. Finally the owner sold out. The elderly geisha who took over decided to close for good.

Nevertheless I wanted to see for myself. Perhaps I could find Inagaki and talk to the old woman who had owned it or at least absorb the atmosphere of this most romantic of flower towns. So one day when I was in the east of the city I made a detour to Yanagibashi.

Willow Bridge itself was still there, linking the two sides of the canal, though it was no longer a delicate wooden construction that geisha tripped across on wooden clogs, sheltering under their parasols. Now it was a swathe of steel girders. From the other side of the Sumida I could make out the tiled roofs of a gracious old house peeking above the concrete wall which edged the river, half-hidden behind overgrown foliage and dwarfed by giant developments. Close by, the little canal was still romantic, with willow trees along each bank and wooden houseboats moored there—though it required eyes which had been trained in the Japanese way of looking, filtering out the high-rises all around, to see it. There were a couple of boathouses but behind the willow trees, where restaurants had once stood, lights twinkling in the water, was a blur of concrete.

When I asked for Inagaki, I was directed to an old house hidden behind a forbidding wall topped with old-fashioned curved tiles, utterly out of place in that landscape of concrete. The heavy wooden doors were locked, bolted, and immovable, as if they had not been opened for a long time. I had been told that I might find the owner in the housing block which loomed beside it. But that door too was locked.

A few days later I met up with a Shimbashi geisha I knew, and told her my sad tale. What had become of those last Yanagibashi geisha, I wondered.

"One started teaching calligraphy," she told me. "Another was a very good shamisen player. These days it's a real problem to find good shamisen players, so I invited her to Shimbashi. But she didn't want to come. They were old. They wanted to retire."

Teahouse Politics

The demise of Yanagibashi left five flower towns in Tokyo: the high-powered joints of Shimbashi and Akasaka; the hilly lanes of Kagurazaka, blazing with neon at night; Yoshicho, which was quietly declining; and down-to-earth Asakusa, in the city's East End. Until two or three years ago it was a matter of dispute which, of Akasaka and Shimbashi, was the classiest of them all. Both had their histories, aficionados, and siren queens.

The country's rulers—the politicians and the bureaucrats—preferred Akasaka. A couple of minutes' purr by limousine from the Diet, it was like having a pleasure quarter in the heart of Capitol Hill, or a stone's throw from the White House. Hidden behind high dun-colored earthen walls and heavy wooden gates amid the bustle and neon of the Akasaka entertainment district, with its nightclubs, cabarets, discos, bars, and tiny restaurants run by ex-geisha, Akasaka's *ryotei* were every bit as grand and exclusive as Shimbashi's. If, however, you had the right connections and were invited to step inside, they had the reputation of being less expensive and formal. Akasaka geisha were said to be mediocre dancers and not quite as classy as the Shimbashi geisha. But then again, they were younger and prettier. That was ample compensation.

The Akasaka teahouses were the scene of much wheeling and dealing. In Japan there is an enormous gulf between surface and reality, daytime and night-time. In the daytime politicians would stand up and read out prepared speeches in the Diet or ask questions which had been submitted a couple of days in advance so as to allow plenty of time to prepare an answer. Businessmen meanwhile would be whiling away the day in board meetings at which nothing was ever decided. It was largely theater, promoting the appearance of democracy.

But night-time was when much of the real business and the real politics took place. With ties loosened and faces flushed, people put inhibitions aside and said what they really thought. In Japan nothing could be done in the way of business or politics or anything that mattered at all without face-to-face contact. Executives and politicians had to know and like the people with whom they were intending to do business. They had to eat together, drink together, get drunk together.

At the topmost levels of society, geisha were a key part of that evening activity. It would not be an overstatement to say that geisha parties were essential to the running of the country. In the Akasaka *ryotei*—as exclusive as elite private clubs, akin to the Harvard or the Yale Club—Japan's political rulers, the Liberal Democratic Party, would discuss matters of state and make deals after unwinding over a meal and several flasks of saké. The geisha, women they had known as friends or lovers for years, knew instinctively when to keep the tone light and when to slip discreetly out of the room. Sometimes the older and wiser among them might join in a conversation or add their commonsensical view to help unravel a knotty problem. It was a little like going home and talking things over with the wife—except that was something a Japanese man, of that generation at any rate, would never do.

Geisha, of course, would never give direct advice. Japan is a country where the ex-geisha wife of a business magnate is much admired for being, as people say, "clever enough never to let a man realize how clever she is." The essence of the feminine ideal is to make a man think that he is the one who has the brilliant ideas. But a geisha might well prod even the finance minister in one direction or another, cooing something along the lines of "You were saying you might raise the interest rates. How clever of you to think of that!"

Bernard Krisher, a veteran American journalist who has lived in Japan for forty years, put it bluntly. "Most Japanese men can't converse with their wives," he said. "But they find that they can with geisha. That's why the geisha system has survived so long. It's more than sex.

"Many people look down on geisha, but they are the only people who can talk on an equal level to the prime minister. They can tease him and joke with him. No one else can do that. They're like cats—dignified and totally independent. They demand your love. You have to take care of them and feed them. But you can't get them to jump on your lap if they don't want to."

Krisher's take on geisha was simple. "They are mistresses," he said, "like a Japanese version of the Colette story.

"What foreigners can't comprehend is that someone will spend two thousand dollars and not even try to take a geisha home. Japanese get embarrassed, having to tell a visiting foreigner that it's just not going to happen. They're not programmed to sleep with someone for money. But if you ask someone five or six times for something, on five or six occasions, finally you can get what you want. The more often you go to a geisha house, the more chance there is that you can probably sleep with someone. I did that a lot in the sixties. I didn't pay. For them too it was a novel experience. They're also human beings and they're women. But it would be on that basis—love, not payment."

But in the end the partying had to stop. Being too closely tied to the country's wheelers and dealers proved to be Akasaka's downfall. The problems began in the mid-nineties when the Ministry of Finance— until then an impregnable bastion of faceless bureaucrats who effectively ran the country—found itself under fire, under suspicion of incompetence and corruption.

For years the MOF had controlled the country's financial institutions, feeding vital information to banks and wielding control over everything from the opening and closing of bank branches to the uniforms the female clerks wore. There were executives at each bank whose job was to wine and dine the relevant MOF officials, often at vast expense, at classy restaurants, exclusive clubs, golf links, and teahouses. But with the Japanese economy on the skids, the public prosecutors decided to take a good look at the MOF's affairs. At the beginning of 1998 they breached the gates of the fortress, took away lorry loads of papers, and arrested four officials, accusing them of accepting bribes from the financial institutions they were paid to oversee.

None of this was directly to do with the geisha. But the Japanese tabloids, scenting blood, took to hanging around the places politicians and bureaucrats were known to frequent, on the lookout for more stories of big spending and, better still, sexual improprieties. Once upon a time such behavior would have been taken for granted and not considered worthy of note. But now it sold papers. And the obvious place for a stakeout was the Akasaka teahouses.

Suddenly the once thriving geisha district became very quiet. When politicians got together, they did so in the more anonymous surroundings of a hotel restaurant or a golf links. In Akasaka business went into a steep decline. Rumors flitted around the small world of the geisha. Business was so bad that one previously famous Akasaka geisha, it was said, was called to teahouses at most twice a month. She had been reduced to appearing on television in kimono fashion shows and had had to move from her palatial apartment to one so cramped it lacked even its own toilet. From 300 geisha in the sixties, the numbers fell to 90, working in 13 *ryotei;* of those, only a few had regular work. Effortlessly Shimbashi floated back to the top of the hierarchy.

The Sophisticated Ladies of Shimbashi

Butterfly
Or falling leaf,
Which ought I to imitate
In my dancing?

Geisha song[3]

Tokyo's flower and willow world is not a clearly delineated geographical area, visibly separate from the real-life world in the way Kyoto's is. I had passed Kanetanaka for years without ever realizing that its sand-colored walls and enormous gates concealed not the palatial private home of a minor prince or the heir to an industrial fortune but one of the

most venerable teahouses in Shimbashi. I had been to kabuki performances in the Shimbashi Embujo without knowing that it had been
built for the Shimbashi geisha to perform their annual dances, which
took place in May. I had walked down innumerable tiny alleys near the
Tsukiji fish market without having the faintest idea that some of the
shabby facades with potted plants lined up outside hid geisha houses.
And if I saw a woman in a kimono flitting down one of these streets, I
would never have guessed she was a geisha. The geisha of Tokyo were
far more discreet and circumspect than their Kyoto counterparts.

Here, one day, I was sitting in the coffee shop of a hotel which I had
never realized before was in the heart of the geisha world, talking to a
glamorous young woman. It had been a matter of the right connections.
I had phoned up and dropped a rather weighty name. I was amazed at
the alacrity with which she said, "Let's have lunch."

"Did you know we still have rickshaws in Shimbashi?" she asked
in a soft, musical voice, after we had placed our orders. "There are two
and two rickshaw men. When I go from one *ryotei* to another I sometimes call them. But I worry what will become of us in the future. Japan
has changed; it's not like the old Japan. Lots of Japanese have never been
to a geisha party; they think we're doing something bad. These days it's
very difficult. If I was doing this for the money I would give up."

Anyone looking at her might have taken Shuko for an executive in
the fashion industry or the young wife of a wealthy man but certainly
not a geisha. Dressed in an exquisitely coordinated beige suit topped
with a floaty jacket, an outfit which had clearly come from a Paris or
Milan couturier, she wore her long hair loose and tumbling around her
shoulders. She had a pale, refined, pretty face, softly oval, with a sensuous mouth which curved into a provocative smile, and almond eyes
brought out with just a hint of makeup. She was lovely in a feminine
way rather than intimidatingly beautiful.

But it was less her appearance than some indefinable presence
that set her apart. She was poised, confident, funny, and charming. She
would, I imagined, be any man's perfect woman—sexy yet motherly.
To me, as a woman, she had another face. We talked girl to girl, though
she still gently, so that I hardly noticed, made sure that my glass was full
and that I had everything I wanted. I was perfectly taken care of, in fact.

She spoke earnestly, seriously, yet managed at the same time to keep the conversation light, interspersing her remarks with smiles and silvery laughter.

The Shimbashi geisha, she told me, prided themselves on their "wifeliness." Within the Tokyo flower and willow world, that was the Shimbashi flavor. The Akasaka geisha were more overtly sexy. They wore more makeup and brighter kimonos. The Shimbashi geisha, conversely, were the embodiment of good taste. Their kimonos were sober and modest, their hair swept into simple buns and their makeup subtle, more suited to the sophisticated and wealthy customers they entertained.

Shuko regularly spent her evenings in the company of some of the country's most powerful and brilliant minds, men who headed industrial conglomerates, banks, financial institutions, and major corporations. To prepare herself, she kept up to date with the news, read the latest books, and went to exhibitions. Not that the guests expected intellectual conversation. They were there to relax, not to have their minds taxed. The geisha party was the one place where a man could let slip the mask which social convention required him to wear. There the company chairman who bore a huge weight of responsibility from morning till night and made mammoth decisions which affected millions of yen or millions of people could, if he wanted, play the fool or be babied by geisha who called him not Mr. Suzuki but by some cozy nickname like Su-chan, as if he were a child. At work he might be a god; but at the geisha party he could have an entirely different face.

But the most important quality was confidentiality. No one would ever have a political or business discussion in a hostess club, where the guests at one table could easily overhear the conversation at another. In a teahouse, each banquet took place in a separate room and the guests never knew who else was present in the teahouse that night. When a guest wanted to go to the toilet, the geisha made sure that he never bumped into a guest from another party on his way; the corridors were always empty. And if a guest happened to be part of two parties on the same evening, when he arrived the second time the geisha never gave the game away. They always greeted him with "How are you, sir? We haven't seen you for such a long time!"

But what if a man, having had a little too much to drink and finding himself surrounded by beautiful women attending to his every need, wanted more? Had there not been times when Shuko herself, enjoying the company of the same brilliant men night after night, had felt drawn to one of them? What of love?

"Many men have asked me to marry them," she smiled with a toss of her long black hair. "Men enjoy our company because we're free spirits. It makes it safe for them. Whenever they spend time with us they can imagine they're having a romance because they know we can't leave our profession. We're caged birds."

Shuko was now out of her twenties, the age by which most Japanese women expect to be married. Did she not worry that she would miss out on what was the Holy Grail of most Japanese women's lives?

"I'm not interested in marriage," she said firmly. She paused, then smiled woman to woman and added wistfully, "But a lover would be nice . . ."

"The trouble is," I said, "when you reach our age, most men are married."

She looked puzzled.

"In the West," I said, sensing a cultural chasm, "we prefer not to have affairs with married men."

"All our customers are married," she replied carelessly. That, of course, would be the pool from which she would take a lover.

A Teahouse Party

There was something afoot when I arrived at Kanetanaka a couple of days later. Usually the quiet backstreet was dark and empty, especially by eight o'clock at night. But that evening there was a line of gleaming limousines with darkened windows filling the road and a crush of young men in dark suits standing around in the doorway. They ignored me as I pushed between them into the entrance hall.

As I was slipping out of my shoes, Shuko came running to greet me, along with a bevy of other geisha, scurrying with tiny steps across the tatami. She had metamorphosed. Her hair was swept into a tidy knot, her face powdered and rouged, her eyes outlined in black, her eyebrows penciled into two immaculate brown moth wings and her mouth the color of a camellia flower. She wore a cornflower-blue kimono of thin silk with a design of white flowers on the sleeves and hem. Her dark-blue obi was decorated with a summery pattern of gingko leaf–shaped fans sprinkled with tiny flowers. On her feet she wore white cotton tabi socks.

Even the way she carried her body had changed. Instead of the glamorous creature with whom I lunched in hotel restaurants and who flew to Milan and Paris for her clothes, she was the embodiment of woman, warm, caring, and attentive. I was the guest and she the hostess. It put a kind of distance between us.

Twittering a welcome, the women led me through the imposing entrance hall, decorated with a gorgeously painted gold screen, and along a corridor to an austerely traditional room with sand-colored walls and tatami mats. The only furniture was a low red-lacquered table with a cushion on each side and two antique wooden armrests topped with padded tapestry, such as samurai would have used. In the *tokonoma,* the alcove which forms the focal point of a Japanese room, was a red camellia blossom artfully placed in a bamboo vase. Taking pride of place on the wall behind it was a scroll with a few words brushed in bold black characters. My host, Mr. Matsumoto, was already there. A regular customer of Shuko's, he had agreed on her suggestion to invite me along to one of his regular get-togethers with the geisha of Shimbashi.

"Good to meet you," he said, rising to his feet and stepping forward to shake my hand. "Shuko has told me all about you!"

I had assumed that anyone who frequented geisha parties, particularly in such a grand setting, must be old; but he could not have been more than fifty. He was a handsome, trim man with a relaxed, cosmopolitan air. His hair was fashionably short, his dark suit discreetly expensive. He was the owner, it transpired, of a highly successful import-export business and spent his life flitting between Japan and the United States. Beyond that, of course, we did not discuss his work or family. After all, we had crossed into the flower and willow world. It would have been unspeakably boorish.

"I've been coming to Kanetanaka for years," he said as we took our places on the cushions, reclining luxuriously like Edo-period daimyo on the armrests. Mine was the place of honor, with my back to the *tokonoma* alcove. "My father brought me when I was a teenager. We are old friends here."

Shuko knelt by my side and filled my cup with saké. One by one the geisha sank gracefully to their knees, bowed their heads so that they practically touched the tatami, and gaily introduced themselves. I was used to Japanese formality. Middle-class women of a certain age at, for example, a tea ceremony, engaged in endless bowing and scraping, bombarding one with language larded with baroque polite forms. It was all rather stiff and uncomfortable. But this was different. These were highly sophisticated women. They observed the formalities, they used formal language, yet their behavior was full of gaiety and laughter. They played with the forms, they were not enslaved by them.

It was a little like being surrounded by a flock of gorgeously plumed birds. Cooing softly, covering their mouths with an elegant hand when they giggled, they chatted and bantered, fluttering about, making sure that saké cups and beer glasses were filled and everything was to our liking. Skillfully they kept the conversation light and merry.

Did I know the difference, they asked, between the way a wife and a geisha wore their kimono? I had to confess that I did not. In Kyoto when a geisha was formally dressed, with her kimono low at the back and swirling about her feet, it was obvious. But among the geisha in this room it was difficult to tell. Their kimonos looked every bit as chaste and modest as a married woman's. Smiling, they explained the telltale signs that communicated to the practiced eye that they were geisha—the kimono tied a little more loosely than a married woman's and a touch more open at the neck to reveal a tantalizing hint of the collar at the throat and a rakish flash of the under-kimono at the hem and cuff; the hair swept back into a glossy helmet with not a strand out of place.

"Geisha wear kimonos all the time, whereas wives wear them only on special occasions," explained a geisha who had introduced herself as Kimie. Poised, elegant, she must have been brushing fifty. Her kimono was a deep blue tinged with gray, the color of the sea on a summer's evening, with a pattern of waves swirling across the sleeves and hem. "We have to carry on all the jobs of everyday life in kimono; so we tie ours a little more loosely."

After that first evening Kimie and I became friends and she told me her story. She had a pedigree stretching back several generations. Her mother had been a famous beauty in her day and the child of another famous beauty. The family kept a geisha house where generations of youthful geisha had lived. Her father had been the head of one of the country's vast industrial conglomerates before the war. During the American occupation he was purged and put under house arrest along with other leaders of society and had been unable to visit Kimie and her mother, who was of course not his wife but his second, third, or fourth "wife"; a man in that position would have had several. Kimie never knew him. When she was three he died. By the time she was growing up, she had another "father," a leading novelist who, like many literary men, enjoyed the louche atmosphere of the geisha districts. He too had a wife and family and stayed over at the geisha house a couple of days a week.

Had she been born in different circumstances, Kimie might have been an academic or a doctor. There was something about her of the bluestocking. She had clearly inherited her father's brilliance. She was not beautiful. Her long-chinned, rather plain face had faded and lost its definition with the passing of the years though, like all the geisha, she had a powerful presence. She was, I later learned, one of the leading women in the Shimbashi community and hinted once that she was "married"—she had a *danna*—though, like all the geisha, her lips were sealed on that score.

A couple of kimono-clad maids rustled in with trays laden with dishes of exquisite delicacies—vegetables carved into miniature sculptures, a wobbling beige cube of mock tofu made of ground sesame, a deep-purple baby eggplant dabbed with mustard-colored miso paste, each arranged like a small landscape on a porcelain dish or costly slab of stoneware. They laid them out before Mr. Matsumoto and myself on the lacquered table top.

It was a little like being at a dinner party where only two of the guests were served. I felt a little uncomfortable as I picked up my chopsticks, then remembered that in traditional Japanese homes the womenfolk do not dine with the guests. I had spent many dull evenings conversing painfully with the husband or father of the friend I had been invited to visit while she scuttled silently in and out of the room, carrying trays of food. On this occasion I was an honorary man—though fortunately there were geisha present to brighten up the conversation.

The second course was *ayu,* a small sweet river trout grilled whole and cunningly arranged on an oblong dish so that it almost looked as if it were still alive and swimming along. Before I had a chance to dig into mine, Kimie, who had taken Shuko's place next to me, took it and expertly filleted it with her chopsticks, then divided it into bite-size pieces. As the guest, it would be unthinkable for me to have to perform even the least taxing of chores, such as filleting my own fish. The meal continued with succulent slices of sashimi and a succession of simmered, steamed, and raw dishes followed by rice and pickles in the traditional Japanese order.

Mr. Matsumoto was talking about what made a geisha sexy.

"It's not physical beauty," he said. "It's not the way they look. It's some indefinable quality, the way in which they interact with men. Take Kimie, for example. She doesn't seem sexy . . ."

"What?" exclaimed Kimie in mock horror. "In that case, I'm leaving right now!"

". . . but when she dances she's extremely sexy."

Kimie smiled, mollified.

"We have a saying in the geisha world," said Shuko. "There are five conditions that make a geisha famous." The other geisha chimed in. "First, to be beautiful but not too beautiful. Shimbashi geisha are homely," they explained. "We wear plain, simple kimonos, like wives." Next, to be able to hold one's drink but never to get drunk. Third, to devote oneself to one's art. Fourth, to be good at talking but better at listening. "That's the secret of the geisha's conversation," they said. Last, to have a good reputation not just in one's own district but throughout the geisha community.

The meal over, the maids cleared the table.

"Please sing for us, Shuko-san," begged Mr. Matsumoto.

"I'm not good enough, I'm embarrassed," demurred Shuko. Finally persuaded, she knelt and, accompanied by a birdlike older geisha on the shamisen, sang a measured melancholy ditty. There was much applause. She bowed, touching her fingers to the tatami, smiling modestly.

Then Kimie was persuaded to dance. In the room there was an expectant silence. She paused, drew breath, and composed her face to an expression of masklike stillness, then raised her fan in a crisp gesture.

As the elderly geisha sang out a plaintive melody, thrumming her shamisen, Kimie painted a story. With a ripple of her fan she created a river where she, pining for her lover, sat gazing at the lanterns bobbing along it. She turned her hand, palm upward, fingers and thumb fused together like a puppet's hand, to the sky. There was a bird, a skylark, hovering overhead, reminding her of the fragility and transience of love. A letter came. She seemed to read it and wept, throwing it aside. Each gesture was perfection, finding movement out of stillness and stillness in the heart of movement, refined, controlled, and magical. With the tiniest angle of her head, glance of her eyes, or graceful twist of her hand she created a whole universe of love, passion, loneliness, sadness, and loss. We watched, transfixed. She was no longer a fading middle-aged woman but a siren, ineffably seductive, for whom any man would happily have risked shipwreck.

In the past, I remembered, geisha had been like the opera singers, ballet dancers, and Hollywood stars of today. In their world they still were. It was as if I had spent the evening in the company of Meryl Streep and Michelle Pfeiffer or Gelsey Kirkland and Jessye Norman, who had fussed over me, poured my drink, filleted my fish, beguiled me with their chatter, then risen to their feet to perform for me. I felt privileged and humbled.

Before the evening was over, there was one last mystery I wanted to solve. Why had there been limousines at the entrance to Kanetanaka? Who were the men in black suits and why were they there? The geisha smiled. On this occasion, just for me, they would put aside their code of secrecy. Prime Minister Keizo Obuchi, they whispered, had been entertaining in a neighboring room that night.

Honorable Swinging Sleeves

One sign that there was demand for the geisha was the development of fake geisha, a development which the geisha themselves tolerated with resignation. There were of course no fake geisha in Shimbashi; it was far too grand for that. But in Asakusa, the East End which had been where the townsmen lived in the old city of Edo, there were fake geisha who performed for ordinary people at the sort of venues where geisha would never normally be seen. They had also recently sometimes been invited to perform alongside the Asakusa geisha and the *taikomochi* jesters.

They were called *furisode-san,* "honorable swinging sleeves," *furisode* being the term for the gorgeous long-sleeved kimono worn by maiko and other young women. The *furisode-san* were poor men's geisha. From the moment they appeared in 1994, they inspired endless articles with headlines like "Goodbye to the geisha!," concluding from their rise that true geisha were dying out. In reality there were only ten or eleven *furisode-san* as against several thousand geisha; but unlike the geisha, who studiously maintained a culture of silence, the *furisode-san* engaged in clamorous self-promotion.

The young women were actually very different from geisha. They were salaried workers earning 250,000 yen ($2,500) a month, worked five days a week, and had to retire when they reached the age of twenty-five. People liked geisha to be young and pretty; one of the problems with real geisha was that so many were old.

Their training in dance and manners lasted three months. Instead of esoteric classical music, they danced to tapes of popular music—big band music, songs by famous chanteuses, folk music, and the catchy songs sung in karaoké bars. Unlike geisha, the *furisode-san* could be hired to entertain anywhere, even in the most humble of establishments—a soba noodle shop, a sushi bar, or an eel restaurant—and they had no *ichigen san* ("no first-timers") policy. They would work for anyone willing to pay for them.

One day I happened to hear of a display of *furisode-san* dancing at the Foreign Correspondents' Club in Tokyo and went along to see it. There were five dancers, each named after a flower or a fruit: Sakura (Cherry Blossom), Komomo (Peach), Botan (Peony), Ichigo (Strawberry), and Ringo (Apple). They wore long-sleeved kimonos like maiko, though a little less fine and costly looking, and their faces were painted white, but without the two-pronged fork of bare flesh at the nape of the neck.

To me, having been immersed in the geisha world for months and seen the best of geisha dancing, they looked like what they were—young girls who had had just three months of dance training. They had none of the crispness or precision which made geisha dancing so seductive and entrancing to watch. It was like taking beginners out of ballet school and asking them to put on a show or comparing a musical at a village hall to Wagner at Bayreuth.

In a way, seeing the *furisode* confirmed everything the geisha had said. Classical geisha dancing was an acquired taste, it demanded an educated eye, and their singing and music were really quite difficult to appreciate. But in the past the flower and willow world had not been the rarefied experience it was today. Though these geisha arts might seem arcane, they had been the popular music and dance of their time, added to which, there had been many more geisha, enough to entertain, mother, and provide lovers for a much wider stratum of society. In the early years of the twentieth century, the heyday of the geisha, ordinary classy gentlemen—like the writer Kafu Nagai, who was far from inordinately rich—had been able to enjoy their company.

The *furisode-san* were accessible and modern, as geisha had been in the past. Perhaps they would inspire a renewed interest in kimono and classical culture, even if they were not as purist as the geisha might like. They might even increase the market for geisha. But what saddened me was the commercial feel of it. These young women were not particularly interested in their "arts"; their training was something to be got out of the way as quickly as possible. They were really just hostesses in period costume.

The Island on the Far Side

In all the years I had been in Tokyo I had never heard of Mukojima, literally "the island on the far side." It was off the English-language map. But when I dipped my toe into the waters of the flower and willow world, I began to hear that there was quite a community of geisha there. While Shimbashi and Akasaka boasted about ninety geisha each, in Mukojima there were almost two hundred.

"It isn't ranked as a flower town," sniffed Shuko when I asked her, looking disdainfully down her pretty nose.

"Why?" I asked; but that is not a question which is ever asked—or answered—in Japan. The Gion geisha spoke with undisguised contempt of Miyagawa-cho and East Gion, but at least they were recognized as geisha districts. How bad could Mukojima be?

Once upon a time Mukojima was "the island on the far side" of the Sumida, though it was certainly not an island any longer. It was further afield even than the Yoshiwara and well beyond the working-class heartland of Asakusa. In fact it barely felt like Tokyo at all. From the station (it was so far out that the subway had risen above ground to become a railway line) I walked the long, straight suburban streets, lined with faceless houses and shops. The place was strangely depopulated. But dotted among the backstreets, discreetly hidden behind high walls, were large prosperous houses that looked remarkably like teahouses.

Down a back alley I came across the geisha house I was looking for, with potted plants in rows along the front and a trellis loaded with wisteria creating a porch. Inside, a couple of young women were lounging in a tatami room, propping themselves on their elbows on the low table and chatting merrily. Neither were beauties; no one would have mistaken them for "high-class courtesans." But they had a straightforward warmth which was hugely refreshing after weeks among the snobbish Gion geisha and the bluestocking geisha of Shimbashi. They were not worried about what image I might have of them as geisha. They were prepared to talk quite candidly about whatever they thought and felt.

"I hated it when I first went to a teahouse party," said one who had introduced herself as Kyoko. At twenty-two, she had an elfin face with a tiny turned-up nose, wide quizzical eyes, and a mischievous smile. "I don't know why. Everyone was perfectly nice to me. I just hated it. I cried. I still sometimes think, 'I hate this. I don't want to go to another teahouse party.' But it's my life. What can I do?"

Kyoko's mother was the owner of the geisha house and had been a famous geisha in her time. She had gone through the geisha training in the Yoshiwara and been a dancer there, which in this environment was akin to having trained in the Royal Ballet; she was a star among the Mukojima geisha. When Kyoko was a child, she was registered at the local primary school under her mother's name. It was perfectly normal in the area; most of the other children were registered under their mothers' names too. It was only when she went on to middle school that she realized there was anything unusual about her.

"One girl asked me, 'Why are you registered under your mother's name?' I went to look. Everyone else was under their father's. 'I wonder why?' I thought. Later my mother told me everything. Round here it's normal. I never think about it. I met my father a while ago. I thought, 'Wow, he's really got old.' He came for my geisha debut. I talked about it with my mother. At first I thought I'd be a waitress. But in the end I decided to be a geisha."

"It's lonely sometimes," said Ayako, a homely woman of thirty-nine in an oversize turquoise T-shirt and black slacks who wore her hair girlishly loose. "When I get back to my apartment at five o'clock in the morning and have a can of beer by myself . . . To be single and living alone when you're in your thirties is kind of strange in Japanese society."

Ayako too had a story to tell. She had become a geisha by accident. Eleven years earlier, she had turned up in Mukojima with her suitcase, thinking she had a job as a waitress in a teahouse. It was only after she had been there for a week that she came across a label with the words "Geisha Union" written on it.

"I thought, 'It can't be! I'm in the geisha world, like on TV!' I wish I'd known about it when I was eighteen, I would have become a geisha straight away."

She had left home to be a fashion stylist and had never dared tell her parents about her change of occupation.

"I once thought I might get married. But it only lasted three seconds," she chuckled. "There was this guy around. Yeah, it lasted three seconds. Then I thought, 'Geisha, geisha, I'll carry on being a geisha. If I get married, that's it. No more freedom. Jail!' I see him from time to time. I never think, 'Should've got married.' When I go home and see my old school friends, I think, 'Lucky escape! I'm glad I'm a geisha.' They all have these children. It looks like really hard work."

"Wives don't have sex appeal," said Kyoko smiling her elfin smile. "You look at a wife, the same age as a single person—no sex appeal at all. It's because they have children. They turn into mothers, they let themselves go. They don't know anything about life. But funnily enough, married guys, in Japan, anyway, seem to know more about life than single guys do. You get a single guy of forty or fifty and you think, 'Something odd there.' My mother often says so."

The witching hour of six o'clock was approaching. Kyoko's mother came out of the kitchen to tell the women to begin their preparations. At first sight she was a frowzy, slatternly woman in her shapeless dress, pink apron, and uncombed bird's nest hair. But then she folded elegantly to her knees, propped her chin on her hand, tilted her head, and looked provocatively out of the corner of her eye. Suddenly one could see the fine bones of the face and the grace of the movements. It would only take a little makeup and a kimono and she could have any man on his knees.

In the kitchen a young woman of twenty-one had arrived and was downing a bowl of rice and boiled beef. She was the *han-gyoku,* the Tokyo equivalent of a maiko. *Han-gyoku* means "half-jewel," "jewel" being "jewel money," a coy euphemism, like "flower money," for the geisha's fee. The *han-gyoku,* being a trainee, was paid half the standard fee.

All around there was frantic painting and dressing. The *han-gyoku* painted her face white—though not as white as a Kyoto maiko and without the erotic tongue of bare flesh at the back of the neck. Then she donned a wig; beginner though she was, her hair was not dressed into a stiff coiffure like a maiko's. Kyoko, meanwhile, had applied eye shadow and eye liner and painted her lips scarlet, then wrapped herself in a summery white kimono and a shimmering silver-and-blue obi embroidered with a burst of pink-and-white chrysanthemums.

On my way back to the station, I dropped into the hairdresser's to say good-bye to Ayako. Gone was the homely, slovenly woman who had sat joking with me. Gazing intently into the mirror as the hairdresser teased the last strands of hair into place, she touched up her face with a powder brush. Her eyes and eyebrows were etched in black, her lips blushed red. In her ink-black kimono, she positively smoldered. These women knew about sex appeal.

It struck me that the Mukojima geisha were more like the geisha of the past. They created a world where men could live out their fantasies, but it was a world open to ordinary men, not just the elite. Most businessmen, successful though they might be, lacked not only the necessary connections to party in Shimbashi but even the desire. After a hard day's work, they wanted to relax, eat, drink, and have a laugh in the company of sexy, flirtatious, kimono-clad women, then get up and belt out a karaoké number or two, rather than watch classical dancing or listen to classical singing.

And despite the low regard in which the Mukojima variety were held by the establishment geisha, they were thriving. Just as geisha seemed on the point of extinction, in Mukojima they offered a service for which there was a demand. They were democratic, they were "people's geisha."

Getting into Hot Water

> How cruel the floating world
> Its solaces how few—
> And soon my unmourned life
> Will vanish with the dew.
> Saikaku Ihara (1642–1693)[4]

The Kyoto *geiko* and the Tokyo geisha were the aristocrats of the flower and willow world, the highly visible tip of the iceberg. But they were not the end of the story. In the past there had been geisha quarters in every town and every district of every city in Japan, covering the spectrum from refined to raunchy. Most cities still maintained a small community. The numbers might be dwindling, the flower towns withering, but they were not yet extinct.

But there was another category of geisha who were quite beyond the pale—the geisha of the hot spring resorts, the *onsen* geisha.

For all their reputation as workaholics, the Japanese are also hedonists of the first order. Without any puritan ethic to restrain them, they have no compunction about indulging the most sybaritic desires. Foremost among those is the desire to soak away one's cares in very hot water. Being a volcanic country prone to earthquakes, Japan is peppered with natural hot springs where water, stinking of sulfur or some other healing mineral, spurts out of the ground. Since time immemorial, taking the waters has been a central part of Japanese life, pursued with an almost religious fervor. Like merry Canterbury pilgrims or characters from a Jane Austen novel, people travel from spa to spa, sampling the waters at each.

The essential spa experience has always been communal. Until Westerners arrived with their hangups about nudity, men and women bathed together without the slightest embarrassment or inhibition. Nowadays, thanks to the intervention of scandalized Victorian missionaries and travelers, baths are divided into ladies' and men's sections in all but the most remote parts of the country. But bathing is still a group activity. Naked as nature intended, without any clothing to mark status or wealth, all vestiges of the formality and hierarchy which bedevil everyday life can gently slip away. Leaving the monochrome world of work, bathers step into a parallel universe of fantasy, fun, and play, not far removed from the flower and willow world.

Such a place is naturally the domain of the geisha. The main customers at spas tend to be groups of men, business associates, or workmates on an overnighter or a long weekend where they bathe together, eat together, get drunk together, hang out in identical yukata—literally "bath wear"—and sleep all together in one big tatami room. A trip to a spa fulfills the same function, in fact, as a Shimbashi teahouse party. It is the ultimate bonding experience.

Unfortunately *onsen* geisha have acquired rather a poor reputation. In fact the very words are sufficient to raise a titter. They are by reputation rather low on arts and high on the ability to entertain in other less salubrious ways. Not to put too fine a point upon it, "*onsen* geisha" is practically synonymous with "prostitute." The high-class geisha of the cities hate to be associated with them in any way—so much so that many call themselves *geiko* rather than geisha. What with the *onsen* geisha, not to mention Westerners with their prurient notions of "geisha gals," the word "geisha" itself has become devalued. Thus, although I regaled my geisha friends with tales of my travels to the classy geisha districts of cities such as Fukuoka and Kanazawa, I never mentioned that I had also been to Atami.

An easy hour's commute from Tokyo, Atami—"Hot Sea"—is Japan's capital of fun, cousin to Coney Island or Las Vegas. Within sight of Mount Fuji and sitting atop a major fault line, its waters contain salt and calcium sulfate, said to be calming for the nerves and beneficial for the skin. Once upon a time guests stayed in picturesque little wooden inns. But these days Atami is far from quaint. The guidebooks use words like "sleazy" and "tacky" to describe it. It is a tourist resort of the most vulgar variety, the kind of place where one would expect to find wild geisha parties and clutches of yukata-clad salarymen lurching up and down the narrow streets in various stages of inebriation. It is not at all the sort of place where any self-respecting Westerner who claimed to have the slightest interest in serious Japanese culture would dream of going.

As the train rounded a bend before pulling into Atami station, I caught a glimpse of the sea sparkling in the distance. But it was soon eclipsed by the jumble of streets and concrete buildings running up and down the hillsides of what had once been a beautiful seaside resort. The sea itself and the streams which ran into it were edged with concrete and the little wooden inns had long since been replaced by multistory concrete slabs. But despite everything there was a gaiety and innocence about the place. It had that heady feeling of a holiday resort entirely devoted to fun.

I finally found my hotel, a particularly large and imposing concrete monolith just off the main road. There kimono-clad women at the door bowed me in and showed me to my room. In proper *onsen* style, I flung off my clothes immediately, put on the starched yukata provided by the hotel, and took the lift down to the enormous communal baths in the basement. I slid open the door to the cedar-walled bathing area. Steam swirled out, as hot and clammy as a tropical jungle. I soaped and rinsed on the tiled floor at the side of the bath, then edged myself gingerly into the savagely hot water. As my body took on the lurid red coloring of a boiled octopus (as the Japanese phrase it), the day's weariness began to evaporate. A few minutes more and I would be ready for a night of partying.

Yuko was the queen of the Atami geisha. A big-boned, handsome woman, she had been a geisha for thirty years. When I first met her she was off duty, in daytime mode, in a dark-blue blouse and plain knee-length gray skirt. She might have been a middle-aged housewife or an office worker. But there was something about her good-time-girl smile, the way she held herself very straight, her hair, which she wore loose and rippling about her shoulders, and her deep-toned gravelly voice which marked her out as different.

Yuko was a survivor. Like most of the Atami geisha, she hailed from the southern island of Kyushu, one of the poorest, most underprivileged parts of the country. She arrived in Atami looking for work and eventually became a geisha.

"My mother and father were angry," she said. "We don't do anything bad in the water trade. But it was very low status."

The water trade—*mizu shobai*—was a phrase normally used solely to refer to bar girls, call girls, prostitutes, and others who made a living by selling their bodies. I had never before heard the geishas' profession referred to in those terms. The grand geisha of Kyoto and Tokyo would have been horrified, I thought. Perhaps for the geisha of Atami the two professions were not as far removed as the Tokyo and Kyoto geisha always insisted they were.

Had she ever married, I wondered. For a moment her face clouded.

"Seventeen years ago," she said slowly. "He wasn't a customer. I had to give up being a geisha. I had a daughter. It didn't last even a year. Then I became a geisha again. I had to leave my daughter at a neighbor's at nights. It was hard.

"I'm not lonely," she added, her cast-iron smile back in place. "I live with my daughter. She doesn't want to be a geisha, she wants to be a nurse. If I'd met someone I liked I might have settled down. But I didn't want a *danna*. If you have a *danna,* you lose your freedom. It's like being a concubine, you have to sleep with them. Some girls like to have one, some don't. If you're popular enough, you don't need one.

"Some people meet nice guys. I haven't, I haven't fallen in love. But I know people who have."

Exactly twenty years ago, she remembered, a guest and a geisha fell desperately in love here in Atami. They had met at a geisha party. But the man was married and had children and couldn't divorce. For four or five years they saw each other as often as they could. Then one day they disappeared. The man had written a note and left it at his house, saying that they had gone to commit suicide together. His family guessed that he was in Atami with the geisha.

"We were all terribly shocked. They sent out search parties, they searched and searched in the woods at the foot of Mount Fuji but they couldn't find them. It must have been five or six years later that they came across the bones. I guess they had taken sleeping pills.

"My generation, people in their forties, we understood. Twenty- or thirty-year-olds wouldn't. They wanted to die in beauty."

Cherry Blossoms and Golf Flags

The geisha of Kyoto, said Yuko, were like "a flower in a high place." Everyone would love the chance to spend time in their company but for most they were completely out of reach. They were too expensive and in any case their doors were open only to the few.

Atami did not have such a long history. But it offered the pleasures of the geisha world to all comers at an affordable price. Admittedly the pleasures were less refined. Nowadays few customers ever asked for a traditional teahouse party with dancing and games. Men no longer wanted or appreciated such things. An evening with geisha in Atami was more likely to be spent chatting and singing karaoké.

Not, of course, that the Atami geisha were prostitutes, she added firmly—perish the thought! In that sense they were very far from *onsen* geisha. The so-called geisha at the hot spring up the road and the ones on the Japan Sea coast—now they were nothing but prostitutes. But in Atami they were decent girls. After all, it was a top government-approved holiday resort. If a man wanted to date a geisha, he could do that, but it would have to be private. Officially sanctioned prostitution was a thing of the past.

No one knew exactly how many *onsen* geisha there were. Geisha were not required to register or to have a license, added to which it could not be denied that there were a fair number of "pillow geisha," women who called themselves geisha but whose dancing and musical skills were far from their most appealing feature. Geisha were part of the *onsen* experience and Japan was peppered with *onsen*; thus it seemed likely that there were far more *onsen* geisha than town geisha, probably several thousand. However, if the situation in Atami was anything to go by, it was a dying profession.

In Atami, unlike less organized *onsen,* there was a register of geisha. It was kept at the Atami Geisha Union and arranged by geisha houses, with a dark cherry blossom symbol to indicate a shamisen player and a pale cherry blossom to indicate a dancer; a small golf flag indicated a golf player. The key thing with golf, of course, was not to be better than the customer, let alone beat him. The geisha's job was to stroll around chatting girlishly, playing just well enough not to frustrate the customer, so that he could feel properly gratified when he won.

But it was becoming harder and harder to make a living as a geisha in Atami. In 1969 there had been 1,200 registered geisha. By 1991 the number had fallen to 800. There were now less than 400; in just eight years the number had halved. Of the 400, 30 had the golf flag beside their name.

"There just wasn't the work," said Yuko. As a result fewer and fewer young women were joining up to become geisha any more and those that did often left to get a "normal" job.

"Twenty years ago, whenever there was a shamisen player along, we'd dance. If you were a good dancer, you carried on dancing no matter how old you were. But these days there are hardly any guests who want to see that kind of thing. There are hardly any guests who can understand our arts. One geisha gave up and became a maid in a hotel. She used to be one of the most famous dancers in Atami.

"But tonight is special. Tonight we'll have a good time. Tonight we're going to have a traditional teahouse party. These guests came four years ago and loved it and asked to have the same kind of party again. There'll be lots of saké. You'll see!"

The Businessmen's Big Night Out

"This way," said Yuko, sliding open the door of a large hotel. She slipped out of her silk-covered sandals and led the way down some stairs into a basement and along a corridor to a closed door. From inside came shouts and raucous laughter. She knelt, slid open the door and, hands to the floor in formal greeting, sang out, "Evening, everybody!"

Yuko in geisha mode was not radically different from Yuko in off-duty mode. She had put on a rather matronly kimono of sheeny green silk and a beige obi with a subtle pattern of chrysanthemums, carefully selected, I thought, to be dressy—it would not do for the guests to think she was not dressing for the occasion—but not intimidatingly glamorous or costly. She had added a little makeup and her hair was swept into a loose bun.

"This is my guest from England," she added, gesturing to me. Kneeling alongside her, I bowed, rose to my feet, and followed her rather awkwardly into the banqueting hall.

It was the size of a village hall, lined with tatami mats, with a stage at one end walled with glimmering gold leaf. Disposed around three sides of the room were fifteen to twenty elderly men in identical indigo-and-white-striped cotton yukata bathrobes. Most sat cross-legged with large expanses of hairy shins and knobbly bare feet on display. In front of each was a small square table of lacquered wood holding a saké cup, a beer glass, and an array of tiny dishes of food.

Sauntering into the room, Yuko settled me in a corner between a couple of grizzled men.

"This is Yamada-san," she said. The ancient craggy-faced gentleman to my right nodded to me, then turned back to his beer. "He's the leader. He'll take care of you."

The men were members of a businessmen's club from one of the wealthier Tokyo boroughs and this was their annual outing. Most were in their sixties and seventies with a good proportion in their eighties.

The oldest was eighty-eight. All were successful, prosperous men, all owned their own businesses and all, as it happened, represented different professions. To my left was a gray-haired fifty-four-year-old solicitor who described himself as the baby of the group.

"People of my age find this kind of thing offensive, especially women," he said, wrinkling his brow severely, anxious to disassociate himself from the unruly oldsters. "That's why there's so few people here. Half the club were against having a geisha party for the annual outing. A lot didn't want to come."

Still, he himself was there and a few minutes later he was laughing as loudly as everyone else.

Besides Yuko, there were three other geisha moving skillfully from group to group, keeping the saké and beer flowing and the conversation sparkling. One was the comedienne, in full regalia with a stiff waxed wig, white face, and ornate gray-and-white kimono with a honeycomb pattern of red-and-mauve chrysanthemums and a red obi. At fifty-something, on her the white makeup looked faintly ghoulish. But as far as she was concerned, that just added to the comic effect. She was the Dolly Parton of the group, shamelessly flaunting her sexuality no matter what her age. But, being Japanese, she revealed not an ample bosom but an ample expanse of back.

Then there was a chubby-faced twenty-one-year-old, bringing a breath of youth to the proceedings. Like the maiko of Kyoto, she was shy and inarticulate; but such naiveté only made her all the more charming. The cast was completed by the shamisen "older sister," a tiny birdlike woman of ninety who spoke hardly at all but proved to have a raucous cackle; she laughed loudest and longest at the dirtiest jokes.

Mr. Yamada, the horse-faced eighty-year-old to my right, had, it transpired, been the most enthusiastic advocate of this particular form of outing. The evening was not far advanced when, twisting a scarf and knotting it rakishly around his head like the lads who carry the portable shrine in a Japanese festival, he grabbed the microphone and began to belt out a song with "older sister" accompanying him on the shamisen. The change of costume released a raffish new persona. He was no longer Mr. Yamada the Company Boss but a wild man who had cast aside all inhibitions for the night. He had brought his wife along. A faded woman with short black hair, she sat on the other side of the room, laughing merrily.

"Did you catch the words?" asked the chubby-faced solicitor, back in disapproval mode. He seemed to have positioned me, a fellow youngster, as his ally for the night. " 'Let's go to Fukagawa.' You know about Fukagawa?"

I knew very well about Fukagawa, once home to the most stylish geisha of all.

"That means, 'Let's go to a whore house!' " he tutted sternly.

Things were hotting up. A beefy man—owner-chairman of a printing company, said the solicitor, my newfound friend—took the stage with his face painted like a doll's, a ribbon tied around his head and his bathrobe pulled up to his knees, revealing a pair of hefty calves. Hand in hand with Yuko, he performed a comic dance, then took a theatrical peek inside her kimono. Then a frail eighty-four-year-old stepped up in an ornate geisha wig with a red pinafore over his yukata and did a creaky arthritic dance. His reward was more than just a peek inside a kimono. To huge applause Yuko rolled on the floor and the tiny old man rolled on top of her. The ancient shamisen player was cackling with laughter.

At eight-thirty the party moved on to the karaoké bar in the basement of the hotel. Still in their cotton yukata bathrobes, the men lounged on leather sofas around small tables in the darkened room.

"I could have any of this lot for thirty thousand yen [$300]," bragged the beefy owner-chairman of a printing company, giving me a nudge. I looked at him, wondering if I had heard right. "Or forty thousand yen [$400] for overnight."

"No, fifty thousand yen [$500]," another guest corrected him.

"That young geisha," leered the printer. "I could definitely have her." He paused and edged closer to me.

"But I don't want to sleep with those old bags," he said with a cheeky smile. "I'd rather sleep with you! What about it? I'm single. Let's get married!"

Smiling, I told him I'd have to get to know him a bit better first. Somehow my role had subtly changed. At the beginning of the evening I had been the observer, asking questions and making notes. But now the men had found a slot for me in the flower and willow world. As far as they were concerned, they had an extra girl—and this one was free! They weren't even being billed at 10,000 yen ($100) an hour for me. What was there to do except be a geisha, laugh, be charming, and flirt, with the unshakable determination to creep off at the end of the evening to my solitary bed.

Another two hours passed. Those members of the party still on their feet stepped into wooden clogs lined up at the entrance to the hotel and headed off in their yukata into the silent neon-lit streets. Occasionally we passed another group of revelers, also in matching hotel-issue yukata, clattering past the darkened shops.

Finally we came to an open restaurant, a window of light along a dark alley. Squeezed around a small table, the men ordered noodles, rice balls, yakitori (chicken kebabs)—simple fare, very different from the elaborate cuisine on offer at the banquet earlier. Saké and beer were still flowing.

As the men belted out a chorus of "Let's go to Yoshiwara," the comedienne stood up, turned to face the wall, and gyrated rhythmically, rubbing her groin against it. Then she grabbed the young solicitor. He tried to resist, then gave in, laughing. She pulled him on top of her, thrashing her arms and legs in simulated ecstasy. "Aah," she groaned, pushing him off and sitting up. "Now I'm going to have a baby. What shall I call it?"

"They're really drunk, that's why they're making so much noise," explained one man.

"They're not that drunk," muttered Yuko.

Mr. Yamada was singing at the top of his voice. "Be quiet," scolded his wife, who was still with the group. "You have the loudest voice of all!"

At one o'clock the evening came to an abrupt end. Farewells were peremptory, the intimacy suddenly over. The men disappeared into the darkness, clattering along the road to their hotel.

"I need to deal with money," said Yuko. She looked tired and a little sad. "Your hotel is that way, up the hill and around the corner. You can find it."

And, having taken care of me so solicitously, she disappeared in the wake of the men, leaving me alone on the dark street. All through the evening she had laughed, bantered, and made sure that everyone was chatting, everyone was happy, and everyone had plenty to drink. Unlike the spoiled young girls who chose to become maiko in Kyoto, the geisha of Atami were working girls not so far removed from the young women from poor families who used to be sold in the bad old prewar days. They had to make a living. Their job was to be eternally bright and cheerful, no matter how they might really feel. Her smile was part of her job. It was for everyone, she had no favorites.

Was she, perhaps, in need of a little extra income, I wondered. But it seemed an ungenerous thought and I put it out of my mind.

Snow Country

> The train came out of the long tunnel into the snow country. The earth lay white under the night sky. The train pulled up at a signal stop. A girl who had been sitting on the other side of the car came over and opened the window in front of Shimamura. The snowy cold poured in.
>
> Yasunari Kawabata (1899–1972)[5]

Not long before I left Japan I took the train through the mountains to the city of Kanazawa on the coast of the Japan Sea, a stretch of country immortalized by the Nobel Prize–winning author Yasunari Kawabata in his 1937 novel, *Snow Country*. The celebrated first sentences evoke a landscape buried deep in snow, white and magical.

When Kawabata was writing, men went on solitary excursions to the Snow Country to take the waters and enjoy the companionship of the beautiful white-skinned geisha. Many formed relationships there. But for the geisha who foolishly allowed themselves to fall in love, it was a lonely existence. They would be left pining for months, waiting for the day when their lover stepped unannounced off a train from Tokyo to spend a few precious hours with them—a poignant image which the words "snow country" also evoke. Kawabata's novel is about one such wealthy dilettante and the geisha who loves him.

Cut off from the bustling southern plains by the impenetrable mountain ranges of the Japan Alps, the cities of the Japan Sea coast developed a distinctive and robust culture. Kanazawa, the capital of the fabulously rich Maeda lords, became famous for its mansions, gardens, and exquisite handicrafts. It was also known for its refined and elegant geisha, rated as highly as the *geiko* of Kyoto.

From the station I took a bus to Higashi-chaya-machi (Eastern "Teahouse Town" or Pleasure Quarter). I had arranged to stay the night in an old geisha house there. The other two geisha districts were Nishi-chaya-machi (Western Pleasure Quarter) and Kazue-machi (Kazue Town). Leaving my bag in a tatami-matted room very similar to the one I had left in Kyoto, I took a stroll along the little main street.

It was clean, neat, and well preserved, quite disturbingly so. Newly paved with tidy rectangular concrete slabs, it was lined with picturesque old houses of dark wood with shiny tiled roofs. Rows of red lanterns hung along the eaves where the upper floor jutted out above the lower. But behind many of the slatted windows of the ground floors were modern interiors. Most of the people on the street were tourists. It was a geisha theme park, sanitized and lifeless.

Still, at least the area had found a way of surviving. Hanami-koji—Flower-Viewing Alley—in Gion was heading in the same direction. Camera-toting tourists prowled the street and there were even restaurants where they could dine, very expensively, on traditional Japanese cuisine and be entertained by maiko. But the street still retained that ancient forbidding geisha flavor. The dark wooden houses were firmly closed. None but the boldest of *ichigen san*—first-timers—would ever dare slide open a door and put a foot inside; and if he did, he would be briskly seen off.

That was the problem. In order to retain its distinctive character, the geisha world had to remain hermetically sealed. It had to be a special world, cocooned in secrecy and mystery. Once the hoi polloi were able to encroach upon the geisha world it would fade away like dew in the sun. The wonder was not that the geisha were disappearing but rather that they had managed to survive for so long.

A Tokyo friend had given me an introduction to the president of a construction company, the kind of man who in the old days would have been the *danna* of a geisha. Having sat me down in a boardroom and given me a formal greeting, he packed me off in a taxi along with one of the vice presidents of the company to meet the gray men who ran the Kanazawa Chamber of Commerce.

The geisha of Kanazawa were dying out, they told me. After the war there had been about 300 geisha in all in Kanazawa. As recently as 1997, there were still 25 in Higashi, 26 in Nishi, and 13 in Kazue. Now, in a mere two years the numbers had dwindled to 19 in Higashi, 19 in Nishi, and 9 in Kazue. Only one new entrant had joined this year. The *danna* system was disappearing, partly because income tax had risen hugely compared to the prewar years, greatly reducing the amount of disposable income. Added to this, there were very few family-owned businesses anymore. Company presidents, answerable to a board of shareholders, could not throw around corporate money in the way that independent owners had been able to.

"Without the support of *danna-san* the geisha cannot go on," they said. But geisha, along with the other traditional arts, were an important part of Kanazawa's heritage. The city officers had decided that they desperately needed to be preserved.

Accordingly, although they could not hope to match the level of sponsorship which a *danna* had been able to offer, they had created a variety of schemes. They had made funds available to support young geisha, to cover the cost of their kimonos and classes and to pay for a dance teacher to visit regularly from Tokyo. They had also created a pension fund for elderly geisha.

The Town Hall had a separate scheme of its own. Through a private donor the city bureaucrats had amassed sufficient funds to provide four or five novice geisha with 300,000 yen ($3,000) for the first year. They would grant a similar sum to the teahouse mother to help support the young geisha and pay for her classes. It was pitifully small. There were, I learned, other cities which subsidized their dwindling geisha communities in the same way—though in Kyoto and Tokyo there was, at the moment at least, no need to do so.

In exchange for subsidies, the Kanazawa geisha consented to a Faustian pact. They agreed to give a certain number of performances of music and dancing for the public for no charge during July and August each year. They even offered to allow the public, thirty at a time, into the hallowed halls of the union building to watch their rehearsals. In fact, they relinquished their mystique.

It explained the theme-park look of the Eastern Pleasure Quarter. The geisha of Kanazawa had become civil servants, part of the tourist heritage, carefully preserved like the pink pickled plums that Japanese women laid out to dry in summer. They would not die out, their dance and music would survive—but at a price. It was profoundly ironic that this was what had become of these women, once queens of a subversive alternative culture. Without an edge of the forbidden, of the erotic, of danger, it was just pretty dancing.

But perhaps it was better that the geisha should survive in some form rather than disappear completely.

chapter 10

saying goodbye

Parting is merely longing,
    never farewell—
The temple bell sounding
    at dawn.
        Geisha song[1]

Geisha in a Neon World

Everyone in the geisha world was worried about the future. The problem was not so much the geisha as the growing gap between them and the rest of society. The geisha did not change. They were stuck in a time warp. But Japan had changed hugely and continued to change at dizzying speed. It was the home of Pokémon, Nintendo, and Sony, where women strove for equality in politics and business, where young women chose not to marry because they did not want to spend the rest of their lives mothering men, and where old women, whose husbands had retired, chose to get divorced. The country was consumed in a tidal wave of concrete, skyscrapers, neon, traffic, and cool youngsters with dyed brown hair who took amphetamines, listened to house and garage music and went to raves. The geisha were utterly out of synch.

People often told me that the geisha embodied everything that made Japan Japan. At their most elevated the geisha lived lives dedicated to beauty. They were human works of art, an absurdly anachronistic notion in an aggressively modern society like Japan. If they disappeared, that whole exquisite world—in which every detail, from the placement of the fan in the tea ceremony to the line of a moth wing eyebrow and the intricate weave of an obi, was studied and perfected with loving attention—would die out with them. There was nowhere else where this aesthetic survived.

As a shamisen teacher who lived her life on the fringes of the geisha world said, "Manners are disappearing in Japan. The only place where the old ways of behavior survive is the flower and willow world. The *okiya* system—the system of bringing up maiko in geisha houses under the strict supervision of the mothers—preserves good manners because it's so strict." If the geisha died out, it would be the end of what made Japan unique, the end of traditional Japanese culture and manners.

Back in Tokyo, I went to pay a last visit to my geisha friends in Shimbashi. They took me backstage at the Shimbashi Embujo, the only theater built specifically for geisha dance. I had been there earlier in the year to see *Azuma Odori,* literally "Dances of the East" (Tokyo being in the east and Kyoto in the west), the Shimbashi geishas' annual dance performance. I could not fail to notice that most of the audience were geisha. Many had come up from Kyoto to see how their rivals were doing.

At the theater, we dropped in on one of the officials, a plump, floppy-wristed man with shiny oiled hair fixed immovably to the top of his round head. In the old days, he said gloomily, Azuma Odori used to be performed for a whole month in spring and a month in autumn. These days it had shrunk to a mere four days at the end of May, carefully timed to take place between seasons of kabuki.

"If the flower and willow world disappears, kimonos will disappear too," he sighed. "Outside the geisha world, people wear kimonos once or twice a year. It's only geisha who wear them every day. Obi, zori [straw sandals], fans, clogs—all the accouterments of the geisha world—will disappear forever. *Gei*—the arts, Japanese classical culture—will disappear. Music, dancing, that whole gracious teahouse way of life, will be lost.

"In the past," he went on, "we had a class system. Now we are democratic. Of course, that's a very good thing; how could anyone say otherwise? But it means that everything is reduced to the same level. What we need is to get young businessmen to come to teahouse parties. But they won't, no matter how rich they get.

"Young people can't understand the charm of the flower and willow world. It's the quietness that makes it interesting. You go into a teahouse and there is a beautiful painting, exquisite flowers, good food, charming geisha. In the old days you would sit quietly and talk to the geisha, how lovely she was, her beautiful kimono, the wonderful tea ceremony, the beautiful piece of craftsmanship you had just bought. But in our modern democratic society, no one knows how to appreciate that kind of thing anymore.

"I hope the flower and willow world survives. Without it life will be lonely and dull. Japan will be just another Hong Kong, nothing but neon.

"The oldest geisha in Shimbashi is ninety. She told me that this is the worst. Worse than after the Great Earthquake, worse than after the war. It's not just that business is bad. It's the end."

Tea and Cakes

Before I left for good I wanted to go back to Kyoto to say farewell to the hairdresser, the printer, the wig maker, everyone at the Haruta geisha house, and all the other geisha house mothers, maiko, and geisha who had come to seem like my enormous extended family. Arriving in the geisha district there from Tokyo was like stepping back in time to a quieter, slower era. For the last time I unpacked my bag in my barely furnished tatami-matted room with the tall narrow mirror and flimsy rack on which to hang my clothes, then went out onto the balcony to watch the maiko clattering along the street and clustering like butterflies in the concrete-lined parking lot in front of the Kaburenjo, giggling and chattering.

Months had passed since I first arrived, all innocence, looking for a way to breach this closed world. I had never realized then how fragile and threatened that world was and is. Now, when I walked the streets of the Kyoto flower towns, I saw the maiko, the geisha, and the "older sisters" with new eyes. To me they were no longer exotic birds but women dedicated to their art who had chosen a life of discipline in order to transmute themselves into creatures of beauty. I had come to respect their silence. That was their iki, their "cool," that gave them their special flavor. I felt proud and humbled that some of these powerful and alluring women had chosen to befriend and confide in me.

I pondered the best gifts to give everyone. For the sharp-tongued mama-san, who had in her abrasive way provided me with a real experience of geisha training, it had to be cakes from Kanshindo. But for others, less concerned about propriety, maybe the best would be something more personal, with a hint of England about it.

Not far from the Haruta geisha house there was a newly opened tea shop, run by a plump, rather pompous man who spent a good ten minutes brewing up each pot of Darjeeling tea, following, he assured me, the strict rules and rituals of the English tea ceremony. He also sold for an exorbitant price small packets of Indian tea, carefully wrapped in pretty flowery cloth bags, and slices of cake each in its own cellophane package. I decided on tea for the "older sisters" and "mothers" and cake or cookies for the maiko.

In the case of the mama-san, the conventions had to be followed to the letter. I phoned her and made an appointment to visit, then arrived promptly with my Kanshindo cakes neatly wrapped in their shop packaging. She was sitting very upright like a ballet dancer, talking to a guest, while the barman leaned on the counter with a deferential smile.

As usual, she was discussing the terrible decline in traditional values.

"It's all a matter of rank," she said regally. "In the old days, when you visited a lord, his wife and all the concubines would be kneeling in order of rank, bowing and greeting the guests. But now rank has disappeared completely. People pay as much attention to what a maid says," she went on with the tiniest exquisite hint of a disdainful wrinkle of the nose, "as to what a lord says.

"Mine is the last generation," she concluded. "There will be no geisha after me."

I remembered that whenever I sat down to pore over books on the history of the Yoshiwara, I was always puzzled as to when exactly the famous pleasure quarter began to decline. Almost as soon as the first brothels were in place back in the early seventeenth century, people started to bemoan the fall in standards. Thereafter generation after generation of writers complained that the courtesans of the old days had been queens, boasting every imaginable accomplishment; those of their own day were lowly creatures in comparison, hardly better than prostitutes. The same thing applied to the geisha. At the beginning of the last century Kafu Nagai made it his personal mission to capture for posterity their last fleeting years. They were, he declared in his novels, already effectively extinct.

I decided I should take into account this eternal tendency to glorify the past and lament the present when listening to the mama-san's complaints. Things might be bad but they were not that bad. With an appropriate show of humility I thanked her profusely for her help and took my leave.

The next day I dropped in to see my neighbor, the beaming and beautiful white-haired ex-geisha, Hara-san. In exchange for the humble tea I gave her, she deluged me with gifts—dainty wooden sandals with bright blue silk-covered thongs, a couple of pairs of white socks, and a delicate wooden hairpin with a tiny chicken carved on the end. Then, laden down with bags of tea and cakes, I made the rounds. In the evening I met up with Mori-san, my raffish drinking companion who had written a book on guide dogs for the blind, and paid a last visit to the mama-san who had told me about her experiences of *mizuage*. I also said good-bye to the plump mistress and jazz-loving master of the coffee shop. They told me to be sure to come back soon. The best time, they said, would be New Year, when everyone would be relaxed and I could enjoy the New Year festivities.

On my last morning, a maiko called Miegiku, who lived in a geisha house a few doors from my inn, suggested that we have a cup of tea together before I took the bus to the station. At twenty-two she was a little older than average, rather serious and thoughtful, not as giggly and little-girlish as the others. She had an intelligent, open face with a pert nose, a pretty smile, and a candid, direct gaze. Unlike other maiko she had gone to high school. That was one very good reason that not many girls were becoming maiko now; to do so meant that they had to drop out of school at fourteen or fifteen. Then she had had to decide between university and maiko training; so she had started her maiko training late, at seventeen.

"I decided this was something I could only do while I was young," she told me. "My father was opposed to it. He knows now that we learn traditional arts but he's still worried. He knows I always say what I think. It's not good to be too outspoken in this world. We're supposed to be cute, not clever."

That day she was wearing a summery pale pink kimono with a pattern of white flowers and a deep mauve obi. Her hair was waxed in the *ofuku* style of the mature maiko. We strolled along together, she shuffling with tiny steps on her wooden clogs, her legs constrained by her tight kimono.

"Let's go to Hankyu," she said, naming one of the department stores in the bustling traffic-filled hub of the city. We crossed the River Kamo by a small bridge, cut through a side street to the store, and took the escalator to the coffee shop.

Miegiku had reached that moment of no return when she had to choose whether to go ahead with the turning of the collar and commit herself to being a geisha or leave the flower and willow world for good.

"Have you decided yet?" I asked.

"I really want to be an English teacher," she confessed. "Sometimes I think I should have gone to university. Customers talk about their children who are students and I wonder if I made a mistake.

"My life has become very narrow. I always have to be so polite; and everyone's always so nice to me. I feel I'm getting selfish. Whenever I'm invited to a party, I know I will definitely be going by taxi and the customer will pay for the taxi and everything. I'm afraid if I stay here too long I will be completely spoiled. It will be more and more difficult to return to normal life.

"It's difficult to make a living nowadays as a geisha. In the old days it was easier, people had *danna*. Nowadays fewer people are interested in teahouse parties. Geisha have no families. They live by themselves. Some of those older sisters must be lonely.

"I'm thinking little by little of giving up and doing a normal job. Being a geisha is not a normal job. It looks so pretty from the outside, always wearing a kimono. But inside it's harsh. If you think of that, it's not so pretty. It's a world of show. I want to go back to normal life."

Sitting on the train as it pulled out of Kyoto, away from the purple hills and crystal streams celebrated by poets for more than a thousand years, I wondered how much longer there would be people around who appreciated that heritage of beauty. There were many reasons why the geisha were fading away—higher taxes, fewer private businesses, more choices for women and, above all, modernization and the changing tastes of the new generation.

Nevertheless Japanese culture—the essential Japaneseness of Japan—had persisted for millennia. Each younger generation was seduced by fashion and modernity; but as they grew older, they always returned to the old ways. In the 1920s young women dressed like flappers. Now many of those same women wore kimonos.

In a few years the baby boomers, who currently considered themselves far too modern and sophisticated to consort with geisha, would have aged into patriarchs. Then Ginza hostess bars and fancy French restaurants might begin to seem a little mundane. Like their fathers and grandfathers before them, perhaps they too would begin to feel that what they now deserved to mark their years and status was the society of those classiest and most exclusive of women—geisha.

The geisha, it seemed to me, might decline but they would not die out. Even if they became very few, they would be all the more valued, like rare precious stones. While there was a demand for them, they would always be there to fill it.

For most people in Japan, there was precious little love or romance to be had anywhere—not in marriage and certainly not in the booming sex industry. But Japanese songs, films, and traditional literature were awash with it, as if in a desperate attempt to inject it into brutally unromantic lives. It was not surprising that such a country should have invented the geisha to embody all the missing romance and love—even if their world too turned out to be only a dream.

glossary

ageya house of assignation, where patrons made appointments with courtesans in the pleasure quarters; precursor of the geisha teahouse.

asobi literally, "play"; time spent with geisha, courtesans, or other entertainers.

awase lined kimono worn in autumn and winter.

biwa four- or five-stringed traditional Japanese lute played with a plectrum.

cha-tate onna "tea-brewing women"—precursors of the geisha.

-chan suffix used for children or intimate friends as in Ken-chan (akin to "cute little Ken" or "Kenny").

chokibune light, swift, single-oared boats, used to take customers along the River Sumida to the Yoshiwara pleasure quarter.

daimyō provincial princes or warlords who governed their own domains but had to swear loyalty to the shogun.

dango round, white rice flour dumplings, steamed on skewers.

danna   literally "husband" or "master"; a male customer or patron of geisha or *tayu*.

Edo   name for Tokyo until 1868; also name of period of Japanese history from 1603 to 1868.

Edokko   "child of Edo"; a native of Edo, Edo born and bred.

enkai   banquet, geisha party (word used by customers but not geisha).

eri   stiff brocade collar or neckband worn under the top layer of kimono.

erikae   "changing of the collar"; ritual marking the transition from maiko to geisha.

furisode   "swinging-sleeve" kimono worn by unmarried girls; term used for fake maiko of Asakusa.

gei   arts or entertainment.

geiko   "arts child"; term for geisha in Kyoto and some other cities.

hakama   traditional starched and pleated man's kimono.

hana-dai   "flower money"; a geisha's wages.

hanamachi   "flower town"; geisha district.

han-gyoku   "half-jewel"; trainee geisha in Tokyo (the equivalent of a maiko in Kyoto).

haori   a loose, square-cut jacket worn over the kimono; adopted by Fukagawa geisha from the late eighteenth century.

hari   "attitude" or "style"; used of the Yoshiwara courtesans of the seventeenth century.

hiki-iwai   celebration of retirement from geisha life.

homu baa   "home bar"; a small private bar in a teahouse.

ichigen san kotowari   "the first-time customer is refused"; the "no strangers" rule followed by geisha.

iki   "chic," "style," or "cool"; originated among the geisha of Edo.

jiutamai   form of classical Japanese dance practiced by geisha, particularly the geisha of Gion, linked to the dance forms of the Noh theater.

joruri   Japanese narrative music.

kabuki   traditional popular theater, characterized by spectacular drama, splendid costumes, and melodramatic performance style; many kabuki plays tell stories of the floating world.

kabuku   "to frolic" or "to be wild or outrageous."

kaburenjo   "music dance practice place"; headquarters of each geisha district, housing a theater, classrooms, and the union offices of that district.

kamuro   child attendant(s) of a courtesan.

karaoké   "empty barrel"; popular evening entertainment in Japan, in which customers sing to recorded accompaniment.

kata   "form"; the proper way of doing something.

katsuyama   the most complex of the maiko's topknot hairstyles, named after a seventeenth-century courtesan who popularized it.

kawaramono   "riverbed folk"; underclass in Edo-period Japan, primarily popular entertainers, including musicians, jesters, actors, and courtesans, who performed in dry riverbeds.

keisei   "castle topplers"; courtesans of legendary beauty.

kemban   the geisha union or registry office; each geisha district has its own kemban.

kiyomoto   form of classical narrative song practiced by geisha.

kokyū   "North-Chinese-barbarian bow"; ancient three-stringed lute played with a bow.

kōshi   second rank of courtesan.

koto   thirteen-stringed classical zither.

ko-uta   "short song"; characteristic geisha songs accompanied by the shamisen.

maiko   "dancing girl"; apprentice geisha in Kyoto.

mama-san   "mother"; owner of a bar.

maneki nekko   lucky "money-beckoning cat."

minarai   "learning by observation"; early stage of geisha training before becoming a maiko.

misedashi   "store opening"; maiko's debut.

mizu shobai   "water trade"; the sex industry.

mizu yokan   eggplant-colored jelly made of aduki beans and eaten in summer.

mizuage   "raising or offering up the waters"; sexual initiation of an apprentice geisha or courtesan.

momme   silver nugget; 1/60 of a *ryo* in Edo-period Japan.

nigo-san   "number two wife"; concubine.

Nihon buyo   "Japanese dance"; the main form of classical Japanese dance practiced by geisha, closely linked to the dance and dramas of kabuki.

Noh   Japanese classical theater, patronized by the samurai classes since the late fourteenth century; considered "respectable" whereas kabuki was not.

obi   wide, stiff sash worn around the waist, over a kimono.

ochaya   "honorable teahouse"; place where banquets are held and geisha work, offering music, dance, and conversation; food, if offered, is brought in from a caterer.

odori-ko   "dancing child"; professional dancing girls.

odori-kai   dance meet.

ofuku   maiko's second hairstyle; in the past it signified that she was no longer a virgin; now the mark of a second-year maiko.

ohayo dosu or *ohayo san dosu*   "good morning" (dialect of Kyoto women, particularly geisha).

oiran   highest rank of courtesan in Edo, from the eighteenth century onward.

oka basho   "hill places"; unlicensed teahouse and brothel areas in old Japan.

okami-san   proprietress of a geisha house or teahouse.

okāsan   "mother"; proprietress of a geisha house.

ōki-ni   "thank you" (Kyoto dialect).

okiya   house where geisha live.

okobo   high wooden clogs worn by maiko.

onē-san   "older sister."

onnagata   male kabuki actors specializing in women's roles.

onsen   spa; hot spring resort.

onsen geisha   geisha who works at a hot spring resort.

otokoshi   "male staff"; geisha's assistant, nowadays usually a middle-aged woman rather than a man.

o-zashiki   "honorable tatami room"; geisha term for a banquet or party.

rabu   Japanese phoneticization of "love."

rakugo   Japanese comic monologue.

ro   loosely woven silk gauze, used to make summer kimonos.

rōnin   "wave men"; lordless samurai.

ryō   currency in Edo-period Japan worth 4 gold nuggets; about $450 in contemporary currency.

ryōtei   high-class Tokyo restaurant, serving Japanese haute cuisine and where geisha can be called to entertain.

saké   "rice wine"; served hot in winter and chilled in summer.

sakko   hairstyle worn for the last month before a maiko graduates to become a geisha.

samurai   warriors who served the warlords of old Japan; highest class in the Tokugawa ranking system.

-san   "Mr." or "Ms."; polite suffix normally added to names.

sancha   teahouse waitresses-*cum*-courtesans in old Japan.

san-san-kudo   "three times three, nine times"; ritual exchange of cups of saké in a wedding ceremony or maiko's ceremony of sisterhood.

sensei   teacher.

seppuku   ritual suicide as practiced by samurai; the English term "hara-kiri" is incorrect.

shamisen   literally "three taste strings" or "strings of three tastes"; three-stringed banjo-like instrument played with a plectrum, associated with kabuki and geisha.

shikitari   tradition, custom.

shikomi   "in training"; first stage in a geisha house, before *minarai*; the new entrant acts as a housemaid, goes to school, and takes her first classes in music and dance.

Shintō   "The Way of the Gods"; native Japanese religion. Shinto places of worship are usually red-painted and referred to as "shrines" to differentiate them from Buddhist temples.

shirabyōshi   "white rhythm"; song and dance performance characterized by a strongly marked rhythm and popular in the twelfth century; the word is also used to refer to the dancer/prostitutes who practiced it.

shōgun   "generalissimo"; military ruler of Japan during the Edo period, nominally under the emperor but in reality all-powerful.

shogunate   the shogun's government.

sui   ideal of "chic" or "sophistication" in seventeenth-century Kyoto and Osaka.

tabi   white linen socks with the big toe separated.

taikomochi   "drum-bearer"; jester or male geisha.

tamago   "egg"; used to refer to *shikomi,* the first stage of maiko training.

tatami   rice straw matting, several inches thick, inset to make the floor of a traditional Japanese room.

tayū   highest rank of courtesan in Kyoto in the seventeenth and early eighteenth centuries.

tokonoma   alcove which forms part of a Japanese room and always contains a flower arrangement and a hanging scroll; the position of honor, where the guest is seated, is in front of the tokonoma.

torii   portal marking the entrance to a Shinto shrine, made of wood, painted red, and shaped rather like a Stonehenge henge.

tsu   a sophisticated man about town, a connoisseur.

tsuzumi   a small hourglass-shaped hand drum.

ukiyo   "the floating world"; a Buddhist term meaning "the transience of all things," adopted to refer to the world of the courtesans.

ukiyo-e   "painting of the floating world"; woodblock print of the courtesans of the pleasure quarters.

waka   classical Japanese poetic form of thirty-one syllables.

ware-shinobu   maiko's first hairstyle.

yakko-shimada   sweeping, elegant maiko hairstyle worn for the New Year celebrations.

yakuza   Japanese Mafia.

yukata   simple cotton kimono used for informal occasions or as a dressing gown-*cum*-nightwear.

notes

Introduction

1. In Longstreet, p. 103.

Chapter 1

1. *"Chireba-koso itodo sakura wa medetakere ukiyo ni nani ka hisashikarubeki,"* in McCullough, *Tales of Ise,* no. 82, p. 125. Author's translation.

2. *"Iro miede utsurou mono wa yo no naka no hito no kokoro no hana ni zo arikeru,"* in Keene, *Anthology of Japanese Literature,* p. 73.

3. *"Hito ni awamu tsuki no naki yo wa omoiokite mune hashiri hi ni kokoro yakeori,"* ibid., p. 74.

4. Just as there are many words for "snow" in Eskimo languages, for "sand" in Arabic, and for "rain" in English, so there are many words for the differing ranks and varieties of prostitute and courtesan in Japanese. The different terms varied city by city and also changed over the centuries. English unfortunately has very few, so I will use "prostitute" to mean low-level sex workers who were freelance and unrecognized by society and "courtesan" for the trained professionals who held a recognized position in society.

5. Shinto is Japan's ancient folk religion, less a set of beliefs than a way of life. In Shinto all nature is sacred. Mountains, rocks, and trees are all deities. The (literally) innumerable Shinto gods coexist with human beings. They will intercede in human affairs to ensure good health or success in school, love, or business if approached in the proper way by the Shinto priests and priestesses who act as intermediaries. Shinto places of worship are referred to as "shrines" to distinguish them from Buddhist temples. They are usually large red-painted buildings with sweeping tiled roofs and a henge-shaped portal (as in Stonehenge), called a *torii*.

6. Ryoi Asai, *Ukiyo Monogatari* (Tales of the Floating World), written after 1661.

7. François Caron, *A True Description of the Mighty Kingdoms of Japan and Siam,* ed. C. R. Boxer (London, 1935). Caron (1600–1673) lived in Japan from 1639 to 1641, where he fathered an illegitimate child.

8. Hiromi, p. 228.

9. Seigle, p. 229.

10. Crihfield, *Ko-uta* no. 22, p. 84.

11. From Joshin Miura's *Keicho Kenmonshu,* 1614, in Seigle, pp. 26–27.

Chapter 2

1. In Scott, p. 162.

2. *Love Suicides at Sonezaki,* tr. by Keene in *Anthology of Japanese Literature,* pp. 375–393.

3. Dazai's story is told in Dazai, *Return to Tsugaru,* and Keene's *Dawn to the West.*

4. T. H. Sanders, *My Japanese Years* (Mills & Born, 1915).

5. In Keene, *Dawn to the West,* p. 403.

6. Arthur Rose-Innes, *English-Japanese Conversation Dictionary* (Tokyo: Meiseisha Publishing Co., 1969).

7. Keene, *Dawn to the West,* p. 65.

8. Saikaku Ihara, *Comrade Loves of the Samurai and Songs of the Geishas,* no. 10, p. 108.

9. Lafcadio Hearn, "The Eternal Feminine," in *Out of the East: Reveries and Studies in New Japan* (Jonathan Cape, 1927), p. 73.

10. David J. Lu, *Inside Corporate Japan: The Art of Fumble-Free Management* (Tokyo: Charles E. Tuttle, 1987), p. 216.

11. Tamura, *The Japanese Bride,* p. 2.

12. Yukiko Tanaka, *Contemporary Portraits of Japanese Women* (Praeger, 1995), p. 45. In 1983, the divorce rate for Japan was half that for the United States—though still double what it had been fifteen years earlier. Since then the number of

divorces has been increasing, with more and more initiated by women; under the Tokugawa divorce could only be initiated by the husband. The total number of divorces in 1992 was nearly 180,000, as opposed to 70,000 in 1962, in a population of 120 million, almost all married. In England and Wales, with a population of 53 million, there were about 160,000 divorces in 1992. More than two thirds of divorces were initiated by the wife.

13. Paul Abrahams, "Time to Sweeten the Pill," *Financial Times* Weekend section, February 27/28, 1999.

Chapter 3

1. Crihfield, *Ko-uta* no. 5, p. 32.

Chapter 4

1. Crihfield, *Ko-uta* no. 23, p. 87.

2. *Keisei Irojamisen* (1701) and *Keisei Kintanki* (1711).

3. From "A Wayward Wife," translated in Hibbett, p. 110.

4. Elisonas, pp. 285, 287.

5. Seigle, p. 171.

6. Seigle, Appendix D.

7. Sansom, p. 485.

8. Hiromi, p. 232.

9. Crihfield, *Ko-uta* no. 17, p. 67. Tatsumi was another name for Fukagawa.

10. *Edo Mumare Uwaki no Kabayaki* (1785), recounted in Seigle, p. 198, and Keene, *World Within Walls,* p. 405.

Chapter 5

1. Saikaku Ihara, *Comrade Loves of the Samurai and Songs of the Geishas,* no. 24, p. 113.

2. Ibid., no. 8, p. 107.

3. Hayasaki, *Gion yoi banashi.*

Chapter 6

1. Gerstle, p. 27.

2. Seigle, p. 216.

3. Yamata, p. 42.

4. Pierre Loti, *Madame Chrysanthème,* p. 216, quoted in Ashmead, p. 219.

5. Quoted in Otaka, ch. 1, Ito Hirobumi.

6. My thanks to Hal Gold for the information and translation, which I have amended. Gilbert and Sullivan never credited their source; in *The Good Opera Guide* (Weidenfeld & Nicolson, 1994), the author Denis Forman mentions the "phoney Japanesy idiom" in which Sullivan's "Miya Sama" chorus is written. Little did he know!

7. A. B. Mitford, "Wanderings in Japan," *Littell's Living Age* CXIII (April 6, 1872), pp. 36–37, quoted in Kido, p. 275.

8. Quoted in Otaka, ch. 1.

9. Material on Ito from Seidensticker, *Low City, High City,* pp. 99–100.

10. Material on Japonisme in Britain, including "The Geisha" by Charles Wilmott from Sato and Watanabe, pp. 37–40.

11. *New York Times,* December 6, 1899, referred to in Kano, pp. 189–202.

12. Louis Fournier, *Kawakami and Sada Yacco* (Paris: Brentano's, 1900), p. 17, quoted in Kano, pp. 189–202.

13. Kano, pp. 189–202.

14. The material on Sada Yakko is primarily from Ezaki, *Jitsuroku Kawakami Sadayako* (see Japanese language bibliography).

Chapter 7

1. Saikaku Ihara, *Comrade Loves of the Samurai and Songs of the Geishas,* no. 12, p. 109.

2. "Ichiriki" in *The Kirin: For Marketing and Culture,* Kirin beer in-house magazine, Spring 1985, pp. 104–111.

3. Ibid.

4. For an extensive discussion of kimonos, a whole study in its own right, see the last chapter of Liza Dalby's *Geisha* and also her *Kimono: Fashioning Culture.* New Haven: Yale University Press, 1993.

Chapter 8

1. *"Kani kaku ni Gion wa koi shi neru toki mo makura no shita o mizu no nagaruru."* Author's translation. Poem inscribed on a stone beside the Shirakawa stream in Gion by Isamu Yoshii, celebrated writer of geisha songs, 1886–1960.

2. Figures taken from Fujimoto, p. 27; see also Hiroshi Misobuchi, *Dance of the Season in Kyoto* (Kyoto Shoin, 1992) and Sato and Watanabe, p. 82.

3. "Gaijin no Shitsuren" in *Osaka Maenichi Shimbun,* March 3, 1903, quoted in Kosakai, *Morgan Oyuki: Ai ni iki, shin ni shisu.*

4. From Kosakai.

5. Quoted in Sato and Watanabe, p. 88. In 1889 the jingoistic Rudyard Kipling wrote: "The Chinaman's a native, that's the look on a native's face, but the Jap isn't a native, and he isn't a Sahib either." Quoted in Tames, p. 86.

6. From Kosakai.

7. From Dalby, pp. 69, 80.

8. Ibid., p. 77.

9. Seidensticker, *Kafu the Scribbler,* p. 119.

10. From Dalby, p. 80.

11. Ibid., pp. 82, 86.

12. *Sumidagawa,* translated in Keene, *Modern Japanese Literature,* p. 197.

13. Seidensticker, *Kafu the Scribbler,* p. 23.

14. Ibid., p. 121.

15. *Geisha in Rivalry (Udekurabe),* tr. Kurt Meissner.

16. Seidensticker, *Kafu the Scribbler,* pp. 86, 87–88.

17. Kafu's *Diary,* vol. xxii, p. 317, quoted in Seidensticker, *Kafu the Scribbler,* p. 165.

18. Mark Gayn's *Diary,* p. 32.

19. Ibid., pp. 232, 212.

20. Kafu's *Diary,* February 25, 27, quoted in Seidensticker, *Tokyo Rising,* p. 186, and *Kafu the Scribbler,* p. 174.

21. From Dalby, p. 182.

Chapter 9

1. Longstreet, pp. 15, 224.

2. "On a Geisha Party at Yanagibashi" by Yodo Yamauchi (1827–1872), former daimyo of Tosa; translated by Donald Keene in *Dawn to the West,* p. 42.

3. Saikaku Ihara, *Comrade Loves of the Samurai and Songs of the Geishas,* no. 13, p. 109.

4. Translated in Hibbett, p. 72.

5. Yasunari Kawabata, *Snow Country,* tr. and with an introduction by Edward G. Seidensticker, Charles E. Tuttle, Tokyo, 1956, p. 3.

Chapter 10

1. Crihfield, *Ko-uta,* no. 20, p. 77.

select bibliography

English Language

Ashmead, John. *The Idea of Japan, 1853–1895: Japan as Described by American and Other Travellers from the West.* Harvard Dissertations in American and English Literature. New York: Garland Publishing Inc., 1987.

Bornoff, Nicholas. *Pink Samurai: Love, Marriage, and Sex in Contemporary Japan.* London: GraftonBooks, 1991./New York: Pocket Books, 1991.

Brown, Sidney Devere and Akiko Hirota, trs. *The Diary of Kido Takayoshi.* Tokyo: University of Tokyo Press, 1983.

Buruma, Ian. *A Japanese Mirror: Heroes and Villains of Japanese Culture.* London: Jonathan Cape Ltd, 1984.

Cobb, Jodi. *Geisha: The Life, the Voices, the Art.* New York: Alfred A. Knopf, 1997.

Crihfield, Liza. *Ko-uta: "Little Songs" of the Geisha World.* Rutland, Vt.: Charles E. Tuttle, 1979.

Dalby, Liza. *Geisha.* Berkeley: University of California Press, 1983; with a new preface: "Twenty-Four Years Later," Berkeley, 1998.

Dazai, Osamu. *Return to Tsugaru.* Tr. James Westerhoven. Tokyo: Kodansha International, 1985.

De Becker, Joseph E. *The Nightless City.* London: Probsthain & Co, 1899.

Elisonas, Jurgis. "Notorious Places, A Brief Excursion into the Narrative Topography of Early Edo." In *Edo and Paris: Urban Life and the State in the Early Modern Era,* eds. James L. McClain, John M. Merriman, and Kaoru Ugawa. Ithaca, N.Y.: Cornell University Press, 1994.

Fujimoto, T. *The Story of the Geisha Girl.* London: T. Werner Laurie Ltd, 1902.

Gayn, Mark. *Japan Diary.* New York: William Sloane Associates, Inc., 1948.

Gerstle, C. Andrew, ed. *18th-Century Japan: Culture and Society.* Sydney: Allen & Unwin, 1989.

Golden, Arthur. *Memoirs of Geisha.* New York: Random House and Chatto & Windus, London, 1997.

Hendry, Joy. *Marriage in Changing Japan: Community and Society.* Rutland, Vt.: Charles E. Tuttle, 1981.

Hibbett, Howard. *The Floating World in Japanese Fiction.* Oxford: Oxford University Press, 1959.

Hiromi, Sone. "Conceptions of Geisha: A Case Study in the City of Miyazu." In *Gender and Japanese History, Volume 1: Religion and Customs/The Body and Sexuality,* eds. Haruko Wakita, Anne Bouchy, and Chizuko Ueno; tr. ed. Gerry Yokota-Murakami. Osaka: Osaka University Press, 1999.

Ihara, Saikaku. *Comrade Loves of the Samurai and Songs of the Geishas.* Tr. E. Powys Mathers. Rutland, Vt.: Charles E. Tuttle, 1972 (first edition 1928).

————. *The Life of an Amorous Man.* Tr. Kengi Hamada. Rutland, Vt.: Charles E. Tuttle, 1963.

————. *The Life of an Amorous Woman and Other Writings.* Tr. Ivan Morris. London: Chapman and Hall, 1963.

Kano, Ayako. "The Role of the Actress in Modern Japan." In *New Directions in the Study of Meiji Japan,* eds. Helen Hardacre and Adam Kern. Leiden: Brill, 1997.

Keene, Donald, ed. *Anthology of Japanese Literature: to the Nineteenth Century.* New York: Grove Press, 1955.

————. *Modern Japanese Literature: From 1868 to Present Day.* New York: Grove Press, 1956.

————. *World Within Walls: Japanese Literature of the Premodern Era 1600–1867.* Rutland, Vt.: Charles E. Tuttle, 1976.

————. *Dawn to the West: Japanese Literature of the Modern Era. Volume 3: Fiction.* New York: Holt, Rinehart, and Winston, 1984.

Kido, Takayoshi. *See* Brown and Hirota.

Kirkwood, Kenneth P. *Renaissance in Japan: A Cultural Survey of the Seventeenth Century.* Tokyo: Charles E. Tuttle, 1970; first published 1938.

Komachi, Ono. See Teele.

Longstreet, Stephen, and Ethel Longstreet. *Yoshiwara: The Pleasure Quarters of Old Tokyo.* Rutland, Vt.: Charles E. Tuttle, 1970.

Loti, Pierre. *Madame Chrysanthème.* Paris: Calman-Levy, 1888. Tr. Laura Ensor. London: George Routledge and Sons Ltd, 1888.

Louis, Lisa. *Butterflies of the Night: Mama-sans, Geisha, Strippers and the Japanese Men They Serve.* New York: Tengu Books, 1992.

McCullough, Helen Craig, tr. *Tales of Ise: Lyrical Episodes from Tenth-Century Japan.* Stanford: Stanford University Press, 1968.

———. *Yoshitsune: A Fifteenth-Century Japanese Chronicle.* Stanford: Stanford University Press, 1966.

Miner, Earl. *An Introduction to Japanese Court Poetry.* Stanford: Stanford University Press, 1968.

Morris, Ivan. *The Nobility of Failure: Tragic Heroes in the History of Japan.* Rutland, Vt.: Charles E. Tuttle, 1975.

Nagai, Kafu. *Geisha in Rivalry.* Tr. Kurt Meissner. Rutland, Vt.: Charles E. Tuttle, 1963.

Nishiyama, Matsunosuke. *Edo Culture: Daily Life and Diversions in Urban Japan, 1600–1868.* Tr., ed., Gerald Groemer. Honolulu: University of Hawaii Press, 1997.

Otaka, Yoshitaka. *Five Political Leaders of Modern Japan.* Tr. Andrew Fraser and Patricia Murray. Tokyo: University of Tokyo Press, 1986.

Saikaku. *See* Ihara, Saikaku.

Sansom, G. B. *Japan: A Short Cultural History.* London: Cresset Press, 1931.

Sato, Tomoko, and Toshio Watanabe, eds. *Japan and Britain: An Aesthetic Dialogue 1850–1930.* London: Lund Humphries, in association with Barbican Art Gallery and the Setagaya Art Museum, 1991.

Scott, A. C. *The Flower and Willow World.* London: Orion Press, 1960.

Screech, Timon. *Sex and the Floating World: Erotic Images in Japan, 1700–1820.* London: Reaktion Books, 1999.

Seidensticker, Edward. *Kafu the Scribbler.* Stanford: Stanford University Press, 1965.

———. *Low City, High City: Tokyo from Edo to the Earthquake, 1867–1923.* New York: Alfred A. Knopf, 1983.

———. *Tokyo Rising: The City Since the Great Earthquake.* New York: Alfred A. Knopf, 1990.

Seigle, Cecilia Segawa. *Yoshiwara: The Glittering World of the Japanese Courtesan.* Honolulu: University of Hawaii Press, 1993.

Statler, Oliver. *Shimoda Story.* New York: Random House, 1969.

Stevenson, John. *Yoshitoshi's Women: The Woodblock-Print Series, Fuzoku Sanjuniso.* Seattle and London: University of Washington Press in association with Avery Press, 1986.

Swinton, Elizabeth de Sabato. *The Women of the Pleasure Quarter: Japanese Paintings and Prints of the Floating World.* New York: Hudson Hills Press, in association with Worcester Art Museum, Worcester, Massachusetts, 1995.

Tames, Richard. *Encounters with Japan.* New York: St. Martin's Press, 1991.

Tamura, Naomi. *The Japanese Bride.* New York: Harper & Brothers, 1904.

Teele, Roy E., Nicholas J. Teele, and H. Rebecca Teele, trs. *Ono no Komachi: Poems, Stories, Noh Plays.* New York: Garland Publishing, 1993.

Waley, Paul. *Tokyo Now and Then.* New York: Weatherhill, 1984.

Yamata, Kikou. *Three Geishas.* Tr. Emma Crawford. London: Cassell & Co Ltd, 1956.

Japanese Language

Ezaki, Atsushi. *Jitsuroku Kawakami Sadayako* (The True Story of Kawakami Sadayakko). Tokyo: Shinjinbutsu Oraisha, 1985.

Hayasaki, Haruyu. *Gion yoi banashi* (A Drunken Story of Gion). Kyoto: Kyoto Shoin, 1991.

Kabuku bi no sekai (Early Seventeenth-Century Genre Paintings: The World of Lively Entertainment). Nagoya: Tokugawa Art Museum, 1997.

Kosakai, Shumi. *Morgan Oyuki: ai ni iki, shin ni shisu* (Oyuki Morgan: To Live for Love and Die for Belief). Tokyo: Kodansha, 1975.

index